PENGUIN BOOKS

**The Motorist and the Law**

John Pritchard is a solicitor in North
and broadcast extensively on legal m
monthly magazine for solicitors. He
bestselling *Penguin Guide to the Law*.

John Pritchard

# The Motorist and the Law

**A Guide to Motorists' Rights**

Penguin Books

Penguin Books Ltd, Harmondsworth, Middlesex, England
Viking Penguin Inc., 40 West 23rd Street, New York, New York 10010, U.S.A.
Penguin Books Australia Ltd, Ringwood, Victoria, Australia
Penguin Books Canada Limited, 2801 John Street, Markham, Ontario, Canada L3R 1B4
Penguin Books (N.Z.) Ltd, 182–190 Wairau Road, Auckland 10, New Zealand

First published 1987

Made and printed in Great Britain by
Cox & Wyman Ltd, Reading
Filmset in Linotron Times by
Rowland Phototypesetting Ltd
Bury St Edmunds, Suffolk

# Contents

# Acknowledgements

This is the 'thank you' page. As such, it is often skipped by the reader, but to the author it is perhaps the most important page of all.

Main thanks must go to Peter Wallis (solicitor, Clerk to the Tonbridge and Malling Justices) who is particularly knowledgeable about road traffic law. He carefully checked through the manuscript. I am particularly grateful to him for his help and constructive suggestions. For any errors that remain, I alone am responsible!

As a practising solicitor my especial thanks must go to my colleagues and clients. To my colleagues (who have pointed out all my mistakes), and to my clients (who have innocently paid for them), my thanks.

# Introduction

This book cannot tell you all there is about motoring law. No one knows all the law, not even the most eminent judge – and certainly not me.

A book of this sort can do no more than introduce the reader to the complexities of motoring law. It should not be forgotten that the motoring law textbooks used by lawyers total thousands of pages! So this book can only summarize the law – it cannot tell you everything!

I hope that the information in this book will be sufficient to point you in the right direction if you have a motoring problem, but there are two cautionary points that should be remembered. Firstly, the law changes quickly – and this is especially true of motoring law. Any part of this book may be out of date when you read it; therefore, do not treat what is written here as being gospel truth. Secondly, remember that 'a little knowledge can be a dangerous thing'. This book presents a condensed view of the law, and it may be that the details that have been omitted are crucial in deciding the answer to your particular legal problem. If in doubt take legal advice.

The law as described here is up to date to the end of 1986, and covers only England and Wales; the law in Scotland and Northern Ireland may differ.

John Pritchard

# Accidents

**Reporting Accidents**

*Do I have to stop if I have an accident? Do I have to report it to the police?*

It all depends upon whether people are injured and damage is caused.

These rules are difficult to follow. The best starting-point is to look at the chart on p. 14.

**1. If someone else is injured** in the accident special rules apply. You must:

1. *Stop.* If you do not stop you will be committing the offence of failing to stop after an accident.

2. *Produce your insurance certificate.* Here you have a choice: you can produce it either at the time of the accident, or later:

(a) *at the time* of the accident you can produce your insurance certificate to a policeman or to anybody 'reasonably requiring' it (e.g. the other motorist or someone injured). In practice few people carry their insurance certificates on them and so they are unable to produce them at the time of the accident. Also it may be that there is no one that the insurance certificate can be shown to – for instance, the other motorist may be too seriously injured to take down the details. If the insurance details are not produced at the time of the accident:

(b) later *you must go to the police.* There are two things to do:

● *you must report* the accident to them 'as soon as reasonably practicable'. How long that will be will depend upon the facts of the case. But, you must report within twenty-four hours – that is the maximum time allowed. In addition:

● *you must produce your insurance certificate* to the police. This does not have to be done straight away. You have at least five days (from the date of the accident) in which to produce the certificate. The five-day period is applied strictly and cannot be extended (see p. 239).

So, you do not have to report the accident to the police if you were able to produce your insurance certificate at the time of the accident. You only need report the accident to the police (and show them your insurance) if you did not produce your insurance details at the time of the accident. Because of this, sensible motorists will always keep their insurance certificates in the car. If they are involved in an accident they may then be able to produce the certificate at the time – and so avoid having to report the accident to the police and produce their insurance certificate to them.

To summarize: if someone else is injured in the accident you must:

● stop
● produce insurance details (and give your name and address). This can be done at the time of the accident. If you cannot produce them then you will have to (1) report the accident to the police within twenty-four hours, and (2) produce your insurance certificate to the police within five days.

Similar rules apply if you were injured. In that case, the other motorist must stop, and then produce their insurance certificate to you. Alternatively, the other motorist will have to report the accident to the police and produce their insurance certificate to them. One final point to note is that if you are the only person injured in the accident you need not produce your insurance details or report it to the police. This is because the law is only concerned with making sure that other people (i.e. people other than you) can claim off an insurance company. In short, if you injure yourself that's your own affair. But if you injure your passengers or anyone else – then these laws apply to you.

**2. If someone else's property is damaged, or an animal is hurt**, less stringent laws apply. You must:

1. *Stop*. If you do not stop you will be committing the offence of failing to stop after an accident.

2. *Give your name and address*. There are two possibilities here.

(a) Firstly, you can simply give your name and address (and that of the vehicle owner) to someone 'reasonably requiring' that information. In other words, if the other car driver or the owner of the property that was damaged asks, you must give the names and addresses. If you do this when you stop after the accident you have fulfilled your legal requirements – the law does not require anything else of you. It is usual to exchange insurance details, but there is no legal requirement for this (the position is different if someone is injured – see above).

(b) If you do not give names and addresses at the time of the accident you must report the accident to the police, and give them your name and address. Often it will not be possible for you to give your name and address at the time of the accident – for instance, you may not be asked for the information and, more likely, there may be no one to ask for it (e.g. if you drive into a parked car at night). When that happens you must tell the police as soon as possible (certainly no later than twenty-four hours afterwards) and give them your name and address. You will not have to produce your insurance certificate.

To summarize: if no one is injured, but someone else's property or animal is damaged, you must:

- stop
- give your name and address. If you do not give your name and address you must report the accident to the police as soon as possible (maximum of twenty-four hours).

It is all rather complicated. In fact it is even more complicated than it may seem at first sight. Firstly, when we talk about an 'animal' we are not talking about all animals! The law says you need only bother to comply with these requirements if you injure a horse, cow, ass, mule, sheep, pig, goat or dog! If you run over a cat, bird or chicken you need not stop, nor need you give your name and address. The second complication is that – for some strange reason – these rules apply only if the damage is to someone's vehicle or to roadside property (i.e. street furniture, traffic lights, street signs, fencing, trees, etc.). In theory you would not have to stop, or give names, if you drove into a piece of furniture that someone had left on the pavement! In practice, of course, these technicalities rarely apply. The basic rule to remember is that you must stop and exchange details if you are involved in an accident.

**3. If only you, or your car, is damaged.** You need not stop. Nor need you give your name and address to anyone else involved, or report the accident to the police (or produce your insurance documents) – see above.

# Accidents: the law on stopping and reporting.

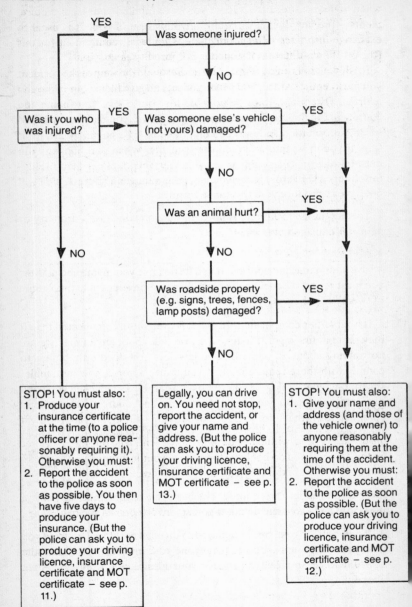

YES — Was someone injured?
↓ NO

Was it you who was injured? — YES → Was someone else's vehicle (not yours) damaged? — YES →
↓ NO

Was an animal hurt? — YES →
↓ NO

Was roadside property (e.g. signs, trees, fences, lamp posts) damaged? — YES →
↓ NO

NO ↓

STOP! You must also:
1. Produce your insurance certificate at the time (to a police officer or anyone reasonably requiring it). Otherwise you must:
2. Report the accident to the police as soon as possible. You then have five days to produce your insurance. (But the police can ask you to produce your driving licence, insurance certificate and MOT certificate – see p. 11.)

Legally, you can drive on. You need not stop, report the accident, or give your name and address. (But the police can ask you to produce your driving licence, insurance certificate and MOT certificate – see p. 13.)

STOP! You must also:
1. Give your name and address (and those of the vehicle owner) to anyone reasonably requiring them at the time of the accident. Otherwise you must:
2. Report the accident to the police as soon as possible. (But the police can ask you to produce your driving licence, insurance certificate and MOT certificate – see p. 12.)

## WHAT'S THE PENALTY?

*For failing to give details after an accident*

*For failing to report an accident to the police*
MAXIMUM PENALTY: four to nine penalty points (plus an endorsement) and a fine of £2,000. Disqualification possible
LIKELY PENALTY: four penalty points and a £50 fine

*For failing to stop after an accident*
MAXIMUM PENALTY: five to nine penalty points (plus an endorsement) and a fine of £2,000. Disqualification possible
LIKELY PENALTY: five penalty points (plus an endorsement) and a fine of about £100. If you are also guilty of failing to give details (or to report to the police), disqualification is likely

*For failing to produce documents to the police within seven days*
MAXIMUM PENALTY: a £400 fine
LIKELY PENALTY: a £30 fine

*(For more on penalties see p. 216)*

### When do I have to produce my insurance certificate, driving licence, log book, etc. after an accident?

If you are involved in an accident in which someone else is injured you must produce your insurance details (see above), but there will be no need to produce your driving licence or your log book. If you produce your insurance certificate at the time of the accident you will not have to produce it to the police (nor will you have to report the accident to the police). Only if you do not produce your insurance details at the time of the accident do you have to notify the police (and produce your insurance to them within five days). In any event, if no one else is injured in the accident you do not have to produce your insurance – either to the people involved in the accident, or to the police.

### But can't the police always ask to see my driving licence and insurance certificate?

The police can often ask to see a motorist's driving licence and insurance certificate. So the police will often be able to ask for these even when the laws for reporting accidents (see above) merely talk about producing insurance or giving names and addresses, etc.

You have to produce your *driving licence, insurance certificate* and *MOT certificate* to a police officer if any of the following apply:

● you are driving on the road, or
● you are suspected of having been involved in an accident, or
● you are suspected of having committed a motoring offence.

In practice, therefore, the police can always ask motorists to produce their licence, insurance or MOT certificate when they are involved in an accident – and when they are reporting an accident to the police at a later date (see above).

If you have to produce any of these documents you normally have seven days in which to do so (see p. 239).

For penalties, and for further information on failure to produce a driving licence, for failure to produce an insurance certificate, and for failure to produce an MOT certificate see p. 242.

### Must I report an accident if I am riding a pedal cycle at the time?

Probably not. The rules on stopping and on reporting accidents (see above) apply only to drivers of 'vehicles' – in other words cars, lorries, motorbikes, etc. They do not apply to pedal cyclists. Of course, responsible cyclists will stop after an accident, and give their name and address to anyone who reasonably requires it.

In fact there is another piece of road traffic law that can be used in this situation. Entirely separate from the normal rules on reporting an accident (see above) is a law which says you must give your name and address to someone who 'reasonably requires it' if that person thinks you have been guilty of careless or reckless driving (or cycling). So, if your careless pedalling (or indeed careless driving) caused an accident, you would have to give your name and address if asked for them – for instance, by the person whose car you pedalled into. If you did not you would be committing an offence. In fact this would apply even if there was not an accident – if you were thought to be guilty of careless or reckless pedalling you would have to give your name and address.

## After the Accident

### What should I do if I am involved in an accident?

Irrespective of the laws on stopping and exchanging names (see p. 11), follow these guidelines:

**Don't**

- shout at (or hit!) the driver
- move any of the vehicles until their positions have been marked or noted
- apologize, offer excuses, or say anything that you might later regret. You should be careful about admitting liability for the accident (see below)
- make a statement to the police. Immediately after the accident you are likely to be flustered and upset. It is better to wait until you have calmed down. However, you must remember that you have to produce your driving licence, insurance certificate and MOT certificate, if asked by the police (see p. 15).

**Do**

- stop
- check whether anyone has been injured
- call the police if the accident is serious. They will probably attend only if someone was injured – but if in doubt call them
- take the names and addresses of everyone involved in the accident. The other drivers must give you their names, addresses and vehicle registration numbers (and also the names and addresses of the owners of the cars if different). If anyone has been injured you can ask them to show their insurance certificates. Similarly you must be prepared to give them this information if they ask for it. In practice it is better to give this information whether or not the law says you have to
- be sure to ask the witnesses for their names and addresses. If you cannot get them – or it looks as though the witnesses are about to drive off – make a note of the registration numbers of the cars they were in. You may be able to use this information later to trace the owners of the cars
- write down any explanations or apologies given by the other motorists – or by witnesses
- make a note of the extent of damage to other vehicles. If you can, make a note of the extent of any injuries
- if there is likely to be any argument about who is to blame try to mark the positions of all the vehicles. Ideally you would do this by marking the wheel positions with a piece of chalk. Realistically, you probably won't have chalk with you – so make a rough sketch plan. If possible pace out distances between cars, kerbs, white lines, etc.

**Afterwards**

- while the facts are still fresh in your mind make a full description of what happened. Note the time, road conditions, road layouts, position of signposts, damage to vehicles, the extent of any other traffic, road markings, any obstructions that might have obscured vision, where the impact occurred, skid marks, etc. If you have a camera it might be helpful to take a photo of the scene of the accident – even if the cars have been moved
- report the accident to your insurance company (see below)
- check whether you have to report the accident to the police (see above).

### *Should I admit liability for the accident if I was to blame for it?*

That's a difficult question to answer! Ideally you should, and in practice you can usually do this without having to worry too much about the consequences. The difficulty is that it is probably a term of your insurance policy that you do not admit liability. Policies often say that 'the insured person shall not make any admission of liability without the previous consent of the Company'. In other words, if you admit liability you will have broken the terms of your policy – and the insurance company could refuse to pay up. Legally they would be fully entitled to do so. In practice insurance companies rarely do this, but take a realistic attitude and appreciate that it is right for guilty motorists to admit liability. But you must be careful. For instance, if you were involved in several accidents, and admitted liability for each of them, you would probably find that your insurance company would say that you had broken the terms of the policy. In that case they would probably pay compensation to the victims of the accidents, and then try to recover the money from you.

The other disadvantage of admitting liability is that the police may use your admission as evidence against you in a careless-driving prosecution. Remember that you do not have to be driving particularly badly to be guilty of careless driving. If you caused an accident, you might well be found guilty of careless driving (see p. 59); so by admitting liability you might bring a careless-driving prosecution on yourself.

Those are the legal considerations. You may however feel there is a more important consideration – that, if you were the cause of the accident, you should say so. After all, if you admit liability it is almost certain that the victim of your bad driving will receive proper compensation. If you have clearly said that the accident was your fault it will be difficult for your insurance company to wriggle out of having to pay up. You may well feel that it is more important that your victim should have proper compensation than that you should worry about these legal technicalities. It is for you to decide.

### Must I tell the insurance company about the accident?

Yes. Your insurance policy will have small print which says you must tell them about the accident. Often there is a fixed time period (usually seven days), or the policy simply says you must report the accident 'as soon as reasonably possible'.

If the accident is at all serious you should definitely tell the insurance company straight away. If you do not tell them they may well say that you have broken the terms of the policy. If that happens they will probably pay out on any valid claim but then expect you to reimburse them.

If the accident is trivial you may think it a waste of time to tell the insurance company. The best advice is always to tell them – if you do that you can't go wrong. If it is obvious that there was no real damage, and no one was injured, you may decide it is simply not worth telling the insurance company – on the basis that it wasn't really an accident at all. But if it should later turn out that you were wrong, that there was damage or injury, you should tell the insurance company straight away. In practice insurance companies take a fairly realistic attitude – if they think you behaved reasonably in not bothering to tell them about the accident (e.g. it didn't seem that anyone was injured) they will not hold this against you.

Bear in mind that simply telling the insurance company about the accident will not affect your no-claims bonus. All you need to do is send them a letter telling them briefly about the accident and saying that, as yet, no claim has been made. If you do not think a claim will be made (because it was a trivial affair) then tell them, and say that you are merely notifying them of the accident because it is a term of your policy. They will realize why you are doing this, and it will not affect your no-claims bonus in any way. You only lose that if a claim is made on the policy – merely reporting an accident is not the same as making a claim (see p. 125).

### Will the police investigate how the accident happened?

It depends how serious the accident was. If someone was injured the police will probably take statements from everyone involved. If you are asked to give a statement you should remember you do not have to give it if you do not want to. It is entirely up to you (but, if you refuse, the police may think you have something to hide!). The police will, as a matter of course, check the driving licences, insurance and MOT certificates of all the drivers and cars involved.

If someone was seriously injured it is possible that the police will do more than this, and try to work out how the accident happened. The police have specially trained Accident Investigation officers who have special techniques for working out what happened at the scene of an accident. For instance, they may be able to use the length of a skid mark as an indication of how fast the car was going; they can calculate thinking times and braking times; they can work out the sequence of pedestrian lights, and calculate how far a person might have been across the road at the time of the accident, etc. Their aim will be to produce a scenario of what probably happened – what each of the drivers did, when they reacted, and when they should have reacted. But these detailed investigations are only carried out in a few serious cases – the police don't have enough officers to do it more often. Similarly the police have vehicle examiners who might carry out a detailed examination of a car involved in a serious accident. This should show whether any defects in the car might have played a part in the accident.

The police inquiries (whether simply the taking of a few statements or a complete accident investigation) goes into a document called a Police Report. When the Police Report is completed the police will decide whether to prosecute anyone.

The Police Report is usually the most detailed information on a road accident, so the lawyers and insurance companies advising the motorists will want to get hold of a copy. It will be invaluable in helping them decide who was to blame for the accident – who was negligent and who has to pay compensation. This, after all, is what the insurance companies are worried about. The police will provide them with copies (the Report costs about £25) once any criminal prosecutions (e.g. careless driving) have been finished.

The upshot is that the results of the police investigations can be used in deciding who was to blame – and which insurance company therefore has to pay out.

### What criminal prosecution might be brought?

It all depends on the facts. In practice it is extremely easy to commit the offence of careless driving (see p. 59), and this charge is often brought against someone who is responsible for an accident. If the police checks showed that someone did not have proper insurance, MOT, etc., prosecutions would be brought for each of those offences (see pp. 122 and 175).

### When will I know if I am going to be prosecuted?

Probably not until some time later. However, it is quite possible that you will receive a Notice of Intended Prosecution within fourteen days of the accident. This is not a definite indication that you will be prosecuted – it is a legal requirement that the police give you a formal warning of possible prosecution for particular motoring offences. See p. 243 for more on the Notice of Intended Prosecution. See p. 245 for time limits on prosecuting.

## Compensation for Accidents

### How do I claim compensation?

The first thing is to contact your insurance company. Whether they will pay you compensation will depend upon the type of insurance that you have:

*Comprehensive cover.* Your insurance company will pay for the damage to your car – irrespective of whether you were to blame for the accident. If you were injured you might be able to claim something off your insurance company. However, you will certainly not be able to claim full compensation. Your comprehensive policy probably says you get a fixed amount if you suffer certain serious injuries (e.g. £1,000 for loss of an arm or £2,000 if you die). These fixed amounts are paid irrespective of your actual losses – for instance, if you lose an arm and so are unable to work your losses are likely to be much more than £1,000. If you want extra compensation you will have to claim off one of the other motorists involved in the accident. Although you may not get full compensation for your injuries, your passengers (and anyone else involved in the accident) will get full compensation – if you were to blame. Another difficulty may be that you have an *excess* on your policy (for instance, you pay the first £50 of any claim). So, even if you have comprehensive cover, you will probably not get 100 per cent reimbursement from the insurance company. You will either have to write off that £50 (or however much) or claim it off the other motorist (and if necessary sue for it).

*Third-party policy.* Your insurance company will not pay you any money. This is because your insurance covers only claims made by other people (e.g. your passengers or other people involved in the accident). If you were to blame for the accident your insurance company will meet their claims. Even if you were not to blame, your insurance company will not give you any compensation. You will have to make a claim against the other motorists involved (who will pass your claim on to their insurance companies). This is so whether you are claiming for injuries or for damage to your car, etc.

So the first thing to do is to contact your insurance company. Even though they may not pay you full compensation it is important that you tell them about the accident – otherwise you may not be fully covered if claims are made against you (see p. 19).

### Should I make a private settlement with the other motorist?

It depends. If a claim is small the motorists will often agree to sort it out between themselves. Motorists who are to blame may well feel it is better to pay a small amount of compensation from their own pockets – rather than claim off their insurance and so risk losing some (or all) of their no-claims bonus. So, if the claim is small, there is no harm in settling it directly with the other motorist.

But do not do this if there is any question of the claim being a large one. For instance, if someone has been injured you should not settle the case privately. Bear in mind that what may seem to be a trivial injury can later have complications (e.g. a simple bump on the head can lead to epilepsy at a later date). So it is most important that you do not settle any claim for injuries without involving your insurance company. However, a small claim for vehicle damage can safely be settled privately, without involving the insurance company.

If you do agree to pay money to the other motorist you should get a receipt for it. Write a letter like this:

I refer to the accident at . . . on . . . when my car was in collision with yours. We have now agreed that I will pay you £... in full and final settlement of any claim that you may have against me as a result of that accident. You will of course appreciate that I do not admit liability for the accident and that this payment is without prejudice to my denial of liability. Please sign the copy of this letter as a record of this agreement.

Yours sincerely

### What if I am injured in the accident?

Injury claims should always be treated seriously. Having said that, there will always be simple cases, where you may, for instance, have had a few grazes and a bit of a shake-up. But if the accident is in any way serious – or could be at a later date – you should take proper legal advice. Bear in mind that a minor collision can still cause serious injuries – many people have suffered from serious whiplash neck injuries from accidents at only 5 or 10 m.p.h.

If you have been injured:

1. Make sure the police are notified of the accident. Try to get them to attend the scene so that they will carry out inquiries.

2. Do everything in the checklist on p. 17.

3. Keep a note of all your expenses arising from the accident (e.g. prescriptions, cost of medicine, phone calls, taxi fares, etc.). Wherever possible get receipts for each of these items. You will be able to include all these items in your claim – but you will have to show that you spent the money, so it is important that you keep a full record (see below).

4. Take legal advice. There is no point in seeing a solicitor straight after the accident. Do not worry if a few months slip by. In practice a solicitor will not be able to take any steps to get compensation until the Police Report of the accident is available – and this will not be for some months (the police will not release it until any criminal prosecutions have been ended – see p. 20).

5. Your solicitor will be able to give you an initial idea of whether or not you have a claim. This will depend upon who was to blame for the accident: in other words, who was negligent – see p. 177 for more on this. The important point to realize is that you will only get compensation if someone else was to blame – and you will certainly not get any compensation if you were solely to blame for the accident.

6. Your solicitor will be more confident about whether or not you can get compensation after receiving the Police Report. If in the solicitor's opinion you have a sound claim – and if you meet the means test – you should be advised to apply for legal aid. See p. 142 for how the legal-aid

system works, and for the rules on financial eligibility. If you are eligible
for legal aid you should certainly apply. If you have the misfortune to go
to a solicitor who does not do legal-aid work you would be better off
going to a different solicitor. The chances are that a solicitor who does
not do legal-aid work does not specialize in personal-injury work (and
also that you will be overcharged!).

7. Your solicitor will make a claim for damages against the other
driver. That driver will pass the claim on to his or her insurance company
and the solicitor will then correspond with the insurance company – not
with the driver. Although the claim is technically brought against the
other motorist, the practical reality is that all dealings are with the
insurance company – and it is they (not the driver) who decide whether
or not to pay up. In practice insurance companies are very reluctant to
admit liability and you should not expect them to do so at this stage.

8. Your solicitor will have to obtain a medical report on your injuries,
and will want a report from a hospital consultant if the injuries were
anything other than trivial. The consultant at the hospital where you
were treated, or quite possibly an independent consultant who has
special experience of personal-injury claims, may be asked to provide
this report. In a serious case both may be approached. Either way, the
solicitor will need to have a detailed medical report which summarizes
your injuries, the extent of your recovery and your likely progress in the
future. There is no point in pressing your solicitor to get a medical report
at too early a stage. It is bound to take some time before your injuries
settle down, and before the doctor can give some sort of realistic
appraisal. Getting a medical report before then is a waste of money. For
instance, if your leg is still in plaster there is no way that the doctor could
provide a useful medical report on your chances of recovery.

9. Your solicitor will also try to work out your financial losses, and
should be able to claim for all the items you have noted on your list of
expenses – with receipts! In addition you will need to claim your loss of
earnings. Your employer will have to give details of what you would
have earned – but you will only get the net figure (i.e. income tax, sick
pay, statutory sick pay, national insurance, etc. will all be deducted).
Any supplementary benefit or unemployment benefit will also have to
be deducted when your wage loss is worked out. So far as the law is
concerned you can only claim for your actual loss – the difference
between what you received and what you would have received had you
been working.

10. If your claim has still not been settled – in practice most are

24

(though the other side may not admit liability) – your solicitor will sue the other motorist. This will be in the High Court if your claim is worth more than £5,000, in your solicitor's view; otherwise in the more informal county court. A different lawyer, called a barrister, will probably prepare the formal court documents for the solicitor. Your formal claim document will be prepared, and in return the other motorist's solicitors will prepare their formal defence. There are then various procedural steps that the solicitors take. At the end of this, if the case is still not settled, your case will go to trial in court. You will have to attend the court and give evidence. Your witnesses will also have to give evidence. At the end the judge will decide who was to blame. If you win your case you will get compensation, and you could also expect to have your legal costs paid by the other side.

### How long does all this take?

It can take a very long time. The vast majority of injury claims are settled by negotiation, and without suing. They may be settled within, say, six months. But the more serious the claim, the more likely it is that it will take longer to settle. This is for two reasons. Firstly, if the injuries are serious it is likely to be longer before the doctors are able to give a definite indication of what sort of recovery will be made. Obviously the case cannot be settled until it is known what the long-term effects of the injury will be. Secondly, the insurance companies will be much more reluctant to settle the claim if a lot of money is involved. They will do what they can to delay. It is quite common for a serious injury case to take three years before it goes to trial – and in a difficult case (e.g. where it is very arguable as to who was to blame, or where the injuries are serious) a delay of four or five years is not unusual.

As a victim you will probably find the whole legal process daunting and dispiriting. You will probably find that the insurance company doctor suggests that you are malingering – that you are not doing all you can to get back to work and that you are exaggerating your injuries. You will find that you have to prove every item of your claim – you will be asked for receipts for the most trivial items. You will have to attend numerous medical examinations. You will sometimes feel as though you were to blame for the accident – not that you were the innocent victim. All in all it is a depressing experience. However, if you want full compensation you will have simply to stick it out and go through the legal minefield. You may find it helpful to get in touch with one of the various victim support groups, where you will be able to discuss your experiences with other victims.

The obvious solution to all of this is to abolish the present negligence system of compensation (i.e. who was to blame?) and replace it with a system of automatic compensation. In other words, all victims would get compensation from the State. See p. 184 for more details of this. Realistically, this is not going to happen. A more feasible reform would be to take personal-injury claims away from the courts. The courts are slow, inefficient, expensive and intimidating. It would be better to have personal-injury claims heard by specialist personal-injury tribunals. These would be similar to the industrial tribunals that hear unfair dismissal claims – informal hearings, before three specialists (e.g. a lawyer, doctor and a lay person). Surely such tribunals would provide more humane – and speedier – justice for victims.

### How will the court decide who was to blame for the accident?

The court will want to work out who was negligent. The judge will try to work out what happened in the accident – how it could have been avoided, who was careless, and who was to blame. Then the judge will apportion blame – not necessarily all on one person. For instance, if two cars were involved the judge might decide that both drivers were partly to blame, and that there was 'contributory negligence' on the part of each driver.

See p. 177 for more on negligence and how the courts try to work out who was to blame for a road accident.

### Can I include the cost of private medical treatment in my claim?

Yes. If you choose to have private medical treatment those bills can be included in your claim. The other motorist's insurance company cannot say that you should have used the free NHS.

### Can I hire a replacement car?

Yes. But it must be a similar car to yours – for instance, the owner of a Mini cannot hire a Rolls!

## *How much will my claim be worth?*

You will probably need a lawyer to tell you this. But your claim will be made up of some or all of the following:

1. *Vehicle damage.* Obviously you will want to include the cost of repairing your car. If your car was a write-off you will want its fair value (see p. 127).

2. *Your losses and expenses.* These would include medical expenses, travel expenses (i.e. the extra cost because you don't have a car), extra phone calls, value of clothes ruined in the accident, etc. In addition you would want to claim any loss of earnings. See above (p. 124) for how the loss of earnings is calculated. If your injuries mean that you will be off work in the future – or that you will earn less – your claim will include compensation for those future losses. Unfortunately the law will not give you full compensation. For instance, if a thirty-year-old man is unable to work he will not get thirty-five years' loss of earnings (i.e. until he is sixty-five). The court will say that he is benefiting by having the money early, besides which he might have died anyway! Realistically, he would probably get fifteen to seventeen years' loss of earnings.

3. *For your injuries.* It is extremely difficult to put a monetary value on an injury. Partly this is because no two injuries are the same in their consequences, and partly because different people take different attitudes to injuries. You will certainly need specialist advice in valuing an injury. Overall most lawyers would agree that English courts put an extremely low monetary value on injuries. Certainly the awards they make are extremely mean when compared to awards made in America. For instance, in this country the amputation of an arm or leg might be worth (say) £25,000, or the loss of an eye about £20,000. Not much is it? The less serious the injury, the more difficult it can be to value it. This is because the smaller the amount, the more open it is to individual interpretation and feeling. The general point to realize is that compensation for injuries is not generous. A rough idea of compensation levels is given by these figures (1985 guidelines issued to compensate victims of criminal attacks):

# The Motorist and the Law

| | |
|---|---:|
| broken nose (displaced) | £700 |
| broken nose (undisplaced) | £150 |
| broken jaw (needs wiring) | £1,250 |
| loss of two front upper teeth (but fixed bridge inserted) | £1,000 |
| loss of two front upper teeth (no bridge inserted) | £1,200 |
| severe face scar (from one ear to edge of mouth) on man | £4,500 |
| severe face scar (from one ear to edge of mouth) on woman | £7,000 |
| loss of one eye | £12,000 |
| total loss of hearing | £32,000 |

## In addition, magistrates' guidelines are:

*Compensation in the magistrates' court: guidelines suggested by the Magistrates Association (1985)*

| Type of injury | Assumption as to pain | Suggested sum |
|---|---|---|
| Graze | Considerable pain for a few days; a little after a week. | £35 |
| Bruise | More variable. Generally speaking, the closer to a bone the more painful. Likely to be painful for a couple of weeks. | £50 |
| Cut | Depends on size and whether stitched. Pain likely to have gone in two weeks. | £50–£150 |
| Sprain | Likely to be painful for three or more weeks. | £75–£150 |
| Fracture | Arms around four weeks. Legs or ribs around six weeks. | £150–£400 |
| Head injury | Headaches unpredictable, average of a month. More serious if knocked out. | £100–£400 |
| Scarring | Important to consider position and likelihood of permanency, especially on face and if young. | £200–£500 |
| Loss of tooth | Depends on position and age of victim. | £60–£150 |

*Note*
1. More compensation is likely if the victim is elderly or infirm, or if the injury is in a particularly sensitive area of the body.
2. Less compensation is likely if there was provocation by the victim or if the injury was less serious than might normally be expected.

Our system of compensation is not generous. As victim you will have to prove every one of your losses. You will be expected to justify every pound that you claim! You will certainly find that being a victim is not a rewarding experience! One trap you should definitely not fall into is to read newspaper reports of damages awards and compare them with yours. Those newspaper reports are usually totally misleading. For instance, suppose two people suffer similar accidents – both lose part of the little finger in the accident. One is a clerk. He is off work for six weeks, but receives full sick pay from his employers during that time. His claim will probably only be worth £1,000 or so. The other victim is an international concert pianist, who is currently earning £50,000 a year. He is aged thirty-five, and could have expected his career to have continued until he was sixty. He too will receive £1,000 for the injury to his finger. But in addition he will be able to claim for his loss of earnings – because he has had to abandon his career as a concert pianist. The court may give him, say, fourteen years' loss of earnings – although it would deduct tax and make an offset for the earnings he now might be able to make as a music teacher. At the end of it the court takes a fairly mean approach – as always – and awards him £200,000. The clerk reads in his newspaper next morning that the court has awarded £200,000 for an identical injury. Not surprisingly the clerk may well think that his solicitor has negligently undersettled the claim – but, in fact, this is not the case.

### How do I find a good accident solicitor?

It is important to choose a solicitor who knows about accident claims called personal-injuries claims by solicitors. Try to find out the name of a specialist solicitor in your area. Bear in mind that the solicitor who did your conveyancing or your divorce may be extremely efficient at those branches of law – but totally useless at a personal-injuries claim. So try to find a specialist. Your local CAB may be able to help you with the name of a suitable solicitor. If you are in the AA or RAC you may find that they are able to give you free legal advice and put you in touch with their solicitors. See p. 299 for details of the AA and RAC schemes.

**Why can't the criminal court give me compensation when the other motorist is prosecuted?**

It would be a good idea if the magistrates' court could order compensation to be paid to the victim (e.g. the person who was injured by the accident, or whose car was damaged). Unfortunately it cannot. Surprisingly magistrates can order compensation in all other cases of injury and damage – but not if the claim is the result of a road accident. So the magistrates do not have the power to award compensation against guilty motorists. The only exception is with a claim for a stolen car; the court can order the thief, if convicted, to pay compensation to the owner (i.e. for damage caused to the car, or its value if it is a total loss).

# Animals

*Who is to blame if an animal causes a road accident?*

As always, it depends on the facts. Bear in mind that when we talk about blame we are not concerned with criminal liability (can someone be prosecuted), but with who is to pay for the damage caused. This is a *civil* claim – suing for damages caused by the negligence of the person in charge of the animal – and is completely separate from the question of prosecution.

The usual rule is that the owners of animals will be liable if they are negligent in the way they looked after the animal. In other words, if an accident was their fault (e.g. they did not take sufficient care when herding cows along the road), they will be liable. On the other hand, if they were not to blame in any way – they did everything that could reasonably be expected of them – they will not be to blame, and so will not have to pay compensation.

However, the motorist must keep a good look-out for animals – and take care when approaching them. As the Highway Code says.

Go slowly when driving past animals. Give them plenty of room and be ready to stop if necessary. Do not frighten the animals by sounding your horn or revving your engine. Watch out for animals being led on your side of the road and be especially careful at a left-hand bend.

*What if a cow causes an accident?*

The normal rules apply – farmers will be liable if they were negligent. If they were not negligent, they will not be liable – and motorists will not get any compensation for their injuries, or for damage to their vehicles:

*A cow was being unloaded from a transporter at Guildford Market. This was being done carefully, and in the proper way. It ran away without any warning, and there was nothing that could be done to stop it. It then took fright – because so many people were shouting and trying to stop it. After a long journey it was panicked by a car horn, and eventually knocked down a pedestrian. The injured pedestrian claimed damages. Held: no one was to blame. The people who had been unloading the cow had not been negligent – they had done all that could reasonably be expected of them, and they could not be criticized. That being so, no one was to blame, so the injured pedestrian did not get any compensation.* Thorp *(1957)*

Each case depends upon its own facts. In particular farmers should be especially careful when taking a herd of cows along a road. Usually it will be necessary to have two people in charge. They must do all they can to warn approaching traffic. As the Highway Code says:

If you are riding or herding animals after sunset, you should wear light-coloured or reflective clothing and carry lights which show white to the front and red to the rear.

If you are herding animals, keep to the left of the road and if there is someone with you send him along the road to warn drivers at places such as bends and brows of hills where they may not be able to see. If your herd is very large, divide it into smaller groups.

A farmer who does not follow this advice, and does not take proper precautions, will be liable if there is an accident:

*A herd of cows had to be moved from a field to the farm, along some narrow country roads. It was a dirty November evening, so the farmer parked her car at the entrance to the field – with headlights on and facing oncoming traffic. She had two farm-hands to help her. One was to go at the front of the herd, and the other at the rear. Neither had lights. A car came along the road and the farmer stood in the road to wave it down, but the driver of the car was confused by the poor visibility – and was blinded by the headlights. She thought there was some kind of robbery or hold-up taking place so she accelerated. She ploughed into one of the herdsmen. His widow sued the car driver, and also the farmer. Held: both the farmer and the car driver were to blame. The car driver should not have accelerated in the way that she did. She was one third to blame. However, the major responsibility lay with the farmer. She should not have left the headlights on so that they dazzled oncoming traffic – and she should have given the herdsmen lights (as suggested by the Highway Code). She was two thirds to blame. So one third of the widow's compensation came from the driver's insurance company; the rest came from the farmer (who, one hopes, was also insured).* Andrews *(1971)*

*A motorist was driving along the main Ilfracombe–Barnstaple road at about 40 m.p.h. Suddenly a cow charged out of an open gateway while it was being taken to the farm for milking. The car driver did all he could to avoid the accident – he jammed on his brakes, but could not avoid hitting the cow. He sued the farmer for the damage caused to his car. Held: the farmer was to blame. He should have not have left his seventeen-year-old son in charge of the cows, but should have had two men to supervise them. The car driver was not to blame in any way – he had not been going at an excessive speed – so he got full compensation from the farmer.* Friend *(1963)*

### What if a dog causes an accident on the road?

The same rules apply. It all depends upon whether or not the owner of the dog is negligent. A negligent owner will be liable to pay compensation. But if there was no negligence the owner will not have to pay compensation to anyone injured, or to anyone whose property was damaged by the dog.

So, it all depends on what is 'reasonable'. All too often motorcyclists are injured when dogs run out on to the road:

*Ms Sudron bought a pedigree puppy. To stop it escaping she had repairs done to her fence and gate. One afternoon, when she was out, her boyfriend did not notice that a visitor to the house had left the front gate open. The puppy darted out and caused a moped to crash. The driver of the moped claimed compensation. Held: Ms Sudron was not liable. She had not been negligent since she had taken all the precautions that could reasonably be expected of a dog owner. The injured moped rider went without any compensation.* Smith *(1982)*

*A motorcyclist was driving along in the evening, at about 40 m.p.h. A golden retriever was in the road, and it swerved and made the motorbike crash. Was the owner liable? Held: yes. There was evidence that the dog had previously got in the way of motorists – a cyclist had even complained about it to the owner. In these circumstances the owner should not have let the dog roam the street. So the dog owner was liable to pay compensation to the motorcyclist.* Howarth *(1953)*

In practice the courts are relatively reluctant to find a dog owner liable. The impression one has is that the courts will only find that there was negligence in a clear-cut case – such as the second example above, where there had been previous warnings to the dog owner. If dog owners know that their dog is a risk to traffic (e.g. it chases motorbikes, or it runs off without warning), they must take care. They should keep it on a lead when they go on the road, and make sure the front gate is locked. But, if there are no clear indications that a dog is dangerous, a court is unlikely to find the dog owner to blame.

One point to bear in mind is that motorists are always insured – so if they have an accident their insurance companies will meet the bill. Similarly most farmers are insured – so if cows, etc. cause accidents an insurance company will probably pay the bill. With dog owners it is different. Relatively few dog owners bother to take out insurance, and

The Motorist and the Law

judges know this. They realize that dog owners who are found to have been negligent will probably have to pay any damages out of their own pockets. Perhaps this explains why courts are reluctant to find dog owners to blame. However, the sensible advice to any dog owner is to make sure that you have adequate insurance.

Finally, dog owners should remember what the Highway Code says: 'Do not let your dog out on its own. When you take it for a walk on the road, keep it on a lead.'

### Is it illegal to drive with a dog loose in the car?

Perhaps. There is no specific criminal offence of having a dog loose in your car when driving along – however dangerous it may be. However, it is blindingly obvious (except, perhaps, to dog owners) that it is danger-ous to have an unrestrained dog climbing about in a moving car. From a practical motoring point of view the sensible advice is to ensure either that the dog is properly trained, so that there is no question of it clambering around the car, or, ideally, that it is tethered to a seat. Bear in mind that, even if the dog does not clamber over you while you are driving, it can still be dangerous – it can block your view from the rear window, and it can even be a distraction to other motorists. As the Highway Code says: 'If you have an animal in your car, keep it under control. Make sure it cannot disturb you while you are driving.'

While there is no specific criminal offence of having an unrestrained dog in a car, the police may be able to bring a charge of careless driving (see p. 59) – for instance, if the dog caused you to crash. Also, in one case, a motorist who allowed her dog to sit on her lap was found guilty of carrying a dangerous load (i.e. the dog!).

One final point. When you are leaving a dog in a car it is important to give it sufficient ventilation. In an extreme case a person who did not give the dog ventilation, and so caused distress to it, could be prosecuted under the cruelty to animals laws, though in practice this would be extremely unlikely.

### What if a horse causes a road accident?

The same principles apply. If negligent, the owner of the horse will have to pay compensation to anyone injured by it:

*The owner of a riding-school organized a gymkhana in a field. When a pony was being saddled it slipped the saddle and bolted. It jumped over a piece of rope that acted as a fence and ran out into the road, causing a car to crash. Was the riding-school owner liable? Held: yes. It was well known that a horse was likely to bolt in fear if the saddle slipped. The precautions to keep horses in the field were inadequate. Therefore full compensation had to be paid to the owner of the damaged car.* Bativala *(1970)*

The same applies if a horse is on the road and it swerves or shies, causing an accident. A horserider who has taken all reasonable precautions (e.g. was keeping well in to the left; the horse was properly trained and not known to be frightened of traffic) will not be liable. On the other hand, a careless horserider (e.g. was riding too quickly; knows that the horse does not like traffic; was riding in the middle of the road, etc.) will be liable if there is an accident. The advice given in the Highway Code should always be followed:

Before riding a horse on the roads, make sure you can control it in traffic. When riding, keep to the left. If you are leading a horse, on foot or while riding another, you should also keep to the left and keep the led animal on your left. In one-way streets proceed only in the direction of the traffic and keep to the left. You must not ride, lead or drive a horse on a footpath or pavement by the side of the road.

If you are riding a horse, you should wear a hard hat.

Similarly motorists must take care when passing horses. In the same way that horseriders will be liable if they are negligent, so will motorists be liable if their negligence causes an accident. Motorists should bear in mind the advice given in the Highway Code about driving slowly when going past animals, giving them plenty of room, and not frightening them. A negligent motorist will have to pay damages:

*A horse was being ridden on a path beside a narrow road. One of the horse's legs was in the road. A car came up from behind, and slowed down when it saw another car coming in the opposite direction. The car then passed, but went very close to the horse – almost brushing it. The horse was frightened; it reared up, and one of its hooves was caught in the car's bumper. It was seriously injured and had to be destroyed. The horse's owner claimed damages from the car driver – for her injuries and also for the value of the horse. Held: the car driver was liable because he had not taken sufficient care when passing the horse. Horses are entitled to be on roads, and motorists must take great care whenever passing them. So the horserider got compensation from the motorist (in practice, of course, from the motorist's insurance company).* Burns *(1969)*

If you are a horse owner, take out insurance, in case you are involved in an accident and found to be liable.

# The Motorist and the Law

### *If I run over an animal, do I have to report it to the police?*

Probably. The general rule is that you must report an accident to the police, within twenty-four hours, if an animal is injured. This is so even if no other property was damaged, or no person was injured. However, the word 'animal' in this context covers only horses, cattle, asses, mules, sheep, pigs, goats or dogs. If you hit any of these animals, and injure it, you must report the accident to the police. Note that animals such as cats and chickens are not included – you do not have to report the running over of one of those to the police. Nor do you have to tell the police if you run over a bird.

For more on reporting accidents to the police see p. 12.

# Brakes

*How frequently should I maintain my brakes?*

All the time! Every part of the braking system must be in good and efficient condition and properly adjusted. If it is not, you are committing an offence. It is as simple as that. The fact that you did not know the brakes were defective will not be a defence. If you are stopped by the police for a vehicle check (see p. 241), and your brakes are found to be defective, you cannot escape prosecution simply by saying you did not know they were defective. Obviously, if there is some hidden defect that you could not reasonably have known about, the court will take this into account when deciding on the severity of the sentence. In practice this means that you would get a lesser fine. Also you might avoid an endorsement and penalty points (see the penalty chart below).

You cannot rely on a recent MOT test as proof that the brakes are satisfactory (see p. 173).

There are very complicated and strict rules on braking systems. The basic requirement is that you should not tamper with the system as

## WHAT'S THE PENALTY?

*For defective brakes*

MAXIMUM PENALTY: a £1,000 fine, plus an endorsement (or even disqualification) and three penalty points. For a goods vehicle (including passenger vehicles with over eight seats) the fine can be up to £2,000

LIKELY PENALTY: a £40–£60 fine (it could be much more in the case of a goods vehicle – say £100 or £150 for a large vehicle). You will also get three penalty points and an endorsement unless you can show you did not know of the defective brakes (see p. 228 for more on this). You may get a £24 fixed penalty ticket instead (see p. 217)

*(For more on penalties see p. 216)*

fitted. You should, of course, also have rear brake lights – both of which must be working. There are restrictions on how bright these lights can be, so you will almost certainly be committing an offence if you wire your foglights up to the brake lights (see p. 151).

*Practical motoring:* **What are the shortest stopping distances?**

It is impossible to say. It all depends upon the type of vehicle involved, the road conditions and the reaction time of the driver. Because of these different factors, all one can do is give general guidance. What the Highway Code says is:

The safe rule is never to get closer than the overall stopping distance shown below. But on the open road, in good conditions, a gap of one yard for each mph of your speed or a two-second time gap may be enough. This will also leave space for an overtaking vehicle to pull in. On wet or icy roads the gap should be at least doubled. Drop back if an overtaking vehicle pulls into the gap in front of you.

*Shortest stopping distances – in feet*

| mph | Thinking distance | Braking distance | Overall stopping distance |
|---|---|---|---|
| 20 | 20 | 20 | 40 |
| 30 | 30 | 45 | 75 |
| 40 | 40 | 80 | 120 |
| 50 | 50 | 125 | 175 |
| 60 | 60 | 180 | 240 |
| 70 | 70 | 245 | 315 |

For most people these distances are meaningless. When you are driving along the road it is extremely difficult to work out the size of the gap between you and the car in front – especially if you are trying to do it in feet and inches! An easier way is to think of the gap in terms of car lengths. If you do this you will probably be amazed at the size of the gap that you should be leaving. For instance, at 30 m.p.h. there should be at least six car lengths between you and the car in front. At 50 m.p.h. there should be at least thirteen car lengths! And at 70 m.p.h. there should be a gap of no less than twenty-three car lengths! And, what is more, those figures should be doubled on wet or icy roads – so, next time you are driving down the motorway at 70 m.p.h. in the rain, check whether there is a gap of forty-six car lengths between you and the vehicle in front!

In practice these minimum stopping distances are ignored by numerous motorists.

*Practical motoring:* **What is the safest way of braking?**

Good braking is gentle and progressive. This means that you should begin braking early – do not wait until the last moment and then brake fiercely. It also means that you should brake progressively; start off with a gentle pressure on the brake pedal and then increase it before you stop. Not only is this more comfortable for you and your passengers (and less wearing on the brakes and the rest of the car), but it is by far the safest way of braking – you are much less likely to skid.

Remember that the brakes are not the only way of slowing down your car. The engine and gears also act as a brake – whenever you take your foot off the accelerator the engine will begin to slow down, and this will help to brake the car. Always use the braking effect of the engine to help bring the car to a smooth and gradual halt.

The Department of Transport manual *Driving* gives good guidance on the best way to stop:

- firstly, check your mirrors
- give any signals that may be necessary
- take your foot off the accelerator (the braking effect of the engine will immediately cause the car to begin to slow down)
- begin to press the brake pedal. Begin by pressing it gently, and then press more firmly
- just before the car stops press the clutch pedal down (otherwise the engine will stall). Do not do this too early – if you do you will lose the braking effect of the engine
- reduce the pressure on the brake pedal just as the car stops (except, obviously, if you are on a hill!). This makes for a smooth and jolt-free stop
- now you have stopped put the gear lever in neutral and apply the handbrake.

*Practical motoring:*
**What is the proper way of doing an 'emergency stop'?**

There is more to an emergency stop than simply slamming your foot on the brake pedal. The important point is that you should be able to stop the vehicle as speedily as possible – but without losing control of it. In practical terms this means:

- have both hands on the steering-wheel throughout
- press the brake pedal firmly – not so hard that you lock any of the wheels. Many learners press too hard and lock the front wheels
- do not put your foot on the clutch until just before you stop (otherwise you lose the helpful braking power of the engine)
- resist the temptation to use the handbrake as an extra means of stopping. Most handbrakes only work the rear wheels – so if you pull on the handbrake lever you will probably lock the rear wheels and get into a skid
- if you are in an emergency do not bother with indicators or other signals.

### Am I legally to blame if I drive into the back of another car?

Normally you will be to blame. After all, rule 46 of the Highway Code says: 'Never drive so fast that you cannot stop well within the distance you can see to be clear.'

When we talk about blame we are not concerned with criminal liability (e.g. can you be prosecuted by the police for careless driving), but with the question of who is to pay for the damage caused. This is a *civil* claim – suing for damages caused by the negligence of a motorist – completely separate from the question of prosecution by the police. A motorist – or, more likely, the motorist's insurance company – will have to pay compensation (i.e. for the damage and injury caused) only if he or she was negligent. See p. 177 for more information on the negligence laws.

The usual rule is that if you drive into the rear of another vehicle you will be liable and must pay full compensation. Usually, of course, your insurance company will meet the bill.

But, contrary to what some motorists believe, this is not a completely hard-and-fast rule. For instance, the driver of the vehicle in front may have done something extremely unexpected, and may thus be partly to blame:

*Ms Thompson was on her moped in a line of traffic. In front of her was a Triumph, and in front of that was a Morris. The Morris pulled up suddenly, to turn right. The Triumph braked fiercely and was able to stop without hitting the Morris. But Ms Thompson – on her moped – could not stop in time and crashed into the back of the Triumph. She was injured, and sued the owner of the Morris (i.e. the car that was going to turn right) for compensation. Could the driver of the Morris escape liability by saying that the accident was Ms Thompson's own fault – after all, shouldn't she have been observing the Highway Code and making sure she was going slowly enough to pull up in time? Held: yes and no. Ms Thompson was partly to blame, but so also was the driver of the Morris. Each was 50/50 to blame; thus, Ms Thompson got 50 per cent of her normal damages.* Thompson *(1973)*

In fact the rear driver may not be to blame at all:

*A bus was travelling behind a lorry. They were about 20–30 feet apart, and both were doing 15 m.p.h. The lorry braked suddenly, to avoid a pedestrian, and came to an almost immediate halt. The driver of the bus reacted straight away, but couldn't stop in time. He drove into the back of the lorry. The owners of the lorry sued the bus company for the damage caused to the lorry. Held: the bus driver was not to blame, and so the lorry company did not receive any compensation. The court decided that a motorist has to be on his guard so that he can deal with all 'traffic exigencies' that can reasonably be anticipated. If an unusual emergency occurs, and he does everything that can be expected of him, he need not be to blame.* Brown *(1945)*

Despite this case the normal rule remains that a motorist who drives into the back of another car will be solely to blame for the accident. Only if it can be shown that the vehicle in front braked extremely suddenly, with no signal or warning, is there any hope that some of the blame can be passed off on to the driver of the other vehicle. In practice, of course, that is likely to be difficult. Certainly if the vehicle in front is simply slowing down – not fiercely braking – the driver of the rear vehicle must expect to be solely to blame if there is an accident:

*A lorry was driving in the slow lane of the motorway, at night. The driver began to reduce his speed – not by braking, but simply by taking his foot off the accelerator. Another lorry drove into the back of him, and that lorry then crossed the central reservation, killing an oncoming car driver. The family of the dead car driver sued both lorry drivers for compensation – they said that both had been negligent and so were liable for damages. The judge who heard the case agreed; he said that the driver of the first lorry was 10 per cent to blame (he should have given warning of his slowing down), and that the driver of the other lorry was 90 per cent to blame. The Court of Appeal disagreed. They overruled this finding, and found the driver of the second lorry to be 100 per cent to blame. The driver of the first lorry had acted perfectly reasonably.* Jungnikel *(1966)*

*Practical motoring:* **What causes a skid?**

A skid is usually caused by bad braking, bad steering or over-acceleration.

Remember that when you apply the brakes you shift the balance of weight of the car forward – so the front tyres grip the ground more and the rear tyres grip less. Further, if you are going round a bend at the time the weight of the car will be thrown on to the outside – in particular the outside front tyre will be taking a lot of the pressure, and the rear inside rear tyre will have least pressure of all. So it is easy to see how careless braking can cause a skid, and why it is important that your braking should be smooth and progressive – never fierce and harsh. The same applies to your steering, and to the way you accelerate.

If you get into a skid it may be possible to drive out of it – provided you have enough room left in which to manoeuvre. If you feel your car beginning to slide, or skid, the first thing to do is to take your foot off the brake pedal. Not surprisingly this is easier said than done! Your natural reaction will be to keep your foot on the brake – don't! Take your foot off the brake, and try to correct the slide by slightly moving the steering-wheel in the same direction as your skid. If this does not work – or if the skid is too serious – you will have to move the steering-wheel more positively. To do this you must 'drive out' of the skid. For instance, if the rear of the car is swinging out to the right, you must steer to the right; if the back of the car is skidding towards the left, you must steer as though you were going to turn left. The idea of this is to bring the front of the vehicle in line with the back and so get out of the skid. It will probably help if you take your foot off the accelerator – but don't do this violently: this is particularly important if it is the front wheels of the car that are beginning to slide and skid.

It is naturally when roads are wet, snowy or icy that you are most likely to get into a skid. Tyre grip is reduced, so you must leave a longer stopping distance. Generally you should allow at least double the normal stopping distance if a road is wet. In snow and ice the position is even worse – on ice, braking distances can be more than ten times the normal dry stopping distance. The answer is to ensure that you drive smoothly, as slowly as is necessary, and that your motoring is progressive. If in doubt remain in a low gear (the natural braking effect of the engine will help you control the vehicle) and avoid all sudden movements of the brakes, steering and accelerator. Plan ahead: get into a lower gear at an early stage and allow your speed to drop without the use of the brakes. If you are going around a corner think ahead – if you reduce speed sufficiently you may be able to get around the corner without having to touch the brakes at all. This will reduce your chances of skidding on any ice or snow.

### Will I be legally to blame if my car skids and causes an accident?

Almost certainly. When deciding who is to blame for an accident (i.e. who was negligent) the courts take the view that motorists must drive in such a way that their vehicle will not get into a skid. Basically if you get into a skid it is up to you to convince the court that the skid was in no way your fault. Needless to say, in practice this is extremely difficult to do. In an exceptional case you may be able to show that the skid was caused by an unknown defect in your steering or tyres – as in the case on p. 185. But, generally, if your car skids you will be found to have been negligent and so have to pay compensation for any damage caused:

*Ms Pratt was driving towards a very slight right-hand bend, at a normal speed. Suddenly her car skidded – crossing the road and hitting a pedestrian on the opposite pavement. Ms Pratt said she had not been negligent in her driving. She herself had a head injury and could not remember the accident, but all the evidence was that she was driving at a reasonable speed, and had not done anything wrong. In short, the accident was totally unexplained. Held: Ms Pratt was to blame. When a skid happens like this it is for the motorist to show that he or she was not to blame. Ms Pratt was unable to do this, and so she was liable in negligence. She had to pay full compensation to the injured pedestrian. (In practice, of course, this would have been paid by her insurance company.)* Brayshaw *(1947)*

# Buying and Selling a Car

*What legal protection do I have when I buy a car?*

It depends who you buy it from. There are different rules for:

- *buying from a dealer* (see p. 44)
- *buying at auction* (see p. 51)
- *buying privately* (see p. 52).

You have more legal rights if you buy from a dealer.


*I have bought a car, and I am not happy with it. What should I do?*

Do not delay – act quickly. The first thing to do is to check what your legal rights are. These will depend upon whether you bought the car from a dealer, or at auction, or privately (see below). The next thing to do is to take the car back to the person who you bought it from – and complain.

You should resist the temptation to carry on using the car and postpone complaining. The longer you leave your complaint, the weaker your position. If you delay there is a danger that you will be taken to have accepted the car with all its faults. That is why you are best off taking the car back straight away.


## Buying from a Dealer

### What rights do I have if I buy a car from a dealer?

If you buy a car from a dealer you have protection under the Sale of Goods Act. This is so whether you buy a new car or a secondhand car.

Under the Sale of Goods Act dealers make three promises to you – whether they want to or not! These promises are:

1. *The car will be fit for its normal use.* Quite simply the car must be fit

for use. Clearly, if the car is broken down and does not go, it is not fit for the purpose for which it was designed, and so the dealer will be in breach of this Sale of Goods Act promise. You will therefore have a claim against the dealer (i.e. to claim compensation by suing for damages).

2. *The car is of 'merchantable quality'.* In effect this means that the car must be of proper quality – bearing in mind the price you paid. For instance, suppose you buy a new car that has a scratch down the side. Clearly the car still works – and so it is fit for its purpose. Thus there has been no breach of dealer's promise no. 1 (above). But it is equally clear that the car is not of proper quality if it has a scratch down the side – the dealer will have broken promise no. 2 because the car is not of 'merchantable quality'. That is a straightforward example, but in practice it can be difficult to agree on whether or not a car is of merchantable quality. Basically what one is saying is that the car must be in reasonable condition for the price paid. It follows that you do not expect a secondhand car to be in such good condition as a new car. Similarly you do not expect an old banger that cost £200 to be in as good condition as a car (of the same year and model) that cost £750. It is all a matter of degree – what do you expect to get for the money? With a new car it is relatively easy to decide whether or not it is of proper quality. It is with secondhand cars that the real problems arise. What the buyer has to do is to prove that the defects were in existence at the time of the sale. This is why it is important that you should complain without delay. The more you delay, the more scope there is for the dealer to say that the defects have developed since you bought the car. Incidentally, the mere fact that you have spent money on repairing and mending the car is not sufficient proof that it was not of 'merchantable quality'. If you buy a secondhand car you must often expect to spend money on it. It all depends on the price, the type of car involved and what you could reasonably expect for the money. After all, all cars go wrong at some time. If you can show that the car was not of proper quality you will have a claim against the dealer (i.e. to claim compensation by suing for damages) for having broken promise no. 2.

3. *The car is as the dealer described it to you.* If dealers make specific promises about a car they will be bound by what they said. For instance, saying that a secondhand car has just been fitted with a replacement engine will make a dealer liable if this turns out not to be so. Similarly, if a car sold as being a 1981 model is in fact a 1980 one, the dealer's promise will have been broken. The law does not stop there – it goes further, and says that the dealer's sales talk must be true. A different Act (not the

Sale of Goods Act but the Misrepresentation Act 1967) makes dealers liable if their sales pitch is untrue. But the law will only intervene if a dealer makes clear statements of fact, on which you rely – merely expressing an opinion is different. For instance, if a dealer said: 'It's a good runner; it'll last for ever', the court will dismiss this as a mere sales pitch. In other words, it is not specific, or factual, enough for the dealer to be pinned down. On the other hand, a statement such as 'I can guarantee you can get 40 m.p.g. from this car' would make the dealer liable if you get much less than 40 m.p.g., as would saying that there is a new exhaust or an overhauled engine, or that there are new brake pads, if any of those claims turns out to be false. These are specific promises, and the dealer will be liable if they are unfounded. In practice it is often difficult to prove just what the dealer did say. This is why it is sensible to take a friend with you when you go to buy a car – the friend can act as a witness as to what the dealer said, if there should be a dispute at a later date. Similarly it is sensible to try and get dealers to commit themselves by putting their promises in writing – although they will probably be extremely reluctant to do so! But if you can prove what a dealer said, and it turns out to be untrue, the dealer will have broken promise no. 3. You will therefore have a claim (i.e. to claim compensation by suing for damages).

To summarize: a dealer who sells you a car makes three promises: that it is fit for use as a car; that it is of proper quality in relation to the price; and that any sales talk is true. If any of these promises are broken you can sue the dealer for compensation.

### Is there any way dealers can wriggle out of these promises?

They may try to. A dealer may say that you were specifically told about any defects, and you bought the car on that basis (e.g. 'But you knew about that, guv, that's why we sold it to you so cheap'). If that is true the dealer will have a defence, and will not be liable to you. If you buy the car knowing of a particular defect you cannot complain about that defect at a later date – but this assumes that you were told the truth. If you were misled as to the extent of the defect ('It'll only cost a fiver to fix') the dealer remains liable.

The other defence that the dealer may raise is to say that you inspected the car, and so you should have noticed any defects in it. To some extent that is true. Dealer's promise no. 2 – that the goods are of proper quality for their price – does not cover defects that you should have seen. In other words, if you inspect the car and fail to notice obvious defects, that is your look-out! What the law says is that you cannot complain about defects that you should reasonably have spotted. This is fair enough, but it should not be taken too far. Unless you are knowledgeable about cars you will only be expected to spot defects that any other lay person would have spotted. For instance, you should be able to spot if the wing is dented, or if the upholstery is torn. On the other hand, only an expert, and not you – as a lay person – could be expected to notice slight wearing sounds in the transmission and interpret them as indicating a fault in the car. Dealers often say that a person who examines a car takes it with all its faults. That is not so – you only take it with the faults that you could reasonably have spotted.

### Can the dealer get me to sign away my legal rights?

Many dealers have receipts that they ask customers to sign. Often the customers do not bother to read them – but if they did they would find that the small print said something like: 'I have inspected the vehicle and satisfied myself as to its condition.' When the unlucky customer comes back with a complaint the car dealer will then try to wave this piece of paper and argue that the customer has no claim. The dealer is wrong!

The law says that the dealer cannot wriggle out of the three promises (see above), which apply whether or not the dealer wants them to. So if you signed a receipt that said those promises were not to apply you could still sue. In other words, your having signed that piece of paper would not be held against you.

The obvious way of avoiding these problems is not to sign any receipt which implies that you are taking the car 'as found', or 'in its present condition'. Simply refuse to sign it. If the dealer refuses to sell you the car unless you sign you could try signing it, but writing in some extra words, making it clear that no faults are visible to you *as a lay person*. This will strengthen your hand, should there be arguments at a later stage.

To conclude, dealers cannot get out of their promises. Although they may argue that you should have realized there were faults, this argument is often not legally justifiable.

The Motorist and the Law

### *How should I complain to the dealer?*

As always, begin with a reasoned complaint. Do not exaggerate the complaints, and do not be rude or abusive. Present your case clearly and reasonably. Do not delay in seeing the dealer – go as soon as you realize there is something wrong with the car. It is often a good idea to have a friend with you. That friend can be a witness as to what was said.

If the dealer will not fix the faults, you must decide what to do next. It is usually sensible to write to the dealer (keeping a copy of the letter) recording the fact that you went in and complained about the defects (which you should list). This will be proof – if needed – at a later date that you did complain straight away.

If you intend to pursue the matter you will need independent evidence (from an expert) to confirm that the car is as faulty as you say it is. Ideally you would obtain an independent engineer's report from a motoring organization such as the AA or RAC. Alternatively you could go to a local garage and ask them to prepare a report. Either way you do need to obtain some written evidence confirming the defects in the car. Once you have done that it is usually a good idea to send a copy of that report to the dealer and ask for the defects to be fixed. You could say that unless the defects are made good within (say) fourteen days you will have them fixed elsewhere.

You should then be safe in having the work done by another garage. You will obviously want to try and recover the cost from the dealer who sold you the car. Provided you obtained independent specialist evidence (e.g. a report from an engineer) you should be able to sue without much difficulty. To do this you will need to sue in the county court. Most claims of this sort do not exceed £500, so you can use the small-claims procedure in your local county court. This procedure is designed to enable you to sue without the help of a lawyer. If you look up 'Courts' in the phone directory you should find the address of your local county court. They will be able to give you a free booklet on *Small Claims in the County Court* which will tell you what the procedure is, and what you need to do next.

Your main concern will probably be to get compensation (i.e. the cost of the repairs). But in addition you could check whether the dealer has broken the criminal laws (see below).

### Is it worth having a guarantee?

If you buy a new car it will probably come with a guarantee or warranty from the manufacturer. That guarantee or warranty is well worth having. If a defect appears within the time limit you should rely upon that guarantee or warranty.

Even with secondhand cars, dealers sometimes offer guarantees or warranties. Once again such a warranty should be accepted. But bear in mind that this guarantee or warranty can never take away the three promises that are made by the dealer (i.e. that the car is fit for use, that it is of proper quality for the price, and that the dealer's sales talk is true – see above).

Often a warranty will say that it covers only the cost of spare parts – labour is excluded. If the dealer would be liable to you under one of the three promises you will have a full claim – for both parts and labour. So you cannot be worse off by accepting the warranty or guarantee.

### Should I pay extra for a warranty?

Most warranties are given free by the manufacturer or dealer. However, it is sometimes possible to pay extra and get an extended warranty. This is not a normal warranty (i.e. from the dealer or manufacturer). In effect you – as the customer – will be taking out an insurance policy with an insurance company. If the car goes wrong the insurance policy will cover the cost. That is the theory – if not the practice.

In practice these extended warranties are often a bad buy. This is because the small print frequently makes them worthless. For instance, these insurance policies may require that the vehicle be regularly serviced, say that they do not cover 'normal wear and tear', impose strict timetables for submitting estimates, exclude 'minor' repairs, etc. In other words, the usual procedure is for these insurance companies to lay down numerous petty restrictions – which can then be rigidly enforced. The end result is that it is usually impossible for the average motorist to make a claim under these policies. They are so badly worded that they are usually not worth paying for. In addition several of the companies that introduced these policies have since gone into liquidation – and the people who paid the premiums have been left without a warranty.

### Is it best to buy from a dealer who is a member of a trade association?

Yes. The mere fact that a dealer is a member of one of the main trade organizations is not a guarantee that you will receive excellent service. This is because most trade associations do not have the resources to vet scrupulously all applicants for membership. However, the mere fact that a dealer is a member of a trade association is usually a good sign!

There is a Code of Practice for members of the Motor Agents Association (MAA) which covers the selling of cars, and also the carrying out of repairs and servicing. In Appendix 3, p. 312, you will find details of the Code of Practice. Check that it has been followed.

The most important part of the Code, for a person buying a car from a dealer, is that:

- the car should have been given a pre-sales inspection, and any defects should be displayed on a checklist. A copy of that checklist should have been given to the buyer
- customers should be given reasonable facilities for independent pre-sale inspection (e.g. a report by the AA)
- wherever possible the dealer should get a signed statement from the previous owner of the car as to its previous mileage. If the mileage cannot be guaranteed the dealer should specifically say so.

There is, of course, much more in the Code (see p. 312). Bear in mind that the Code only applies to members of the Association. The Code also sets out a procedure for dealing with complaints, and it offers low-cost arbitration as an alternative to court proceedings.

### Does it affect my legal rights if I buy a car on credit?

No. In fact, you may be legally better off if you buy through credit. There are three possibilities:

1. *If the dealer arranged the credit.* If the dealer arranged HP, a credit sale, etc. for you through a finance company, the finance company will be jointly liable with the dealer for any defects. In other words, you can sue the finance company if the dealer breaks any of the dealer's promises (see above). In practice, few motorists do this, but it is nice to know that – at the end of the day – if you cannot get your money off the dealer (e.g. who has gone bankrupt or disappeared) you will be able to get your money from the finance company.

2. *You used a credit card.* If you used a credit card, your credit card

company (e.g. Access or Barclaycard) will be jointly liable with the dealer. The same principles apply as with (1.). The credit card company will be equally liable with the dealer if the dealer has broken any of the three dealer's promises. For instance, if the dealer goes bankrupt, or disappears, you will be able to recover your compensation from the credit card company. (This applies only if the car cost more than £100 and less than £15,000.)

3. *If you fixed up your own credit arrangements.* If you arranged the finance yourself (e.g. by borrowing from a friend, or through a general overdraft from the bank or a second mortgage on your house) you will still have your normal rights against the dealer, but you will not have any additional rights against the person you borrowed the money from. For instance, although you may have borrowed the money from your bank they will not be liable in any way – even though they would have been liable if they had lent the money to you through their credit card organization (i.e. as in (2.) above).

Many people buy cars through HP, etc. arranged through finance companies. Similarly many people pay for car repairs, etc. through credit cards. However, very few of these motorists realize that the finance company or credit card company may be equally liable with the garage or dealer. In practical terms the finance company or credit card company will not want to be involved in the day-to-day handling of your complaint. They will simply refer it to the garage or the dealer. However, you may find that the finance company or credit card company puts pressure on the dealer to settle the complaint, so it may be a good tactical move to involve these companies even if you do not really intend to pursue your claim against them.

## Buying at Auction

### What are my legal rights if I buy a car at auction?

You have virtually none. The chances are that you will have no legal redress if you make a bad buy.

In theory the Sale of Goods Act applies if you buy a car at auction. Thus the normal three dealer's promises apply (see p. 44). But the big difference between buying at auction and buying from a dealer is that those three promises can be excluded. And in practice they always are!

All car auctioneers draw up standard terms and conditions which make it clear that neither they nor the person selling the car is liable for any defects, and that the usual promises do not apply. We have seen (p. 47) that a car dealer or garage cannot use small print to exclude the three promises. But an auctioneer can – and always does.

A further complication is that the auctioneer is not the seller, but just the agent for the seller. So under no circumstances could you have a claim against the auctioneer – your claim would be against the seller. However, there is no legal requirement for the auctioneer to tell you the identity of the seller. Sometimes you will be able to find this out through the registration document, but it is often the case that vehicles are put into auction by dealers (whose names are not on the registration document). Thus you could find that you buy a car in auction and are unable to find out who the seller was – and so you have no one to sue! If this happens your only hope is to contact the last registered keeper (i.e. the person in the registration book) and try and find out who the vehicle was sold to.

Buying in auction is therefore a risky business. On the positive side, you can save a lot of money on the price of your car; on the negative side, you could make a bad buy and then find you have no legal remedy.

## Buying Privately

### What legal rights do I have if I buy a car from a private individual?

Very few. It is important to realize that if you buy a car privately (i.e. from someone who is not a dealer) you do not get the same legal rights as you do if you buy from a dealer (see p. 44). We have seen that dealers promise three things: that the car is fit for use as a car; that it is of proper quality in relation to its price; and that their sales talk is true. If you buy from a private individual the only promise that will apply is that the sales talk must be true. In particular you will not have a promise that the car is of proper quality in relation to its price.

As regards sales talk, similar principles apply for private sellers as for dealers (see p. 45). If someone selling you a car makes false statements – by saying, for instance, that the car has a new clutch when it does not – you will have a claim against them. Similarly if they say the car has only done 25,000 miles – but they have turned the clock back from 50,000 to 25,000 – you will also have a claim against them.

In practice the difficulty usually lies in proving what the seller said – in producing evidence that promises were in fact made. This is why it is sensible to have a friend with you when you buy a car. He or she can be a witness as to what was promised.

The point to realize is that you cannot take the car back merely because you think you paid too much for it, or because it has since gone wrong. If you buy privately it is for you to check the vehicle out before you buy it (e.g. arrange an AA inspection). If you do not do this, and the car goes wrong, you will have no one to blame but yourself – unless the seller made specific promises about the car. But even then those promises must be relevant to your complaints. For example, if the person selling told you that the car had a new exhaust, and then shortly afterwards the clutch went, you would not have a substantial claim against them. True, you might be able to claim the cost of a new exhaust, but you could not claim the cost of a new clutch – because no promises about the clutch were made.

### I bought a secondhand car privately. How do I go about making a complaint?

You begin in the same way as you would when making a complaint to a garage (see p. 48). Make a reasoned complaint to the seller. Do this without delay.

If the seller will not make you a reasonable offer (e.g. some money back) it is a sensible idea to make a record of your complaint, by means of a letter.

Next you will have to decide whether or not a legal remedy is open to you against the seller. Remember that there will be a legal remedy only if some promise was made about the car that has turned out to be false. You will not have a remedy merely because the car is not such a good buy as you thought it was. If you have simply paid over the odds, or the car has gone wrong since then, that is your bad luck. However, if you do think you have a legal claim against the seller (i.e. because a promise turned out to be untrue) you should consider suing. Get a report from an independent garage (or the AA, or RAC) and then sue in the county court.

In fact, private sellers will often not realize how little legal responsibility they have when selling a car. It follows that it is often possible to negotiate with a seller even when the seller is not strictly liable, so it is always worth having a go at making a complaint (e.g. if a car has developed faults after it has been sold, in which case, though not legally liable, the seller may be morally liable!).

### What if a dealer pretends to be selling cars privately?

The motor trade is full of part-time dealers. These are people who regularly buy cars, and then sell them through small adverts – posing as private individuals.

Deciding whether a person is 'a dealer' or a private individual comes down to a question of degree. But the chances are that someone who has several cars, and is regularly buying and selling cars, will be a dealer – whether or not they have an official garage business.

If the person selling the car is a dealer, the normal dealer's promises (see p. 44) will apply. The mere fact that someone is selling a car through a small advert, and posing as a private individual, does not make it a private sale – such dealers will be bound in the usual way. This is obviously to the advantage of the buyer, who will have more legal rights against a dealer than against a private individual.

Finally, a dealer who is placing adverts in a paper and pretending to be a private individual is committing a criminal offence. If you have bought a car off someone who you suspect was really a dealer complain to the Trading Standards Office. They may be able to prosecute. In fact, if you are having trouble with the seller, threatening to make a report to the Trading Standards Office may be helpful when you are trying to negotiate a settlement!

## General Problems

### What happens if I buy a car that is stolen?

You will end up the loser.

You cannot buy a car without the owner's consent. Even if you act honestly and innocently you will not acquire ownership of the car.

When the police realize that the car is stolen they will impound it. It will then be handed back to its rightful owner – the person it was stolen from, not you.

The only legal remedy you will have is to sue whoever sold you the car. You will obviously have a valid claim against them for the money you paid for the car. In practice, of course, that remedy is likely to be worthless – people who sell stolen cars generally give false names and addresses and are untraceable! You are likely, therefore, to end up car-less and having lost your money.

To minimize the chances of buying a stolen car you should always insist that the person selling the car has the registration book. The registration book is not proof that the registered keeper is in fact the vehicle's owner, but it is usually a sound starting-point. If whoever is selling you the car is definitely the person named in the registration book, the chances are that they do own the vehicle. On the other hand, if their name does not appear in the registration document you should certainly ask for further proof.

### What if I buy a car that is on HP?

It is surprisingly easy to buy a car that is on HP and sell it to someone else. What happens if you are the innocent person who buys the car that is subject to an HP agreement? Fortunately you will be legally protected. The law says that in this special situation you can keep the car – provided you have no reason to know that it was on HP.

In this situation the finance company (i.e. the company that provides the HP) will be the loser. Their only remedy is to sue whoever sold you the car (i.e. the person who took out the HP). If they cannot recover compensation from this quarter they will bear the loss – not you. Provided you acted innocently you can keep the car.

You may find that the finance company writes to you asking you to return the car. If this happens you should firmly repudiate their claim, and point out that you bought the car innocently and in good faith. In these circumstances the car remains yours. If they persist in their claim consult a solicitor.

But this special protection will not apply if you bought a car from someone who stole it. In other words, if a car on HP is stolen, and you have the bad luck to buy it from a thief, you will not be legally protected. In that case, you will have lost your money, and your only claim will be against the thief who stole the car. Also, the special HP protection applies only to private individuals – so if you are a trader who innocently buys a car on HP you will not be protected: the car will belong to the HP company, not you.

### What if I buy a new car, and it has defects?

The position is the same as with any purchase from a dealer (see p. 44). You will have a claim against the dealer if the car is defective.

Often customers will want to return the car and ask for a replacement vehicle – or, indeed, for their money back. Unfortunately the law is not clear as to when they can do this. The general principle adopted by the law is to say that customers can do this, provided they have not 'accepted' the defects in the vehicle. So if you act quickly, and take the car back straight away, you are entitled to cancel the deal and have your money back. On the other hand, if you delay (for instance, you simply hope that the defects will sort themselves out) you will be taken to have 'accepted' the defects and it will be too late to reject the car. Your legal remedy will then be simply to seek compensation in the usual way (i.e. damages for the cost of repair, etc.).

It can be extremely difficult to decide whether or not a customer has 'accepted' the vehicle with its defects. Anyone faced with this difficult situation should take legal advice. In the meantime the car should be rejected straight away – do not delay at all.

### Do I have any legal remedy if I paid too much for the car?

No. All too often you can buy a car and then discover that you could have bought a similar car for a cheaper price elsewhere. Or you can look in various trade magazines and see that you have paid more than the list price. In this situation you will have no legal remedy. If you buy a car it is for you to check out prices before you buy. If you contract to buy a car at a particular price you will be bound by that contract. Unless the car has defects you will not have any legal grounds for complaining.

### Is it legal to turn back the milometer?

Private individuals who turn back the milometer (odometer is the proper word) will usually not be committing a criminal offence – but buyers may well be able to claim damages (i.e. compensation) if they find out that the mileage figure is incorrect.

'Clocking' by dealers, on the other hand, is a criminal offence. Dealers who sell a car having turned back the milometer will almost certainly be committing an offence under the Trade Descriptions Act 1968. This is so even if they put a large disclaimer on the milometer making it clear that the buyer should not rely on the stated mileage reading.

However, the milometer may have been turned back by a previous owner. When this happens a dealer may – in all innocence – sell the vehicle with a false mileage reading. Once again the chances are that such dealers will be committing an offence – even though they have acted innocently. The only defence they can raise is to show that they have acted 'with due diligence' and that they disclaimed the accuracy of the milometer. In practice this means that there must be a clear warning sign stuck to the milometer – the law says that the sign must be as 'bold, precise and compelling' as the milometer itself – simply putting up a small sign saying 'mileage not guaranteed' is not good enough. There must be a bold sign beside the milometer which clearly says that the milometer reading may not be accurate. Of course, if a dealer knows that the milometer reading is wrong (either through being the one who turned the clock back, or through knowing that someone else did), this simple disclaimer will not be good enough.

The law imposes strict standards on dealers. So if a dealer does claim to have sold the vehicle innocently, and not to have known that it had been clocked, the court will expect to be shown that the dealer 'took all reasonable precautions and exercised all due diligence' – in other words, that efforts were made to contact previous owners to check the correct mileage. Dealers who cannot do this are likely to be found guilty under the Trade Descriptions Act.

What is the best advice to help dealers avoid any risk of prosecution? Their best bet is probably to wind the clock back to zero and then put a sticker over the milometer stating that it has been taken back to zero because the true mileage is not known, and so that customers will not rely upon the stated mileage as being correct. There is a Code of Practice for the motor industry which has been approved by the Office of Fair Trading. This says:

● all descriptions, whether used in advertisements or in negotiations regarding the sale of used cars, should be honest and truthful. Terms which are likely to be misunderstood by the consumer and which are not capable of exact definition should be avoided

● copies of relevant written information provided by previous owners regarding the history of cars should be passed on to the consumer. This may include service records, repair invoices, inspection reports, handbooks and copy of warranty, as applicable

● reasonable steps should be taken to verify the recorded mileage of a used car

● unless the seller is satisfied that the quoted mileage of a used car is accurate, such mileage should not be quoted in advertisements, discussions or negotiations or in any documents related to the supply of the used car

● dealers should pass on any known facts about a previous odometer reading to a prospective customer, and if a disclaimer is used it should be in the following form:

1. WE DO NOT GUARANTEE THE ACCURACY OF THE RECORDED MILEAGE.

2. To the best of our knowledge and belief, however, the reading is CORRECT/ INCORRECT (strike out whichever does not apply).

A dealer found guilty of clocking can be prosecuted and fined up to £2,000. In practice the level of likely fines varies considerably. If the magistrates think the dealer deliberately clocked the vehicle, and misled the customer, the fine may be heavy – the court will probably want to make sure that the dealer loses all the profit made out of the transaction. In addition the court may make a compensation order, requiring the dealer to pay compensation to the customer. This might be assessed on the basis of the difference in value between the vehicle with a high mileage and the quoted mileage.

### Is it illegal to sell a defective vehicle?

It is a criminal offence to sell any motor vehicle if it has certain defects. This applies even if the vehicle is being sold by a private individual – private sales are covered in the same way as trade sales. The only exception is when the vehicle is sold as a non-runner.

The Road Traffic Act covers any defect in the brakes, steering, tyres, etc. that may be dangerous. In addition the various compulsory lights and reflectors (see p. 150) must be working (unless the seller reasonably believes that the vehicle will not be used on the road at night until those lighting defects have been fixed).

This law is more strictly worded than most people would appreciate. To sell a vehicle which has one of these defects is to commit an offence – whether or not the seller knew of the defects – and can lead to prosecution in the magistrates' court and a fine of up to £2,000 (but no penalty points, endorsement or disqualification can be ordered).

In practice prosecutions against private sellers are rare. However, if you are selling a car, and you are doubtful about its condition, it would be best to get the buyer to sign a piece of paper confirming that it is sold as a non-runner. By doing this you will ensure that you cannot be prosecuted for selling an unroadworthy vehicle.

If you buy an unroadworthy vehicle, and want to claim compensation from the seller, you may be able to use the threat of criminal proceedings as a lever in your negotiations.

# Careless Driving

### What is careless driving?

It is very easy to commit the offence of careless driving. As a rough-and-ready guide one can say that all motorists are expected to follow the Highway Code. Any motorist who does not is quite likely to have committed the criminal offence of careless driving, and so could be prosecuted by the police. For instance, when there has been an accident the police will often bring a careless-driving charge against the person who seemed to be to blame. If the driving seems to have been particularly bad it is possible that a charge of reckless driving (see p. 256) will be brought instead.

### How do I know if I am being prosecuted for careless driving?

When you receive the summons from the police look at it carefully. If it says that you were driving '. . . contrary to section 3 of the Road Traffic Act 1972 . . .', you are being prosecuted for careless driving.

Confusingly some people often refer to careless driving by a different name, *driving without due care and attention*, and it can also be called *inconsiderate driving*. To all intents and purposes these mean the same as careless driving.

### What sort of driving counts as careless driving?

As we have seen, the best starting-point is the Highway Code, which sets out a standard of driving that is expected of reasonable drivers. So there will be some grounds for thinking that a motorist who has not followed the Highway Code has been guilty of careless driving. This is so whether or not an accident has happened. However, it does not follow that such a motorist is automatically guilty of the criminal offence of careless driving – each case will depend upon its own facts.

Careless driving is judged on the basis of what the reasonable, prudent, competent motorist would have done in a particular situation. If a competent motorist would have behaved differently, that the particular motorist was doing his or her incompetent best will not be a defence against a charge of careless driving. For instance, a learner driver who crashes into a lamp post will probably be guilty of careless driving – the fact is that a prudent and competent driver would not crash into a lamp post! The same criterion applies if the motorist has got a headache, or is not feeling particularly well, or even has a hangover!

It is impossible to give a list of what amounts to careless driving. No two cases are the same. But cases in which motorists have been convicted of careless driving include:

- indicating left, and then turning right
- coming out of a side road without looking properly
- crossing a white line in the middle of the road
- continually kissing or petting the front-seat passenger
- playing with the dog
- falling asleep at the wheel
- having a dizzy spell because the motorist forgot to take diabetes pills.

But a motorist who was not to blame in any way for an accident cannot be guilty of careless driving. For instance, suppose you are driving your car when a wasp suddenly starts flying in front of your face. If you crash, the court is unlikely to say that you were guilty of careless driving. After all, any reasonable and competent motorist might have crashed in that situation. However, the court would look at the facts of the accident carefully. For instance, if you had seen the wasp in the car some time earlier, but had not stopped to get rid of it, they might feel that you had been careless. Similarly you might be held to have been careless if you had continued driving while you were being attacked by the wasp. But if you were simply attacked by a wasp, without warning, you are likely to be acquitted of a careless-driving charge. So not every accident leads to a careless-driving prosecution – even if it is a serious accident.

*Mr Jones was a lorry driver. He was driving his articulated lorry along the motorway at night. The lorry was in good condition, and had been regularly serviced; as far as Mr Jones knew, there was nothing wrong with it. But for some reason all the lights on the lorry suddenly failed – leaving Mr Jones driving at speed in complete darkness. Mr Jones did not panic, but did what he thought was best in the circumstances – he pulled over to the hard shoulder. Unfortunately, a broken-down car was parked on the hard shoulder, and the lorry crashed into it. The police prosecuted Mr Jones for careless driving. Was he guilty? The court decided that he was not guilty. What he had done was reasonable, and he could not be criticized. After all, no one would have thought of prosecuting him had he not crashed into the stationary vehicle – and yet there was no way he could have known it was there. What he did was reasonable. The test for deciding whether a person was guilty of careless driving was to ask 'was it reasonable in the circumstances for the motorist to act as he did?'. On that basis, Mr Jones was not guilty.* Chief Constable of Avon (1985)

Sometimes a motorist will be involved in an accident and there will be no evidence as to what happened. For instance, the police might turn up at the scene of an accident to find that a car has left the road and crashed into a telegraph pole. The driver may have no recollection of what happened, or may simply claim to the police to have no idea what occurred. Can a prosecution for careless driving be brought? The answer will usually be yes. Although it is for the police to prove their case in any prosecution, the court will probably take the view that cars do not crash into telegraph poles unless someone has been careless. So unless the motorist can come up with a convincing explanation of what happened (e.g. by proving that the car brakes failed or that it was necessary to swerve to avoid an accident), a conviction for careless driving is likely.

### What is the difference between careless driving and inconsiderate driving?

Not much – they are basically the same. Sometimes the police will prosecute for inconsiderate driving, but usually they will choose careless driving. Inconsiderate driving would cover the motorist who stupidly drives through puddles, so splashing pedestrians. There is a technical difference between the two charges. With careless driving the police do not have to show that the careless driving caused problems to any other motorists. With inconsiderate driving it is different. Then the police must show that someone else was inconvenienced. Because of technicalities like this there are relatively few prosecutions for inconsiderate driving. Most are for careless driving.

### What is the difference between careless driving and reckless driving?

Put simply, bad driving is careless driving, but really bad driving is reckless driving! It is all a matter of degree. As we have seen, you can be guilty of careless driving even though you didn't deliberately cause an accident – in other words, you were simply careless. If you were totally careless – in other words, you didn't give a damn what happened – that would be reckless driving. For instance, someone who was involved in an accident when they were doing 10 m.p.h. more than the speed limit would probably be prosecuted for careless driving. On the other hand, doing 30 or 40 m.p.h. more than the speed limit might result in a charge of reckless driving.

Relatively few reckless-driving charges are brought, compared to the number brought for careless driving. A common tactic of the police is to prosecute a motorist for both careless driving and reckless driving. Because the consequences of a conviction for reckless driving are much more serious, the average motorist will then agree to plead guilty to the careless-driving charge if, in return, the police drop the reckless-driving charge. Such deals are not uncommon.

See p. 256 for more on reckless driving.

### What should I do if I am being prosecuted for careless driving?

Think about the following:

1. *Have the police followed the rules?* The police should have:

● given you warning that you might be prosecuted (see p. 243)
● issued the court summons within six months of the offence (see p. 245).

If you think they have broken either of these rules you should take legal advice.

2. *Are you guilty?* Read the section above to see whether you think you are guilty or not. Bear in mind that a lot of motorists are prosecuted for careless driving and relatively few are acquitted. After all, it is very easy to commit the offence! If you are clearly guilty there is no point in pleading not guilty – the court will probably not look at the facts of the case with a fine toothcomb, or examine all the possibilities, but will take a fairly rough-and-ready approach. Once again, if you are not sure about the position you should think about getting legal advice.

3. *What's the penalty?* Look at the chart below for details. Despite the high maximum fine that is possible, in practice the magistrates are likely to impose a fine of around £60, and they will also impose some penalty points (between two and five, depending on seriousness). If you already

have penalty points remember that twelve points in three years would probably result in your losing your licence (see p. 223). Thus, if it is particularly important to you that you do not have any more penalty points, you should definitely take legal advice.

4. *Do you need legal advice?* You can probably get legal advice from your local CAB, solicitor or perhaps from the AA and RAC. See p. 142 for sources of legal advice. Most careless-driving prosecutions are straightforward but you should not hesitate to take legal advice if there are complications.

5. *Check the rules on prosecution and conviction, and also on endorsement, fines and disqualification.* See p. 243 for prosecution; p. 251 for conviction; p. 223 for endorsement; p. 222 for fines; and p. 232 for disqualification.

---

## WHAT'S THE PENALTY?

*For careless driving*

MAXIMUM PENALTY: two to five penalty points (and an endorsement) plus a maximum fine of £1,000. Disqualification possible

LIKELY PENALTY: three penalty points (and an endorsement) and a fine of £60 or so – could be more for a serious offence. Disqualification is only likely for a persistent offender

*(For more on penalties see p. 216)*

---

# Children

**What is the youngest age for riding a bike or driving a car?**

|  | Minimum ages |
|---|---|
| Bike | no minimum age |
| Moped* | 16 |
| Invalid carriage | 16 |
| Motorcycle | 17 |
| Car or small goods vehicle** | 17 |
| Agricultural tractor | 17 |
| Medium-sized goods vehicle*** | 18 |
| HGVs and other vehicles | 21 |

| | |
|---|---|
| * *moped:* | not over 50 cc; maximum design speed not over 30 m.p.h.; kerbside weight not over 250 kilograms. But if first used before August 1977, there is a wider definition (i.e. not over 50 cc, and has pedals). |
| ** *small goods vehicle:* | not to carry more than nine people, and maximum weight not over 3·5 tonnes. |
| *** *medium-sized goods vehicle:* | not to carry more than nine people, and maximum weight not over 7·5 tonnes. |

**When is a child old enough to commit a crime?**

*0–10:* A child under ten cannot commit a criminal offence. If the child does something wrong it cannot be prosecuted. So, a nine-year-old who steals a car, and then goes for a joy-ride in it, cannot be prosecuted. In practice a child that commits numerous offences, or who is clearly beyond control, would be put in the care of the local authority.

*10–14:* A child between ten and fourteen can be guilty of a crime, but only if it can be shown to have known that what it was doing was 'wrong'. This is rather a vague test – in practice it means that the child must have realized it was doing something that was not right, even if it did not know that there was a law against it. The courts take a fairly robust view; the closer the child is to fourteen, the more likely it is that the court will decide that it was doing 'wrong'.

*14–17:* The child is treated in the same way as an adult. In other words, if it commits an offence it will be prosecuted. The only difference will be that it will be treated as a juvenile, and so be tried in a juvenile court (which is more informal, and less legalistic).

*Over 17:* Once the child reaches seventeen it is treated in the same way as an adult. In other words, it will not be tried in a juvenile court but in a magistrates' court or a crown court.

In addition there are various sentences for people aged under twenty-one that cannot be imposed upon adults (e.g. being sent to a detention centre or placed under a supervision order). For more information on children and crime, see the *Penguin Guide to the Law*.

### What are the seat belt laws for children?

They are basically the same as the rules for grown-ups. So a child who is a front-seat passenger must wear its seat belt. If it does not an offence is committed. If the child is under fourteen it is the driver who commits the offence (not the child); if the child is over fourteen it is the child who commits the offence – and who is prosecuted – not the driver.

If a baby under twelve months old is in the front passenger seat it must be in a child restraint seat. Otherwise the driver commits an offence. Surprisingly, there is no law requiring that a baby, in the back of a car, be in a baby seat, or be otherwise strapped in.

For more details see p. 272.

### A child is injured in a car driven by its parent. Does the parent have to pay compensation to the child?

Yes. The fact that the accident victim is the child of the driver is irrelevant. The same principles apply as with any other road accident compensation claim. In other words, if the motorist was to blame, compensation has to be paid. When we talk about blame we are not concerned with criminal liability (e.g. can someone be prosecuted by the police), but with the question of who is to pay for the damage caused. This is a *civil* claim – suing for damages caused by the negligence of a motorist – completely separate from the question of prosecution. A motorist – or, more likely, the motorist's insurance company – will have to pay compensation (i.e. for the damage and injury caused) only if he or she was negligent. See p. 177 for more information on the negligence laws.

If a child is injured it will almost certainly have been a passenger, and there is virtually no way in which the passenger could realistically have been to blame for the accident. So that child – as an innocent passenger – will almost certainly have a 100 per cent claim against someone else. Whoever caused the accident will have to pay compensation to the child. Often the negligent driver will have been the child's own parent. On the other hand, the accident might have been caused by another driver who drove into the parent's car. In that case the child's claim would be against the other driver – although it could choose simply to sue the parent if it wished. Either way the child cannot have been to blame, and so is bound to have a claim for damages. This claim will be for the injury suffered (i.e. compensation for the pain, scars, etc.) and for the cost of any hospital treatment (although in practice most people get free treatment under the NHS).

At first sight it may seem absurd that a child can sue its parent just because the parent caused an accident. But it is a sensible piece of law. The important point to remember is that the parent will almost certainly be insured – and even if he or she is not insured a compensation fund will meet the claim (see p. 130). So the reality of the situation is that the child is claiming off the insurance company, and not personally off its parent.

All too often one finds that, when a child has been injured in an accident in its parent's car, no one bothers to claim damages for the child. Usually this is because of plain ignorance. Not unnaturally the parents do not think they can make a claim against themselves and the child goes uncompensated. Whenever a child is injured in a car a compensation claim should be made.

### What if a child is knocked down in the road. Can it claim compensation?

Perhaps yes, and perhaps no – it all depends on the circumstances. Once again we are talking about who was to blame for the accident. If someone else was to blame, that person will have to pay compensation. Remember that we are not concerned with criminal liability (e.g. can someone be prosecuted for careless driving) but with whether someone – through their insurance company – will have to pay compensation.

The law operates on the basis of 'negligence'. Turn to pp. 177–86 for case histories on what amounts to negligence. The important point to realize is that the law only offers compensation if someone else was negligent. If the victim caused the accident (e.g. by simply running into the path of a car) no compensation will be paid. With children this is often a problem.

To some extent the courts try to find that the drivers were negligent when children are involved. Obviously they want to avoid seeing an injured child go without any compensation. But the courts are to a large extent restricted by the present negligence laws.

What the courts do is to say that careful drivers will be on the look-out for children – and if they see any children they will be taking great care, in case the child runs out without warning. In other words drivers should anticipate that children are unpredictable, and that they do not have a complete sense of road safety:

*Mrs Prudence was waiting at a pedestrian crossing with three children. As they were waiting, her three-year-old ran out without any warning and was hit by a car. She sued on behalf of the three-year-old. The motorist said that he was not to blame in any way – the child had run out without any warning. Held: the motorist was totally to blame for the accident. He had seen the mother and children, and should have realized that there was a chance of a three-year-old running out in this way. In any event they were waiting at a crossing and so he should have stopped to let them cross – he should not have assumed that they would wait for him to pass. So the three-year-old got full compensation (from the motorist's insurance company).*
Prudence *(1966)*

*A motorcyclist was doing 50 m.p.h. in a 30 m.p.h. area. A seven-year-old ran out into the road, from behind a parked car. There was no way the motorcyclist could avoid an accident. Was the motorcyclist negligent, or was the accident the boy's own fault? Held: the careful motorist will appreciate that seven-year-olds run out from behind cars and vans without warning. If the motorcyclist had been going at a proper speed he might have been able to swerve or brake to avoid the collision. So the child got full compensation (from the motorcyclist's insurance company).*
Jones *(1969)*

So the courts will say that prudent motorists are on their guard for children. In effect the courts try to find the motorist negligent – they do all they can to help the child within the confines of the restrictive laws that we have. However, there does come a time when the courts are unable to justify a finding of negligence against the motorist, and they have to leave the child uncompensated:

*A five-year-old boy ran out into the road from behind a parked car; he was running to an ice-cream van on the other side of the road. He was seriously injured by a passing car – even though the car was only travelling at 15 m.p.h. He sued (through his parents), arguing that the motorist had been negligent. Held: the motorist had not been negligent, and so the little boy was not entitled to any compensation. The motorist could only have avoided hitting the boy by driving at 5 m.p.h. It was not reasonable to expect that, so he was not liable. Thus the injured five-year-old went without compensation.* Kite *(1983)*

The age of the child becomes important when it is being decided whether or not the child was to blame. The normal rule is that victims who were in part to blame will lose part of their damages – this is called contributory negligence (see p. 178). Applying this concept to young children obviously causes problems. What the courts say is that a very young child cannot be guilty of contributory negligence – it cannot be expected to think in terms of road safety, and therefore cannot be to blame. So a young child would not expect to have any of its damages deducted for its own carelessness.

Once the child is a teenager the position is different. Then the courts say that the child should have road sense and can be to blame for an accident. For instance, if a fifteen-year-old runs out into the road it will almost certainly lose some (or even all) of its damages.

The real problems come with children who are not very young, and who are yet not teenagers. There comes a dividing point at which one has to start saying that the child is blameworthy – in other words it can be guilty of contributory negligence. The difficulties arise in deciding where the dividing line is. Obviously each case must be decided on its own facts. As a rough-and-ready guide one can probably say that a child who is aged six cannot be to blame in any way – whereas a child aged twelve or more can be to blame. It is the few years in between that really cause the arguments:

*A nine-year-old boy was pedalling along the road. He negligently rode into a pile of hardcore that had wrongly been left in the road by builders. He sued. The builders (through their insurance company) said that the boy was negligent. He should have looked where he was going. In response the boy's solicitors said that the child was too young – at nine – to be guilty of any contributory negligence. Held: the boy was not too young to be guilty of contributory negligence. On the facts, 20 per cent contributory negligence was found (i.e. he got 80 per cent of his normal damages).* Minter *(1983)*

# Commercial Vehicles

### What is a goods vehicle?

A goods vehicle is *any* vehicle that was either designed to carry goods or has since been adapted so it can carry goods. For instance, any van or lorry used in a business will clearly be a goods vehicle since it was designed to carry goods. On the other hand a business car will not count as a goods vehicle since it will not normally have been designed or adapted for carrying goods.

### What is a heavy goods vehicle (HGV)?

An HGV is any goods vehicle with a weight limit of over 7·5 tonnes. Also included are all articulated vehicles (even if – which is unlikely – they can carry less than 7·5 tonnes).

### Do goods vehicles pay more road tax?

Some do, some don't. Most light vehicles (e.g. small vans) are taxed in the same way as private motor cars. Only if the vehicle weighs more than 1,525 kilograms do different road tax rules apply.

It follows that for most small businesses the effect of running a trade vehicle (e.g. a small van) will not be increased road tax but merely increased insurance premiums (because insurance companies tend to charge more for goods vehicles than for private vehicles).

### When is an operator's licence needed?

A goods vehicle operator's licence is needed only if the vehicle's unladen weight is over 1,525 kilograms. In practice, therefore, most light vans, estate cars, etc. are exempted.

*I use a small van in my business. Do I need any special licences?*

No, provided the van does not weigh more than 1,525 kilograms. If it weighs more than this you will need an operator's licence, and you will also have to pay a different scale of road tax.

## What is an HGV licence?

It is an additional licence that you need before you can drive an HGV. You cannot get an HGV licence if you are under twenty-one.

As an HGV learner you will of course have to display L-plates, and you can only drive when accompanied by the holder of a full HGV licence. HGV drivers who are disqualified must give up both their ordinary driving licence and their HGV driving licence (i.e. they are not just disqualified for the ordinary driving licence). Any endorsements will normally go in the ordinary licence (even if they happen during work hours) and will not go in the HGV licence.

## What are the speed limits for commercial vehicles?

| Speed limits for commercial vehicles, m.p.h. | | | |
|---|---|---|---|
| | Motorway | Dual carriageway | Other roads |
| Goods vehicles | | | |
| weight not over 7·5 tonnes | 70 | 60 | 50 |
| weight over 7·5 tonnes | 60 | 50 | 40 |
| Articulated vehicles | | | |
| weight not over 7·5 tonnes | 60 | 60 | 50 |
| weight over 7·5 tonnes | 60 | 50 | 50 |
| Car-derived van* | 70 | 70 | 60 |
| Coach (if over eight seats, or over 3·05 tonnes) | | | |
| not over 12 metres long | 70 | 60 | 50 |
| over 12 metres long | 60 | 60 | 50 |
| Trailer or caravan | 60 | 60 | 50 |
| Agricultural vehicle | | 40 | 40 |

* i.e. van based on a car (up to 2 tonnes laden), such as an Escort, Astra or Metro van.

Note that small vans based on cars (e.g. an Escort van) have the same maximum speeds as an ordinary car – there are not lower speed limits just because it is a van. One other small point to mention is that it used to be the case that caravans towed by cars could only go at 50 m.p.h. if a '50' sticker was put on the back of the caravan. That rule has now been changed, and there is no need for the caravan to have a '50' plate (the speed limit is 60 m.p.h. on motorways and dual carriageways, and 50 m.p.h. on other roads).

### How many hours can a commercial vehicle be driven for?

For commercial goods vehicles the answer is generally no more than eight or ten hours a day – for vehicles over 3·5 tonnes it is eight hours, for those under 3·5 tonnes (and coaches with under sixteen seats) it is ten hours.*

But there are extremely complicated rules (based on EEC regulations) which set down rest periods, weekly driving limits, etc. They are difficult to follow but the table below summarizes them.

Bear in mind that these hours restrictions only apply to goods vehicles (e.g. lorries, articulated lorries, etc.) and PSVs (i.e. coaches, buses, etc.). See p. 69 for what is a goods vehicle; see p. 163 for what is a PSV. In addition these restrictions apply only to commercial operations. In practice there is no question of the police ever enforcing these laws against vehicles used by community groups, youth clubs, charities, societies, etc., or indeed for school trips. If the trip is not a money-making exercise it will not be regarded as commercial, and the hours

| | Drivers' hours | |
|---|---|---|
| | Goods vehicles over 3·5 tonnes | Goods vehicles under 3·5 tonnes or coaches for under sixteen people |
| Daily driving | 8 | 10 |
| Weekly driving | 48 | no limit |
| Fortnightly driving | 92 | no limit |
| Continuous driving | 4 | no limit |
| Weekly rest | 29 | 24 |
| Continuous duty | 5½ | 5½ |
| Daily rest | 11 | 11 |
| Daily duty | 11 | 11 |
| Daily spread-out | 12½ | 12½ |
| Weekly duty | 60 | 60 |
| Break | ½ | ½ |

* Note: these hourly restrictions will change soon.

rules will not apply. Thus a local group that hires a coach for the day is not subject to the driver's hours restrictions. See also 'Minibuses', p. 161.

The rules on drivers' hours are absurdly complicated and difficult to follow. The table above is no more than a rough guide – there are numerous detailed exemptions and special rules that can apply.

### When must a tachograph be fitted?

A tachograph is a device that combines speedometer, mileometer and a clock. It records speed, the hours driven and rest periods. Tachographs must be checked for accuracy every two years, and recalibrated every six years (a plaque inside the tachograph is marked at each inspection so that the police can easily check whether the rules are being complied with).

The basic rule is that any commercial vehicle (used to carry goods or passengers) must use a tachograph, with the following exceptions:

• the vehicle is constructed to carry no more than fifteen people (including the driver – i.e. fourteen passengers), provided it is going to be used solely in the UK. If it will be used on the Continent the maximum number is nine people (including the driver)
• goods vehicles of no more than 3·5 tonnes (including the weight of any trailer)
• buses on a regular passenger service
• vehicles used by the emergency services, and public utilities
• tractors, provided the maximum speed does not exceed 30 m.p.h.
• local agricultural and forest machinery
• circus and funfair vehicles
• specialized breakdown vehicles
• any vehicle which is being used for a local road test, or is being repaired or maintained
• any vehicle being used to transport live animals between farms and local markets (or to transport animal carcasses that are not intended for human consumption)
• specialized vehicles designed for local markets, mobile banking, mobile churches, mobile libraries, mobile exhibitions and door-to-door selling.

If a vehicle does not come within any of these categories a tachograph must be fitted and used. However, all goods vehicles (except those that do have tachographs) must have a Driver's Record Book, which summarizes the hours driven, etc. Because these records are not recorded automatically by the tachograph they are notoriously unreliable!

### Is it the driver's or the employer's job to keep tachograph records?

Both. Employers must make sure that the tachograph is working properly, and that the seals on it are not broken. The employer must also make sure that drivers are given sufficient sheets; in addition employers must keep drivers' sheets for at least a year. For their part all drivers and crew members must see that the tachograph is kept working properly, and that record sheets are handed in to their employer. Conversely the employer must chase up the driver for the work records, if necessary. All too often what happens is that the driver will disconnect the tachograph, or tamper with it, and the question then arises of whether the employer is liable, with the driver, for a breach of the tachograph regulations. As the law stands, the employer will nearly always be liable as well. Penalties for tachograph offences include a maximum fine of up to £1,000 (£2,000 if falsifying of records is involved). No endorsements or points are imposed, but a goods vehicle operator's licence could be suspended or withdrawn by the licensing authority.

Needless to say, some drivers try to fiddle the tachograph. Nearly always such ploys are doomed to failure. For instance, merely bending back the needle (so that all the recorded mileages are slower) will not work – because when the lorry is stationary it will be recorded as going at less than 0 m.p.h.! Similarly, burning the records – to avoid prosecution – will not work. One driver who did this was sent to prison for three weeks for attempting to pervert the course of justice!

### What are the maximum widths and lengths of vehicle loads?

There are detailed restrictions. Basically the overall width of the vehicle or load must not be more than 2·9 metres (except in the case of loose agricultural produce, such as hay). Wider loads are allowed but special notice will have to be given to the police.

As regards length, the maximum (of vehicle and/or load) is 18·3 metres. But there are exceptions. If in doubt check with the police.

There are also overhang restrictions on loads. Generally no part of the load can project more than 0·305 metres from the side; front overhang cannot be more than 1·83 metres, and rear overhang not more than 1·07 metres. Once again there are various exceptions, and longer loads are allowed if notice is given to the police. In addition there are restrictions upon the maximum overhang (i.e. the distance between the rear of the vehicle and the back axle). For most motor cars the overhang at the back cannot be more than 60 per cent of the distance between the front and rear axles. So if you have a lorry you may run into difficulties if you put down the tailboard and use that for carrying loads – you should check that you will not be exceeding the length and overhang rules.

Bear in mind, also, that it may be necessary to put lights on overhanging loads. This will normally be necessary if the overhang to front or side is more than 12 inches, or 3½ feet from the rear.

These rules apply to private cars as well as trade vehicles. If, as a private motorist, you decide to carry (for instance) a large piece of furniture in your boot, and that furniture protrudes from the end of the vehicle, you will have to comply with all the rules set out above. In any event you should make sure that it is securely attached, otherwise you will be guilty of carrying a dangerous load.

There is a specific offence of carrying a load that is dangerous, or which is likely to cause a nuisance to other people. This is the charge that will be brought against the owner of a lorry that sheds its load, but it should be remembered that it applies to private motorists as well. If you do not load the roof rack on your car carefully, or if you let items protrude from your boot, you can face prosecution for having a dangerous load. In addition if you were overloading the car, or using it in a totally inappropriate way (e.g. carrying items that were so large that they should really have gone in a van), you can be prosecuted for the separate offence of putting your car to an unsuitable use. (Once again, you will be guilty if it causes danger or a nuisance.)

The figures quoted here for overhangs, etc. are for rough guidance only. There are various other exemptions and restrictions that can apply.

## What is a dual-purpose vehicle?

A dual-purpose vehicle can carry passengers or goods. Despite the fact that it is a goods vehicle, a dual-purpose vehicle will count as a private vehicle for speed limit purposes (i.e. 70 m.p.h. on motorways and dual carriageways, and 60 m.p.h. on other roads). Also there will be no need for an operator's licence.

A dual-purpose vehicle must not have an unladen weight of over 2,040 kilograms. In addition it must either be a four-wheel drive vehicle (either permanently, or with a four-wheel drive facility) or meet each of the following requirements:

- have a permanent, fixed, rigid roof
- have a row of seats (with upholstered back-rests) for at least two passengers behind the driver's seat. The distance between the steering-wheel and the back of the rear seats must be at least one third of the distance between the steering-wheel and the end of the van's floor
- there must be side windows (at least 1,850 square centimetres on each side) and a rear window, or windows, of at least 770 square centimetres.

## Does the law expect the driver of a goods vehicle to be more careful than the driver of a private car?

Not necessarily. The law expects a proper standard of driving from all drivers – irrespective of the kind of vehicle they are driving. But heavy goods vehicles, such as lorries, do present particular hazards to other road users – and their drivers should be aware of those hazards.

*The driver of a large articulated lorry was waiting to cross a dual carriageway, to get into a farm. It was dawn, and visibility was only 50–100 yards. He waited until the road was clear, and until he could see no headlights; then he pulled across. Headlights appeared, and a car crashed, at speed, into the lorry. The car driver was killed. The estate of the dead car driver sued the owners of the lorry for their driver's negligence. Held: the lorry driver was wholly to blame. An articulated vehicle of this length (50 feet) would take about twelve seconds to cross the dual carriageway and would totally block it. With visibility as poor as it was this was an unacceptably dangerous manoeuvre. Although the lorry needed to get into the farm, it should not have tried to do so by this route. Instead the lorry should have continued up the main road, until it came to a bridge or slip road that would have enabled it to cross safely to the other side of the dual carriageway. The lorry driver was 100 per cent to blame, and so the estate of the dead car driver recovered full compensation.* Lancaster (1979)

The Motorist and the Law

The same might apply if a lorry reversed into a road at night. It all depends upon the particular facts – but lorry drivers must appreciate that what would be a simple manoeuvre in a car can be highly dangerous in a lorry. They should also remember that a lorry may not be visible from the side, however efficient its front and rear lights.

# Cyclists

*Must a cyclist stop at traffic lights?*

Yes. Pedal cyclists are subject to the normal motoring laws – as if they were car drivers. If, as a cyclist, you jump the traffic lights you will be prosecuted in the same way as a car driver, and you will face exactly the same penalties as a car driver (except that you will not face penalty points, endorsement or disqualification – even if you have a car driving licence you cannot get points, etc. for an offence committed on a bike).

Can you get around these traffic laws simply by getting off your bike and then wheeling it through the traffic lights? Surprisingly lawyers are not clear as to whether you can. The likely answer is that this dodge would work – you would be treated as a pedestrian if you were pushing your bike, and so you could go through traffic lights, across pedestrian crossings, etc. On the other hand, if you had one foot on a pedal and one on the ground (i.e. you were scooting) you would probably be treated as a cyclist, not a pedestrian, and so the traffic light laws would apply to you.

Obviously there are some laws affecting cars that cannot apply to bikes – for instance, the construction and use regulations (i.e. the detailed regulations about design of steering, brakes, lights, etc.). There are no similar detailed rules for bikes, except that:

• brakes must be fitted and working properly. There must be brakes on both wheels (unless one of the wheels has a fixed drive). The police are entitled to check a bike's brakes
• it is an offence for a dealer to sell a bike that does not meet British Standards for design safety.

Otherwise there are no specific safety laws laid down. For instance, you could ride a pedal cycle with unsafe steering and not be committing an offence, though it would of course be an offence to drive a car with unsafe steering.

Surprisingly the rules concerning overtaking on a white line apply to bikes – not just cars!

### Can I park my bike wherever I like?

No. There are some controls on parking bikes – but very few. You do not, for example, have to bother about yellow lines – they do not apply to you. The only parking restrictions that you will face are on:

- leaving your bike in a dangerous position
- leaving your bike on a footpath
- leaving your bike on a clearway.

You can, for instance, chain your bike to railings outside a building, or to signposts. Only if you come within one of the three exceptions above, will you be committing a criminal offence. For instance, if you chain your bike to a railing it may well be that your bike will be on the footpath. If so, you would be guilty of a criminal offence. But if the railings were on private property (for instance, the forecourt of a building) you would not be committing an offence by chaining your bike to them. However annoyed the owner of the building might be, there is nothing much – from the legal point of view – that he or she could do about it!

### What are the rules on lights?

The same rules on lighting up apply to bikes as do to cars. Therefore:

- lights must be used during the 'hours of darkness' (i.e. half an hour after sunset to half an hour before sunrise). The rules are the same as those for cars (see p. 153).
- lights must be used when there is poor visibility. The same rules apply as with cars – lights are needed if visibility is 'seriously reduced', even in daytime (see p. 153).

Your bike does not need lights when it is parked, or if you are pushing it along. Nor need you worry if you have a dynamo light, which means that your lights will go out when you are caught in a traffic jam or waiting at traffic lights. There is a specific law that exempts bikes from the need to display lights when stationary owing to traffic and signs – provided the bike is as near as possible to the left-hand side of the road.

The only lights required at law are a white light at the front and a red light and reflector at the rear, though the sensible cyclist will look upon these as the absolute minimum of lights that should be used – it is wise to have reflective stripes, wear bright-coloured clothing, and have additional lights.

### Is there such an offence as careless pedalling?

We have already seen that there is an offence of careless driving that can be brought against car drivers. There is a similar offence for cyclists – cycling 'without due care and attention' (i.e. careless pedalling).

In practice relatively few prosecutions are brought. The sort of pedalling that would be covered by this offence would include the cyclist who pedals on the pavement, who swerves in front of a car causing it to crash, or a group of cyclists riding more than two abreast. However, there is also a separate charge of inconsiderate cycling that may be brought in these cases.

There is also the more serious charge of reckless cycling. This covers the really serious cycling offender (e.g. who runs down a child or old person while pedalling on the pavement). The same basic principles apply as with reckless driving of cars (see p. 256 – and p. 61 for the difference between careless and reckless).

In addition there are specific laws prohibiting:

• carrying a passenger on a bike (unless it is constructed or adapted to carry a passenger – for instance, a tandem, or a bike with a child seat fitted to it). So it is illegal for a child to give a lift to another child by allowing it to ride on the crossbar
• taking hold of another vehicle while on a bike. In effect this prevents cyclists from getting a tow
• racing on the highway.

### Can one be drunk in charge of a bike?

Yes. The normal breathalyser laws do not apply to cyclists, but there is an offence of cycling while unfit through drink or drugs.

Drunk cyclists are not asked to blow into a bag or machine, as a motorist would be. Instead they will be prosecuted if there is sufficient evidence to show that they are under the influence – for instance, if the police doctor can give evidence that the cyclist could not walk along a straight line, speak coherently, and so on.

The important point is that drunk cyclists cannot lose their licence – all they can face is a fine. Even if they have a licence for a car it cannot be endorsed, or taken away from them, because of a drunk-cycling conviction.

---

## WHAT'S THE PENALTY?

*For riding a bike with defective brakes*

*For reckless cycling*

*For riding on a footpath or pavement*

*For riding while unfit through drink or drugs*

*For disobeying a police constable's or a traffic warden's sign*

*For disobeying traffic signs, traffic lights, white lines, etc.*

*For pedestrian crossing offences (failing to give precedence to a pedestrian; overtaking)*

MAXIMUM PENALTY: a £400 fine

LIKELY PENALTY: a fine of £10–£20 for no brakes. Reckless pedalling is regarded seriously – there would be at least a £50 fine. Drunk pedalling would probably bring a £40–£50 fine. Disobeying a police officer's or a traffic warden's sign and traffic signs, and pedestrian crossing offences would probably result in a £15–£25 fine (more for serious cases)

*For not having lights at night*

*For not having lights in poor visibility*

MAXIMUM PENALTY: a £1,000 fine

LIKELY PENALTY: a £10 fine

*For careless cycling*

*For inconsiderate cycling*

*For holding on to another vehicle*

*For carrying a passenger*

*For unauthorized racing*

MAXIMUM PENALTY: a £50 fine

LIKELY PENALTY: a £10–£20 fine

*(For more on penalties see p. 216.)*

---

Finally, the drunk cyclist cannot avoid conviction by pedalling along the pavement or footpath. It is just as much an offence to be pedalling on the footpath or pavement while under the influence as it is on the road.

When it comes to penalties for cycling offences, much will depend upon the age of the cyclist. In the case of a young child a minimal penalty may be imposed. Note that a child's parents can be prosecuted if they knew (or should have known) that brakes or lights were defective.

### What happens if a child cyclist causes an accident?

The normal rules as to blame apply. When we talk about blame we are not concerned with criminal liability (e.g. can someone be prosecuted by the police), but with the question of who is to pay for the damage caused. This is a *civil* claim – suing for damages caused by the negligence of a cyclist – completely separate from the question of prosecution. A cyclist will have to pay compensation (i.e. for the damage and injury caused) only if he or she was negligent. See p. 177 for more information on negligence.

Difficulties arise when it is a young child that causes the accident. Very young children cannot be held responsible for their actions, and so cannot be said to have been negligent. It therefore follows that a motorist cannot sue that child. See p. 68 for more on the responsibility of children.

The point to grasp is that, if a child cyclist causes an accident, the people injured (e.g. the motorists and their cars) may go without compensation. This is because the courts may decide that the child is not legally responsible in view of its young age. When that happens, there is no one for the motorist to sue, and no one to get compensation from.

Even if the child is old enough (e.g. fourteen or fifteen) to be sued, it would probably be a waste of time. This is because the child would almost certainly not have enough money to pay any damages or legal costs that might be awarded against it. The child's parents would not have to meet the claim (unless they were to blame – for instance, if they had known that the child's brakes were defective). The end result, therefore, is that in practice it is almost impossible to recover damages against a young cyclist who causes an accident – unless the sums involved are trivial.

### *What if a young cyclist is injured in a road accident?*

Here we are dealing with the other side of the coin. If the child cyclist can show that the motorist was to blame, it will get full compensation. But, if it cannot be shown that the motorist was to blame, the child will not be entitled to any compensation.

The real problems arise with children who behave recklessly as a result of their young age. The general rule is that the courts expect motorists to be on the look-out for bad behaviour from children (e.g. you should take extreme care when overtaking a young cyclist). But if the child does something totally unpredictable the motorist cannot be criticized – and will not have to pay compensation (see p. 67).

### *Practical cycling:* **What advice does the Highway Code give to cyclists?**

Every cyclist should read the Highway Code. It is full of common-sense advice. Particular points are:

Make sure your cycle is safe to ride. At night you must have front and rear lamps and a rear reflector. Your brakes, lamps and reflector must be kept in proper working order. Make sure your tyres are in good condition and are properly pumped up. It is a good idea to fit a bell to your cycle and to use it, if necessary, to warn other people on the road that you are coming.

Before starting to ride, always look round and make sure that it is safe to move away from the kerb. Before turning right or left, moving out to pass or pulling up at the kerb, always glance behind and make sure it is safe. Give a clear arm signal to show what you intend to do.

Do not ride more than two side by side. Ride in single file on busy narrow roads. You must not ride on a footpath or pavement by the side of the road.

On busy roads and at night, if you want to turn right it is often safer to stop first on the left-hand side of the road. Wait for a safe gap in the traffic before you start to turn.

Where there is a bus lane next to the left-hand kerb for buses going in the same direction as the traffic flow, signs will show that you may use the bus lane. You must not use other bus lanes.

When you are riding:

a    always keep both hands on the handlebar unless you are signalling;
b    always keep both feet on the pedals;
c    do not hold on to another vehicle or another cyclist;

*d*   do not carry a passenger unless your cycle has been built or altered to carry one;

*e*   do not ride close behind another vehicle;

*f*   do not carry anything which might affect your balance or become entangled with the wheels or chain;

*g*   do not lead an animal;

*h*   wear light-coloured or reflective and fluorescent clothing.

# Disabled Drivers

*I have an orange badge. Can I park anywhere I like?*

No. If you are disabled and have an orange badge you are exempt from some parking restrictions – but not all.

---

*An orange-badge holder can park:*

| | |
|---|---|
| in a meter bay | for free, and for any length of time |
| where limited parking time is allowed (e.g. half an hour only) | with no time restriction |
| on dotted, single or double yellow lines | in England and Wales, for up to two hours (provided a special parking disc showing the time of parking is displayed). In Scotland there is no time limit. In central London special rules apply (below) |
| in areas marked as specially reserved for disabled people | with no time limit |

---

But as an orange-badge holder you can never park in a bus lane, or in a place where there is a ban on loading or unloading.

In central London different rules apply. In the City of London, Westminster, Kensington and Chelsea, and Camden (south of Euston Road) the usual privileges do not apply, and instead there are local schemes with slightly different rules.

As an orange-badge holder you can use toll bridges and toll tunnels for free (e.g. the Severn Bridge and the Dartford Tunnel). Private toll bridges and roads are not covered. In addition an orange badge is valid for parking concessions in many foreign countries – details from the Department of Transport, the AA or the RAC.

One final point to note is that these parking concessions do not give you, as an orange-badge holder, *carte blanche* to break the normal laws. For instance, if you park your car so that it is blocking the road you will be guilty of obstruction whether or not you have an orange badge.

### How do I apply for an orange badge?

You apply to your local authority. Usually it is the Social Services Department that deals with applications, although in some councils it is the Borough Surveyor's Department. You will have to fill in a form, and pay a fee of up to £2. You will also have to produce evidence that you are eligible for an orange badge – for most people this will be a blind registration book, or a copy of a mobility allowance order book.

The badge will be valid for three years, and must be displayed on the windscreen of the car when you are using it (i.e. whether you, as the disabled person, are the driver or passenger). It should be taken off if you are not using the car.

To qualify for an orange badge you must be receiving mobility allowance (below), or be any of the following:

• using a vehicle supplied by a government department (e.g. the DHSS) or getting a grant towards the cost of running your own car
• registered as blind
• have a 'permanent and substantial disability which causes inability to walk or very considerable inability in walking'.

It is up to the local authority to decide whether you meet these criteria. In practice arguments tend to arise when a person is claiming an orange badge because of difficulty with walking. In marginal cases the council will write to the GP and ask for his or her views. Normally the council will follow the GP's opinion. Note that there is no right of appeal if the application for an orange badge is refused.

### Who can use an orange badge?

The orange badge can be used if the disabled person is in the car, as either driver or passenger – it need not be the disabled person who is driving. But the disabled person must be riding in the vehicle – the orange badge could not be used, for instance, by a husband doing the shopping for his disabled wife (unless, of course, she came with him in the car).

When the car is not being used by the disabled person the orange badge must be taken off the windscreen.

## What about misuse of orange badges and parking bays for disabled people?

A non-disabled person who parks in a space that has been specially reserved for disabled people will be committing a parking offence. Similarly, if someone uses an orange badge to which they are not entitled (for instance because the disabled person is not a passenger in the car), they will also be committing an offence.

There are controls on the misuse of orange badges. In particular the local authority that issued the orange badge will be told of any parking offence by the badge holder – in other words, of any occasion where parking was not authorized by the orange badge (for instance, if the car was parked in a bus lane). If the local authority decides that the orange badge is being persistently misused (which they will probably do if there have been three such parking offences) they can withdraw the orange badge. Note that the police are supposed to tell the local authority even if no prosecution is brought, and even if no parking ticket is issued. Similarly the orange badge will be withdrawn if the badge holder is allowing it to be used by someone else.

---

### WHAT'S THE PENALTY?

*For improper use of an orange badge*
    MAXIMUM PENALTY: a £400 fine
    LIKELY PENALTY: a £20 fine (if misuse is persistent the council may withdraw the orange badge)

*For wrongly parking in a disabled persons' parking area*
    MAXIMUM PENALTY: a £400 fine
    LIKELY PENALTY: a £25 fine, but you may get away with a £12 fixed penalty ticket (see p. 217)

*(For more on penalties see p. 216)*

---

## What road tax concessions are there for the disabled?

Some disabled people are exempt from having to pay the annual road tax (see p. 260 for the law on road tax). In particular anyone receiving mobility allowance (see p. 88) can claim exemption from road tax – either for themselves or for someone else (e.g. a relative) whom they nominate instead. Similarly any disabled person who receives a motor vehicle from a government department (e.g. the DHSS) is likely to be exempt from road tax. In addition a disabled passenger who is receiving attendance allowance, as well as having 'severe walking difficulties', can apply for exemption from road tax. In this case the vehicle will have to be registered in the name of the disabled person – although this can usually be done without any difficulty.

To claim the exemption you need to apply for a certificate of exemption from the DHSS. This certificate is then sent with the usual road tax application form (form V10), and road tax is applied for in the usual way (see p. 261). Normally the road tax will be issued without any difficulty; exceptionally the road tax licensing authority may decide that the vehicle is not going to be used by the disabled person and so refuse to issue an exemption.

A disabled person can get exemption from road tax even though he or she does not own the vehicle. This applies to a disabled person who is receiving a mobility allowance. For instance, if the disabled person is a child it will be possible to have the parent's vehicle exempt from road tax, provided it can be shown that the car is used *solely* for the benefit of the disabled child. In practice deciding whether or not the vehicle is only used by the disabled person is a grey area – there have been cases when licensing authorities have allowed exemption even though the vehicle is also used by the person caring for the disabled person in travelling to and from work. No firm guidance can be given on this point – obviously the concern of the licensing authority is to stop abuse, but they will normally be satisfied if it can be shown that the primary use of the vehicle is to assist the disabled person, even if that is not the exclusive use. Unlike with an orange badge there is no need for the disabled person to be in the car when it is being used – it would be legitimate for it to be used to collect the shopping or do other errands for him or her. It is all a matter of how often use of the car is attributable to the disabled person.

If road tax exemption is granted it would – in theory at least – be illegal to use it for any purpose that is not connected with the disabled person. If the car were used by someone else for a private trip it should, strictly speaking, be taxed during that time! Of course, this is a theoretical approach to the law and the police would never prosecute – unless there was a blatant misuse of the road tax exemption.

The Motorist and the Law

*What is mobility allowance?*

Mobility allowance is a cash benefit (currently about £22 per week) which is designed to help severely disabled people to become more mobile. The money received is not taxable.

Mobility allowance can be awarded to anyone between the ages of five and sixty-five who is unable (or virtually unable) to walk because of a physical condition.

Apart from the importance of the weekly money, the fact that someone receives mobility benefit will often automatically entitle them to other benefits. For instance, the entitlement to an orange badge, or exemption from road tax (above), will usually be automatic if the disabled person is receiving mobility benefit.

Before 1976 it was possible to get invalid cars, or even allowances towards the cost of running a car. That scheme has now been phased out and instead applicants receive mobility benefit. Most people who are still under the pre-1976 scheme will be better advised to change and claim mobility allowance instead.

*What other concessions are there for disabled drivers?*

There are various concessions available. A disabled person would find it worth while obtaining a copy of an excellent guide from the Department of Transport, Freepost, Ruislip, Middlesex (the booklet is free; so is the postage). The booklet is called *Door to Door*. It lists all the benefits that are available. In particular disabled people should be aware of the following:

*Motability*. This is a voluntary organization (government funded) which is encouraging disabled people to buy or lease a car. There are two schemes on offer; one is for leasing cars, the other is for buying on HP. With buying or leasing, the mobility allowance is paid direct by the DHSS to Motability Finance Ltd, to cover the payments. If the vehicle is bought on HP the mobility allowance will go straight to the disabled person. Bear in mind that, if a vehicle is leased (not bought on HP), it does not belong to the disabled person at the end of the lease. Full details are in free leaflets from Motability, Boundary House, 91–93 Charterhouse Street, London EC1.

*Seat belts*. A disabled person may be exempted from wearing seat belts (see p. 272).

*Learner drivers*. The normal minimum age for applying for a driving licence is seventeen. A disabled teenager who is receiving mobility allowance can apply at sixteen.

*Discounts* on cars and wheelchairs may be available to people on mobility allowance. The Royal Association for Disability and Rehabilitation (RADAR) has negotiated concessionary discounts with many motor manufacturers. It may, therefore, be a good idea to contact RADAR for an up-to-date list of the concessions generally available. These are of course entirely concessionary and discretionary. Full details from RADAR, 25 Mortimer St, London W1, and the Disabled Living Foundation, 380 Harrow Rd, London W9.

*Public transport.* British Rail, and many other travel authorities, offer special rates for disabled people (e.g. a half-price Travel Card). In addition people on mobility allowance (and other severely disabled people) may be able to get help with the cost of their fares (e.g. public transport or taxi) to work. Details from the Manpower Services Commission, Selkirk House, High Holborn, London WC1 (01-836 1213).

*Rate relief.* Many disabled people can claim rate relief. As far as motoring is concerned note that rate relief is available on a garage, carport or parking space for a disabled person's vehicle. Further information from your local council, or from the Department of the Environment, 2 Marsham St, London SW1 (01-212 3434) (who have a free leaflet called *Rate Relief for Disabled Persons*).

### I am disabled. Can I get a driving licence?

It depends on the extent of your disability. See p. 132 for the rules on learners, and p. 92 for driving licences. It is possible for a driving licence to be issued subject to appropriate conditions (e.g. someone with a false right arm may have a driving licence limiting them to driving automatic vehicles, with all emergency controls and switches fitted to the left-hand side of the steering-wheel only).

# Driving Licences

### When do I need a licence?

The general rule is that you need a licence to drive any motor vehicle on the roads. However, there is one exception – you do not need a licence to drive an electrically assisted pedal cycle (these cannot go at more than 15 m.p.h.).

### At what age can I drive?

You need to be seventeen to get a licence to drive a car or motor-bike. For mopeds the minimum age is sixteen. See p. 64 for more information on minimum ages.

### How do I apply for a licence?

Get an application form (D1) from a post office. Complete this and send it to the Driver and Vehicle Licensing Centre at Swansea. If it is your first application for a licence use the postcode SA99 1AD; if it is not your first application for a licence use postcode SA99 1AB.

If this is your first application you must wait until you receive your provisional licence before you start driving. Otherwise you will be driving without a licence. It usually takes about three weeks for the application to be processed (unless you have a medical condition, in which case it is likely to take longer). On the other hand, if you have held a licence before (and are not disqualified from driving and you are in good health) you can drive as soon as your application is received by the DVLC; you do not have to wait until you receive the licence back in the post.

The fee for a provisional licence is £10; the fee for a full licence (which you can get after you have passed your test) is a further £10. When you get your first provisional licence you will also be sent a free copy of the

Highway Code, a kidney donor card and two booklets on *Your Driving Test* and *Get Expert Instruction*.

### What is a provisional licence?

Anyone who is learning to drive must obtain a provisional licence. See 'Learners' (pp. 132–41) for the rules on learning to drive. In fact, if you wanted to, you could simply drive throughout your life on a provisional licence and never take the test! This is because a provisional licence will normally last until you are aged seventy. In practice most people want a full licence so they can drive without L-plates, and without an accompanying driver.

But there are special rules for motorbikes. Motorbikes come within Group D and these provisional licences are valid for only two years; what is more, when the licence expires it cannot then be renewed for at least one year. So if you take out a provisional motorcycle licence you will have to pass your test within two years, or alternatively take your bike off the road for a year and then (after a year's wait) apply for another two-year provisional licence. The only exception to this would be if you already held another licence (e.g. a full licence for driving a car will automatically be treated as a provisional licence for riding a motorbike, and you will not have to worry about that licence expiring after two years – see p. 133 for further information).

If you want to ride a motorbike you should also remember that there are restrictions on the size of bike that you can ride while you have a provisional licence (i.e. while you are a learner) – see p. 135.

### How do I get a full driving licence?

The simple answer is that you must have passed the driving test within the last ten years.

But you can also apply for a new licence if you have previously held a full British licence (including Northern Ireland, the Isle of Man and Channel Islands) within the last ten years (for instance, you might have been disqualified – see p. 232). Also you may be able to obtain a full licence if you have become resident in Britain within the last year (provided you hold a full licence from an EEC country, Australia, Gibraltar, Hong Kong, Kenya, New Zealand, Norway, Singapore, Spain, Sweden or Switzerland).

### Do I have to tell the DVLC about any physical or mental problems I may have?

It depends on how serious the condition is. There are numerous conditions that must be reported to the DVLC, such as giddiness, fainting, epilepsy, diabetes, high blood pressure, arthritis, alcoholism, etc. It is up to you to tell the DVLC about anything that may affect your ability to drive safely. Similarly, if your condition worsens after the time when you were granted a licence, it is up to you to notify the DVLC. They will then make medical inquiries (they will probably contact your GP) and the result may be that you are given a licence for only a short period of time, or perhaps that you are even refused a licence. If this happens you can apply to your local magistrates' court for that decision to be reviewed. See a solicitor for help (tell the solicitor you want to apply under s.90 Road Traffic Act 1972 for a review of a revocation of driving licence). You will almost certainly have to produce medical evidence to establish that you are fit to drive.

The DVLC is automatically told of drunk drivers with excessively high blood/alcohol readings (over 150 milligrams in 100 millilitres of blood). A licence is unlikely to be granted to someone who has had two drunk-driving convictions of over 200 milligrams in their blood within a ten-year period.

### Must I tell the DVLC if I wear glasses or contact lenses?

As always you must tell them of anything that makes you unfit to drive. As regards eyesight there are standards laid down. You must be able to read in good daylight (wearing your glasses or contact lenses) a car numberplate from 75 feet (67 feet if the numbers are the smaller ones, 3⅛ inches in height). If you cannot do this you should not be driving.

If you can pass these eyesight tests only when wearing your glasses or contact lenses you will commit an offence if you drive without wearing them.

### What do the codes on my licence mean?

If you look at your licence you will see that at the top it says whether it is a full or a provisional licence. It then says the dates during which it is valid; you will almost certainly find that it is valid until the date of your seventieth birthday.

The licence says that you are 'hereby licensed to drive motor vehicles of groups . . .', and you will see a long, narrow box containing various letters. Those are the group letters, identifying the different types of vehicle – see the table below. For instance, category A covers motor cars; category B covers automatic cars, etc.; category D covers motorbikes; category E covers mopeds.

The number of your driving licence, which is in the top left-hand corner of the licence, will be based on your name and age – the police can find out a lot simply by knowing your driving licence number.

The first five letters will be the first five letters of your name. The next six figures will be based on your birthday (in year, month, day order). For instance, a man born on 10 November 1960 would have the figures 601110; a woman with the same birthday would have 5 added to the second number (i.e. 651110). After these numbers there should be two letters; these are normally the first two initials of the name. Finally there is a number 9 together with two more letters. For instance, the number

| To drive | You need a licence for group | You are already covered if your existing licence includes groups |
| --- | --- | --- |
| A moped | E | A, B, C or D |
| A motor bicycle (with or without side-car) or scooter | D | |
| A motor car, goods vehicle or bus (manual and automatic) | A | |
| A motor car, goods vehicle or bus (with automatic transmission only) | B | A |
| To drive HGVs or PSVs (except minibuses) an extra licence is needed | | |
| A motor tricycle, three-wheeled car or van | C | A or D |
| Special vehicles | | |
| An invalid carriage | J | |
| An agricultural tractor | F | A or B |
| A mowing machine or pedestrian-controlled vehicle | K | A, B, C or F |
| A road roller | G | |
| A tracked vehicle | H | |
| An electrically propelled vehicle | L | Group containing vehicle type |
| A duty-exempt vehicle | N | Group containing vehicle type |

of Brian Thomas Smith, born 10 November 1960, would be SMITH601110BT9 (plus two more letters).

## What if I lose my licence?

Apply to the DVLC for a duplicate licence. This will cost you £3; apply on form D1 (from any post office). The same applies if the licence is stolen or accidentally destroyed.

## Do I ever have to return my licence to the DVLC?

Yes, if you change your name (e.g. through marriage) or you change your address. There is a maximim penalty of £50 for failing to tell the DVLC about moving or changing your address.

---

### WHAT'S THE PENALTY?

*For no driving licence*

MAXIMUM PENALTY: a £400 fine, plus an endorsement (and even disqualification) and two penalty points if you had not passed the driving test (or were too young to have taken it). Endorsement and penalty points are only possible if the laws on learner drivers are not complied with (so, for instance, motorists who have passed their test and not renewed their licence cannot be given an endorsement or penalty points)

LIKELY PENALTY: a £10 fine for simply forgetting to renew a driving licence. In the more serious case of a motorist who has not passed the driving test, the likely penalty is a £40 fine, with an endorsement and two penalty points. You may get a £24 fixed penalty ticket (plus penalty points) instead (see p. 217)

*For not signing a driving licence*

MAXIMUM PENALTY: a £400 fine

LIKELY PENALTY: a £5 or £10 fine

*For not notifying the DVLC of a change of address or name*

MAXIMUM PENALTY: a £400 fine

LIKELY PENALTY: a £5–£10 fine

*(For more on penalties see p. 216)*

---

*When can the police ask to see my licence?*

The police can demand to see your licence if you are driving, or if they think you were involved in an accident (see pp. 15 and 239).


*What is an international driving permit?*

This is a document that allows you to drive abroad. In fact an ordinary full driving licence will usually be good enough for most Western European (and several Eastern European) countries. Otherwise you will probably need an international driving permit which can be obtained from either the A A, the R A C or the Irish R A C (you need not be a member, but will need the application form and a passport photograph, plus a fee of £1.50 – quote your driving licence number, or produce it if you are applying in person). The permit will last for one year.

You cannot use an international driving permit issued in Britain in place of a full driving licence (e.g. if your licence has expired you cannot rely on your international driving permit).

Foreigners coming to drive in this country can use their own national driving licences or an international driving permit for up to a year. Foreigners who have become resident in this country may be able to swap their foreign driving licence for a British driving licence. But they must do this within one year of becoming resident in this country, and this provision only applies to citizens of certain countries (see p. 91).


*What should I do when I receive my driving licence?*

Check that it is correct (does it cover the right groups of vehicles? – see p. 93) and then sign it – if you do not sign it you are committing an offence. See above for the penalties.

# Drunk Driving

### What is the penalty for drunk driving?

Nearly always it is a fine, plus at least twelve months' disqualification. Only rarely can a motorist hope to escape disqualification (see below).

If you have been breathalysed, and found to be over the limit, your chances of escaping disqualification are minimal. You may read in the press about technical defences, and about clever lawyers being able to have drunk-driving charges dismissed, but in practice this is extremely rare. The harsh reality is that if you are prosecuted for drunk driving you have very little chance of keeping your licence.

The drunk-driving laws were overhauled in 1983. Before that time it was possible to raise one of several technical defences. Also the laws imposed on the police were stricter – they had to follow rigid procedures, and the slightest mistake could result in the breath test being held invalid. That has all changed. Now the courts take a more robust view, and minor procedural mistakes will not be held against the police.

If you have been breathalysed, and you are reading this chapter in the hope of finding an escape from disqualification, think again. You may have been 'unlucky' to have been caught (there is only a 1 in 250 chance of being caught), but it is an extremely serious offence. Drunk drivers cause numerous accidents and kill many people each year. Did you know that one in every three drivers killed in accidents are over the limit at the time of death?

### What drunk-driving charges can be brought?

There are two main charges. Firstly, there is the prosecution for failing the breath test – driving 'with alcohol over the prescribed limit'. This is the charge that is used against the vast majority of drunk drivers. Secondly, there is a separate charge that is a survivor of the days before breath tests were invented, and it does not depend upon the motorist having failed a breath test. This is the 'driving while unfit' offence (i.e. driving 'when unfit through drink or drugs'). Relatively few motorists are prosecuted under this provision.

With both a breathalyser and a driving while unfit charge the court *must* disqualify for at least twelve months. With a drunk in charge prosecution the court need not do this – it has a discretion, and so the motorist may be more likely to get away without being disqualified.

These then are the two main drunk-driving charges. Because of the breath test procedure there are other charges that can be brought against motorists who have tried to avoid conviction by not co-operating with the police:

- refusing to take the breath test
- refusing to give a specimen (i.e. blood, urine or breath).

### When can the police carry out a breath test?

The police have extensive powers to ask motorists to take breath tests. In theory there is no power to impose random breath tests, but in practice the police are usually able to find a legal justification for imposing one.

The law says there are two occasions when a breath test can be required:

- when the police suspect an offence has been committed
- when there has been an accident.

1. *When the police suspect an offence has been committed.* The police can stop you, and ask you to take a breath test, if they think either that you have committed a moving traffic offence or that you have been drinking. This is in fact an extremely wide-ranging power. The phrase 'moving traffic offence' means any traffic offence committed while you are 'moving'. Thus, if a motoring offence is committed, the police can ask you to take a breath test (however trivial the offence may be). Also, if the police reasonably suspect that you have any alcohol in your bloodstream (note that they need not suspect you of having excess alcohol) – if, for example, your driving is in any way erratic – they can ask you to take a breath test. Furthermore, if you are stopped by the police – even without reasonable cause – they can ask you to take a breath test if they can smell alcohol on you. This is because you will still be treated as 'driving' even when the car is stationary. So if the police

then have grounds for thinking that you have alcohol in your bloodstream (e.g. they can smell alcohol on your breath) they can demand that you take a breath test.

The combined effect of these rules is that the police have extensive powers to ask motorists to take breath tests. Any offence – however trivial – gives them that right; any flaw in your driving that may indicate alcohol in the bloodstream gives them that right; if they can get you to stop, and can then smell alcohol on your breath, they can impose a test.

2. *When there has been an accident.* If your vehicle has been involved in an accident, and the police reasonably suspect that you were to blame, they can demand that you take a breath test (even if they had no grounds for thinking that you have been drinking). On the other hand, if you were clearly innocent of blame, and could not have been liable for the accident in any way, the police cannot breathalyse you. However, if they smelt alcohol on your breath they would be entitled to give you a breath test (see (1.) above).

Problems can arise when there is a considerable time-lag between the accident and the breath test. Generally, however, the courts take a fairly robust view and will insist that a police constable is entitled to demand a breath test even when there has been a considerable delay since the time of the accident.

### What if the police trick me, or pressurize me, into taking a breath test?

Here we are dealing with the situation in which the police were not entitled to require you to take a breath test. Unfortunately you agreed to be breathalysed and now find that that breath test is being used against you in a drunk-driving prosecution. Can you argue that the police should never have asked you for a breath test in the first place? The answer is no. The courts have made it quite clear that, even when a breath test is illegally administered (i.e. the police were not justified in imposing it), the courts will not ignore the results. If you have been found to be over the limit you can be prosecuted. The principle is the same as for other criminals: for example, someone who has committed a burglary cannot escape conviction merely because the circumstances of their arrest give grounds for complaint against the police – the courts would still convict them of burglary. Similarly, if you were drunk while driving a car you cannot escape liability merely because the breath test was wrongly imposed:

*Mr Fox had an accident at Raglan. No other vehicle was involved. He drove home, with his passenger, and they went indoors. The police heard about the accident and went to Mr Fox's home. They knocked on the door but received no reply. However, they could tell that the men were inside so they broke in. They then asked Mr Fox to take a breath test. He refused, and was taken to the police station. There he eventually gave specimens of breath, which were over the limit, and he was charged with drunk driving. When he came up for trial he argued that the police were not entitled to break into his home and ask him to take a breath test.*

*Held: Mr Fox was right. The police should not have broken into his home. The only occasions when the police can trespass, i.e. go into someone's home uninvited (but remember, we are talking here about* motoring *offences only), are when they think someone has been injured, or property damaged, in an accident. Here they had no grounds for believing that either Mr Fox or the passenger was injured. Therefore they were trespassers and were not lawfully in the house, and were not entitled to ask him to take the breath test.*

*However, the fact remained that Mr Fox had given a sample at the police station and had been found to be over the limit. The court decided that the evidence of the sample could be admitted. So, despite the fact that the police had acted illegally, Mr Fox was convicted of drunk driving.* Fox *(1984)*

### What if the police call at my house and ask me to take a breath test?

See what happened to Mr Fox (above). The answer is that if you let the police in, and you end up taking a breath test (or giving a sample at the police station), you will be prosecuted if you are over the limit. The tricky question is: can you refuse to let the police in? As will be seen from Mr Fox's case the police can only trespass (i.e. break into your house) in certain circumstances. One of these is if they believe you have been involved in an accident in which someone was injured. But if there was no injury the general rule is that they cannot force their way into your house. In those circumstances, if you refuse them access, and you stick by any refusal to take a breath test (or give a sample), you cannot be prosecuted. But if the police can get at you without trespassing (e.g. you open the front door and they grab you without their stepping inside!) they will have acted legally.

We are obviously getting into complicated areas of law here. How can you, as a motorist, be expected to know the fine details of when the police can, or cannot, enter your home? If you are put in this situation you will have a difficult decision to make. If the police are acting legally in breaking into your home, and you then refuse to be breathalysed or give a sample, you will definitely be convicted of refusing to take the breath test and will probably lose your licence (see below). On the other hand, if you correctly believe that the police do not have any right to be in your house you cannot be convicted of refusing to take the breath test. As a general point you should bear in mind that the courts do not like acquitting drunk drivers (or suspected drunk drivers) because of legal technicalities. You would find that the court was not sympathetic to your arguments and would probably do everything it could to justify the police action.

### Can the police carry out random breath tests?

In theory, no. For instance, the police cannot simply wait outside a pub car park and then breathalyse every motorist who comes out. Similarly they cannot set up road blocks to breathalyse motorists at random. However, in practical terms the police have sufficient powers to be able to enforce the drunk-driving laws. If you read the section on p. 97 you will see that the police have extensive powers for requiring motorists to take breath tests. In any event, if you do take a breath test (whether or not the police were acting legally), that breath test can be used against you – in other words, you can be prosecuted for drunk driving on the basis of having failed the breath test even if the test was illegal. How many motorists have the nerve to refuse to take a breath test when stopped by the police? Anyone who thinks the police cannot carry out random breath tests should read this case:

*A policeman was being trained in how to operate the breathalyser. What better way than to train him on passing motorists? So the police stopped cars – at random – and then asked the drivers to take breath tests. Legally they had no justification for doing this (see p. 97).*

*One of the drivers was Mr Dash. He stopped, and took the breath test. He failed it. Could he be validly convicted of drunk driving? Not surprisingly he argued that the police had not followed the law. The police were not saying there was any suspicion of him having had alcohol in his body, and there was no suspicion of him having committed a traffic offence. How then could he be properly breathalysed? The court dismissed this argument. The results of a breath test would only be ignored if 'malpractice' could be shown. Random stopping of vehicles was not wrong.* Chief Constable of Gwent *(1985)*

So, random stopping is allowed, but random breath tests are not. But if the police randomly stop and then, for instance, smell alcohol, they can give a breath test.

*What is the procedure in an excess-alcohol charge?*

There are three separate steps:

1. *You are asked to take the breath test.* This is when you are stopped by the police; you will be asked to take a roadside breath test. If you fail the test (or if you refuse to take it) you will be arrested and taken to the police station. If you pass the test (i.e. you are not over the limit) that will usually be the end of the matter, and you will not have to go to the police station.

If you should fail the breath test:

2. *You give a sample at the police station.* Normally you simply give another one or two breath specimens (into a machine) at the police station. The Intoximeter machine needs two breath specimens. The print-out from that machine will provide the evidence against you if you are prosecuted for drunk driving. Occasionally you will be able to give a blood or urine sample instead.

If you fail this test:

3. *You will be prosecuted for driving with excess alcohol.* If you refuse to take that second test you will be prosecuted for failing to provide a specimen. The penalties for both offences are the same – either way you will almost certainly lose your licence for at least a year.

There are, then, two tests: the roadside breath test and a further test (usually a breath test) at the police station.

*How is the roadside breath test carried out?*

You will be asked to blow into a bag or machine. Different police forces use different equipment. There are two main types of *machine* in use – the Intoximeter and the Camic Breath Analyser. These machines are generally accepted to be more reliable than bags, and the results less open to argument. The main problems arise when the motorist does not blow hard enough. The most common type of *bag* is still the Alcotest 80. With this the breath test cannot be taken until at least twenty minutes after the suspect has been stopped by the police. The suspect blows into the bag (in a single breath of between ten and twenty seconds). The amount of alcohol will be shown by the extent to which the crystals in the bag change to green – if the green stain extends beyond the yellow ring on the tube the motorist has failed the test.

The roadside breath test is no more than a preliminary screening test.

It is aimed at weeding out those who are clearly not over the limit. Failure to pass the roadside breath test does not mean that a prosecution for drunk driving will follow – that will depend upon the results of the second test, at the police station.

### What happens if I refuse to take the roadside breath test?

You will be arrested and taken to the police station.

If you run off, to avoid being caught, the police can follow you. If someone else was injured in an accident they could, if necessary, break into your home to arrest you.

Failure to take the breath test is an offence. If you look at the penalty chart on p. 110 you will see that the penalty for refusing to take a roadside breath test is different from that for all the other excess-alcohol offences: the maximum fine is only £400, and the magistrates need not automatically disqualify, although there would be four penalty points (and an endorsement) if no disqualification were imposed. With the other excess-alcohol charges the magistrates *must* disqualify for at least twelve months. However, do not be misled into thinking that you will be better off by refusing to take the breath test. If you do so you will normally be arrested and taken to the police station. There you will be asked to provide a sample (i.e. usually another breath test). If you again refuse you will be charged with the separate offence of 'failing to provide a specimen of blood, urine or breath'. This charge does carry automatic disqualification for at least twelve months. The end result therefore is that there is usually nothing to gain by refusing to take the breath test (or the second test in the police station).

### How is the test at the police station carried out?

You will only have to go to the police station and give a sample (usually another breath test) if you have already failed the roadside breath test.

The police can ask you to give either a blood, a urine or a breath sample. In practice it is nearly always a breath sample that is required (i.e. a breath test). However, the police can opt to ask you for a blood or urine sample instead. For instance, they might do this if they think you are not well enough to breathe properly into the machine.

The police should follow the operating instructions for the breath machine carefully. If they do not the test will be invalid – and they will not be able to prosecute you. In practice, of course, it is very rare for the police to make mistakes when using these machines.

The police officer should begin by typing in the name of the police station and his or her own name, together with your name and perhaps your date of birth. The machines automatically log the time, and check themselves against simulated breath samples produced by a simulating machine attached to the main testing machine. In addition the police officer will put a new mouthpiece on the breath tube. The spring-loaded tube should then be pulled out of the machine to at least half its length. The next stage is for the police operator to tell you that you have to give two breath samples, and you have three minutes in which to give them. It is not good enough to give one sample. The police officer will also tell you that if you do not give these samples you will be liable to prosecution.

You will be told when the machine is ready to use. You then have three minutes. If you blow in sufficient air (one and a half litres) an electronic star will probably appear on the machine. It can be difficult to blow into the machine, but the experienced police officer should know when the machine is working properly and when the driver is blowing in properly (this can usually be told from the sound of the air). If you have difficulty blowing into the machine you should say so – tell the police officer what is happening and ask for a written record to be made.

At the end of the test the machine will provide a print-out in triplicate. Usually one copy will be given to you on the spot. If for some reason it is not, it must be sent to you so that it arrives at least seven days before the date of the court hearing. Both you and the police officer should sign the print-out.

If you fail the test you cannot demand another try. But if both the breath tests (i.e. the roadside breath test and the test you have just taken in the police station) give a reading of no more than 50, you might find it worth claiming a blood or urine test instead – in which case that test will replace the breath test readings. This is your right. Note that you cannot decide whether it is to be a blood or a urine test – the police decide which of the two it is to be. If they do take a blood or urine sample you can demand that you be given part of the sample (so you can have it tested elsewhere if you wish). But the police are not bound to offer you this sample – it is up to you to ask for it.

And that's all there is to it!

### How much is it safe to drink?

Do not think that the legal limit is a 'safe' limit. Research shows that someone who is just under the legal limit is four times more likely to have an accident than someone who has not drunk at all.

It is impossible to say how much you can drink without going over the limit. However, there are rough guidelines. If you regard a half pint of beer, a glass of wine, a normal glass of sherry, and a single gin or whisky (pub measures) as all being 'one unit' of alcohol, then the general rule is not to drink more than three units. Four units within half an hour can put some people over the legal limit. So, one and a half pints of beer is a normal allowable amount. Other tests show that a man of 70 kg (about 11 stone) will be over the limit after five units (i.e. two and a half pints, or five single scotches). For the average woman the limit is reached after about 60 per cent of what the average man can drink. So the man's five units would only be three units for a woman (i.e. one and a half pints, or three glasses of wine). But these are rough guides only: much depends on body weight and the speed of drinking. Thus, the best advice is to stick to the rule of three – only three units of alcohol.

### What is the legal limit?

Blood, urine and breath levels are measured in different ways, so different figures are given for the alcohol content – but they all mean the same thing. For instance, you might have a reading of 52 on breath, 159 on urine and 120 on blood – but they would all show that you were well over the alcohol limit (in fact you would be half as much again over it!).

In the old days alcohol levels were always by reference to blood. Thus the standard test was up to 80 milligrams of alcohol in 100 millilitres of blood. This 80 milligram limit remains the same. However, these days breath tests are used far more frequently than blood tests, and the relevant limit for a breath test is 35 micrograms of alcohol in 100 millilitres of breath. If you were to be prosecuted for excess alcohol your alcohol level would almost certainly be on the basis of a breath test – were you over 35 micrograms or not?

If it is urine that is checked, the relevant level is 107 milligrams of alcohol in 100 millilitres of urine.

Although these are the limits laid down by the law, the police, in practice, impose a stricter standard. To avoid arguments the police will normally only prosecute when both breath readings are over 40 micrograms, which is 5 micrograms more than the law's figure of 35. So if your breath readings are in the 35–40 microgram region you will have been over the limit, but you will not be prosecuted. With a blood test the police normally deduct 6 milligrams from the reading (e.g. if your reading is 85 milligrams it will be counted as 79 – so you will not be over the legal limit of 80 milligrams). If your reading is over 100 milligrams, a figure of 6 per cent is deducted (e.g. if your reading is 150 milligrams it will be counted as a reading of 141).

It is impossible to give accurate guidance as to how much drink will take an individual over these limits. As a general guide one can say that an eleven-stone man who drinks a couple of pints of beer, or half a bottle of red wine, or four ounces of spirits, will be at the limit. However, this assumes that he drinks it all within a few minutes. If the drinks are spread over a longer period of time, the reading will not be so high. But remember that the amount of food in the body (i.e. did you have an empty stomach?) can also be relevant.

### What defences are there to an excess-alcohol charge?

Very few! Under the old, pre-1982 laws there were various technical defences that could be raised. These have largely been abolished – the law has been simplified, with the result that there are fewer defences available.

It is easier to talk about what defences are *not* available. It is not a defence to say that:

'*I may have been over the limit, but it didn't affect my driving.*' This is no defence. If you were over the limit you are guilty.

'*But I only drove a short way.*' This is not a defence. If you were over the limit you are guilty. Only exceptionally have motorists been able to raise this argument successfully – for instance, when a motorist moved his car a few yards to remove it from a point of danger. As a general rule, it is a hopeless defence.

'*I tried blowing into the machine, but I couldn't blow hard enough.*' Once again, this is not a defence. If you cannot cope with the machine that is your problem. You will be guilty of failing to take a breath test (or provide a sample).

'*But the police should never have breathalysed me in the first place.*' Bad luck. Even if the police were not entitled to breathalyse you, the breath test can be used against you on an excess-alcohol charge (see p. 98). If you were over the limit you are guilty.

'*But someone laced my drinks.*' Once again – bad luck. If you were over the limit you are guilty of the offence. The mere fact that this was not your fault – because someone else laced your drinks – will not mean that you have a defence. But it may be relevant when it is decided whether or not you should be disqualified (see below). Incidentally, the friend who laced your drinks might be guilty of an offence!

'*I'll use the "hip-flask" defence!*' You can try, but you will probably fail! Before the drunk-driving laws were reformed in 1983 the hip-flask defence was fairly popular. What happened was that the motorist would have a quick drink between being stopped by the police and taking the breath test, and then argue that the breath test result was distorted by the hip-flask drink! Although the courts did narrow down the scope of the defence it still remained a successful ploy – determined drinkers would keep a hip-flask in the car, ready for consumption if stopped by the police! Not surprisingly the 1983 changes resulted in this loophole being tightened up. Now, if you want to argue the hip-flask defence, you will have to prove that you did take the extra drink, and that it took you over the limit. So it will be for you actually to *prove* that you would have been under the limit if you had not had that drink. In practice this is extremely difficult. To do it you would have to call an expert scientist as a witness at your trial – who would give evidence on the amount of drink you had from the hip-flask, and the effect it would have had upon you. You would probably also have to call evidence from colleagues, etc. as to the amount of drink you had had earlier in the day, so as to show that that would not have taken you over the limit. In practical terms this is extremely difficult to do – and the end result is that the hip-flask defence is only rarely available. Incidentally some lawyers have said that a motorist who deliberately drinks from a hip-flask – to avoid a drunk-driving conviction – could be guilty of obstructing the police in the execution of their duty!

'*But the police would not let me call my solicitor.*' You should have been allowed to call your solicitor, but there was no need for the police to wait until your solicitor arrived. Alcohol levels reduce as time passes – so you cannot use delaying tactics (e.g. asking for your solicitor to be present). If you refuse to take the breath test until your solicitor is there you will be guilty of failing to take the breath test, or of refusing to provide a sample.

'*But I was in the pub car park when I was stopped.*' This is probably not a defence. You must not have excess alcohol in your bloodstream if you are driving either on a public road or in a public place. The word 'public' does not mean that it should not be private – if private property is generally open to the public (e.g. a pub car park, a cinema car park, etc.) the excess-alcohol laws apply. So the test is whether the property is generally open to the public. If it was entirely private property (e.g. your own front drive or a friend's field) the excess-alcohol laws would not apply.

You can see from the above that there are virtually no defences to an excess-alcohol charge. If you were over the limit, and the machine was working properly, you will almost certainly be found guilty. And you will almost certainly lose your licence for twelve months.

### *I have been told that the best thing to do is to run away if the police should ever want to breath test me. Is that true?*

It sounds a very risky thing to do! If you run away before the police ask you to take the breath test you cannot be charged with failing to take the breath test. However, you may be guilty of obstructing the police. On the other hand, if you have been asked to take the breath test, and you then run away, you will automatically be guilty of the offence of failing to take the breath test. Although disqualification is not automatic for this offence, in practice the courts treat it very seriously – you would almost certainly end up with the same penalty (if not a more severe penalty) than if you had failed the breath tests and were over the limit.

If you have been involved in an accident you should stop (see p. 11 for the rules on when you must stop after an accident). If you run away from the scene of an accident you may well be committing an offence.

To summarize: if you run away from the police, or from the scene of an accident, you may well be committing an offence. However, by doing so it is true to say that you may avoid an excess-alcohol prosecution. On the other hand, you may not – all too often people who run away are caught and then face prosecution for excess alcohol and for the additional offences!

### Is the offence of drunken driving different from the excess-alcohol charge?

Yes. The excess-alcohol charges are concerned with breathalysers, breath tests, samples, etc. We have dealt with these points above. But in the days before breathalysers there was a different charge that was brought against drunk motorists – 'driving when unfit through drink or drugs'. This is generally known as drunken driving or driving when unfit.

When the breathalyser laws were introduced the offence of excess alcohol was introduced. But, the old drunken-driving offence was also kept. Thus there are now two charges that can be used against drunk motorists – excess alcohol or drunken driving.

Drunken driving is proved without the use of a breath test. There is no need for the police to show that you were totally incapable – they must just show that you were unfit to drive through excess alcohol or drugs. For instance, erratic driving, colliding with a lamp post for no apparent reason, your state and condition (e.g. slurred speech, staggering, seeming confused) will all be sufficient evidence. Often this will be proved by a police officer describing the state in which you were found, or by a police doctor describing the results of an examination of you (e.g. you were unable to walk in a straight line or to touch your nose with your finger).

The drunken-driving charge can be used against a motorist who is unfit through drugs. It can also be used against glue sniffers.

The penalties for drunken driving are the same as those for excess alcohol. If you have been driving after drinking too much alcohol you will almost certainly lose your licence for at least a year – whether you are charged with excess alcohol or drunken driving.

### Can I have my case tried before a jury?

No. All motoring offences involving drinking drivers have to be heard in the magistrates' court. This means that they will be heard by magistrates, and not by a jury (as would be the case in the Crown Court).

### What are the penalties for driving with too much drink?

The penalty chart on p. 110 sets out the maximum penalties and the likely penalties.

The important point to note is that you can normally expect to be disqualified. It is extremely difficult to avoid disqualification – over 97 per cent of convicted excess-alcohol drivers are disqualified.

Disqualification will normally be for at least twelve months. It can be for longer – the court has a complete discretion. The only way that you, as the motorist, can avoid disqualification is if you can show the court that there were mitigating circumstances. See p. 229 for an explanation of what can amount to mitigating circumstances. The classic example is the motorist who is a professional driver, and who will be thrown out of work if disqualified from driving. However, bear in mind that the courts are not sympathetic to drunk drivers, and are reluctant to find mitigating circumstances.

If it is your second drunk-driving conviction in ten years the minimum period of disqualification is three years (not twelve months). Your chances of showing mitigating circumstances in such a case are slim!

For most motorists conviction results in twelve months' disqualification. But the period can be longer if the motorist was well over the limit. For instance, some courts think in terms of eighteen months' disqualification if the breath reading was 65 micrograms or so; two years if 90; three years if over 110. Obviously these are very rough-and-ready guidelines – each court is different, and each case is viewed on an individual basis. However, if you were grossly over the legal limit (e.g. a 100 microgram breath reading) the court might consider ordering you to take the driving test again, at the end of your period of disqualification.

For what it means to be disqualified see p. 235.

In addition to being disqualified you can expect a fine. Generally the fine will not be large – the courts realize that disqualification is usually a severe enough penalty. Probably one can think in terms of a fine of £200 or so, although that amount may be increased if you were way over the limit.

Normally you will not get any penalty points. This is because penalty points are not imposed if you are disqualified. In other words, penalty points are an alternative to disqualification. If you are lucky enough to avoid disqualification you will almost certainly receive four penalty points. The only exception would be when you could show that there were 'special reasons' why you should not have an endorsement and penalty points. This is extremely difficult to do – see p. 226 for an explanation of what can amount to special reasons. In practice you are almost bound to be disqualified – in which case you will not get any points, and your existing penalty points (if any) will be wiped out. So when your period of disqualification ends you will start again with a clean licence.

Prison is also a possibility. The maximum term is six months. In practice very few motorists are sent to prison. One option that has been gaining popularity amongst magistrates is for the motorist to be held in police cells (not in prison) for up to four days. See p. 237 for more on this. In effect the courts have power to order detention for up to four

---

### WHAT'S THE PENALTY?

*For driving with excess alcohol*

*For drunken driving*

*For a driver failing to supply a breath/blood/urine sample*

MAXIMUM PENALTY: disqualification for at least twelve months. In addition there may be a maximum fine of £2,000 and up to six months in prison. If there is no disqualification, four penalty points (and an endorsement) will be imposed

LIKELY PENALTY: twelve months' disqualification plus a £200 fine (see above)

*For refusing to take the roadside breath test*

MAXIMUM PENALTY: the court can disqualify. A maximum fine of £400. If no disqualification is imposed, there will be four penalty points and an endorsement

LIKELY PENALTY: twelve months' disqualification and a £200 fine (see above)

*For in charge (i.e. not driving) with excess alcohol*

*For in charge (i.e. not driving) when unfit*

*For in charge (i.e. not driving) and failing to provide a blood/ breath/urine specimen*

MAXIMUM PENALTY: disqualification is discretionary, i.e. there is no automatic disqualification for at least twelve months in 'in charge' cases. A maximum fine of £1,000. A prison sentence of up to three months can be imposed. If there is no disqualification ten penalty points (and an endorsement) will be given

LIKELY PENALTY: twelve months' disqualification and a £100 fine

*(For more on penalties see p. 216)*

---

days, although this power is not widely used. Its use tends to increase around Christmas time, as a warning to other motorists! Otherwise some courts like to use it as a short, sharp shock for motorists who are over twice the limit, or who have a previous drunk-driving conviction. They take the view that a night in the cells will often be the best way of bringing home the seriousness of the offence to a motorist. This is not an alternative to disqualification – apart from being held in the cells the motorist will normally also receive the minimum twelve months' disqualification.

In effect, most motorists who drink too much will end up losing their licence for at least twelve months.

### *I am facing a drunk-driving charge. Should I take legal advice?*

It is probably worth taking specialist legal advice (see p. 142).

However, the advice you will probably be given is that there is no defence to the charge. If this is the case – as it almost certainly will be – you may feel there is no point in retaining a lawyer, who is unlikely to be able to increase your chances of being acquitted, to represent you at the trial. However, what a lawyer may be able to do is to reduce the amount of your fine, and perhaps argue why you should not be disqualified. But bear in mind that the vast majority of motorists are disqualified, and only if you can show clear 'special reasons' (see p. 226) can you hope to avoid disqualification. If your legal adviser thinks that you might have mitigating circumstances it is certainly worth employing a solicitor to argue your case before the magistrates. For instance, if you are a professional driver and you will lose your job if you lose your licence it is certainly worth paying a solicitor to represent you.

Otherwise there is probably little point in your paying a lawyer to represent you, because in the vast majority of cases there is nothing that even the most brilliant lawyer can do to help the motorist avoid twelve months' disqualification and a fine of about £200. Incidentally, you are unlikely to get legal aid. Only if you can show that you have a legal defence (extremely unlikely), or that there are mitigating circumstances that might mean you can avoid disqualification (relatively rare), will you have a chance of getting legal aid.

# Insurance

### What is the difference between a proposal form, a cover note, an insurance certificate, and an insurance policy?

*The proposal form* is the form that you complete for the insurance company. You should set out all the details of yourself, your driving record, etc. It is important that you fill in this form accurately – if you do not your insurance may be invalid (see p. 115).

*The cover note* is a temporary insurance certificate issued by the insurance company. It will probably be valid for a short period only (e.g. one month) and give you less cover than the policy that you will get (see p. 117).

*The insurance certificate* sets out a basic summary of your insurance details. This is usually in a standard form, printed on one sheet of paper. This is the document that you will have to produce to the police if you are stopped, and you will also have to produce it when applying to renew your road tax (see below).

*The insurance policy* – which you will probably never read – is the lengthy document that sets out the full details of your insurance, including all the ways that the insurance company can avoid liability!

### What insurance must I have?

The Road Traffic Act 1972 sets out the bare minimum. Under this Act you must have insurance to meet claims by people injured (including passengers in your car) in traffic accidents on public roads. If you do not have that insurance you will be committing an offence (see p. 122).

If you have an insurance policy that is limited to this cover only it will be called a 'Road Traffic Act only' policy. In fact it is extremely unlikely that you have such a policy – very few motorists rely upon such an inadequate level of cover. Most opt for comprehensive, and others go for some kind of third-party cover. These other types of policy give more cover than under the Road Traffic Act only policy. Most importantly they will insure you against damage to other people's property and vehicles – not just against liability for injuries. So if you drive into another car, and have a Road Traffic Act policy, you will merely be covered for compensation you would have to pay for injuries caused to the people in the car. You would not be covered for the damage to the car. On the other hand, if you had a third-party policy you would be covered for both the injuries and the damage to the car.

### What is a third-party policy?

A third-party policy is more comprehensive than a Road Traffic Act only policy. In fact there are two types of third-party policy – 'third party' and 'third-party fire and theft'. The extent of the cover given by these policies is set out in the table below. The obvious difference between the two is that third-party fire and theft covers fire in your vehicle, or theft from it (for instance, if the radio is stolen).

In practice about one third of motorists have some kind of third-party cover.

### What is comprehensive cover?

As you would expect, this gives considerably more cover than a third-party policy. In particular it covers accidental damage to your car – so you can recover the cost of repairs even if you were to blame for an accident.

In addition claims for broken windscreens are frequently included in the policy (although there will often be a maximum liability of, say, £50). You will probably find that the policy also gives you (and perhaps your husband or wife) personal-accident benefits, so you receive a lump sum if you are personally injured. Personal possessions will probably also come within the scope of the insurance cover (e.g. clothing, rugs, cameras), although there will usually be a limit of, say, £100 for claims.

Different insurers offer different cover with their comprehensive policies – so you will have to check on what is available. For instance, some insurance companies provide additional benefits (e.g. fire damage to a garage, travel and accommodation expenses if you are involved in an accident, hire charges if you need to hire a replacement vehicle).

# The Motorist and the Law

1. Liability for injuries to other people, arising from accidents caused by your car on public roads or elsewhere. Legal costs incurred with your insurance company's consent in connection with a claim against you will also be paid.

2. Liability for injuries to passengers in your car.

3. Liability for passengers in your car in respect of accidents caused by them – for example, the careless opening of a door causing injury to a passer-by or damage to their property.

4. Liability for damage to other people's property. For example, if you are involved in an accident which causes damage to another car, your insurance company will pay all or part of the cost of repairs to the other car, depending on the extent to which you are legally to blame.

5. Liability for injuries to other people or damage to their property caused by a trailer or caravan attached to your car.

6. Fire or theft but if your car is not normally kept in a locked garage at night your insurer may exclude theft, make theft cover subject to special conditions or charge an extra premium.

7. Accidental damage to your car but not wear and tear, depreciation, loss of use, mechanical or electrical breakdown and punctures. If, at the time of the accident, your car is being driven by or is in the charge of someone who holds a provisional licence or has held a full licence for less than a year, or who is under twenty-five years old, you will usually have to pay for damage to your car up to a maximum stated in your policy. This 'excess' will generally be from £25 upwards.

8. Accidents to yourself and perhaps your wife or husband, resulting in death or loss of sight and/or limbs, up to stated amounts. This applies to all journeys in your private car or in any other car not belonging to you whether you are driving or not. This benefit applies only to policies in the name of an individual.

9. Medical expenses up to a stated amount incurred by you or your passengers as a result of an accident involving your car.

10. Loss of or damage to rugs, clothing and personal effects up to a stated amount while they are in the car.

COMPREHENSIVE Sections 1 to 10

THIRD PARTY FIRE AND THEFT Sections 1 to 6

THIRD PARTY Sections 1 to 5

**ACT ONLY**
This type of cover is restricted to liability for injuries to other people, including your passengers, in traffic accidents on public roads. Act only policies are limited to the minimum compulsory requirements of the Road Traffic Act 1972.

### Is it important to fill in the proposal form accurately?

Yes. It is vital that you fill in the insurance proposal form with great care – and that it is totally accurate.

Insurance companies are lucky. They benefit from a rule of law that says that the customer (i.e. you) must disclose *everything* to the insurance company – even if you are not asked! The legal duty is with you to disclose *anything* that might influence the insurer's decision on whether to insure you, and on the amount of premium to charge you. So you must tell the insurance company of *anything* that is relevant to your cover and the amount of your premium. If you do not do this your insurance may be invalid.

The Law Reports are full of cases of people who did not tell their insurance company all the facts. Those unfortunate people found that they were uninsured. However, it is true to say that the courts are slowly beginning to realize that this is an extremely unfair rule, and they are now taking a tougher line with insurance companies who try to evade liability in this way. But in the meantime the law remains that you – as the customer – must disclose *everything* to the insurance company – even if they do not ask you about it! For instance:

*The motorist did not disclose that a previous proposal for a different type of insurance policy had been turned down. His insurance was invalid.*

*Mrs Dunn did not tell the insurance company that her husband was driving the car and that he had a bad accident record. Her insurance was invalid.*

*Mr Holmes filled in the proposal form on the basis that he was a 'dealer'. In fact he was a bookmaker, but he knew the company would not want to insure him if they knew this. His insurance was invalid.*

Even if you innocently make a mistake when filling in the proposal form this mistake can lead to the insurance being invalid! For instance:

*Mr Hunt completed an insurance proposal form. One of the questions was: 'Has anyone who to your knowledge will drive the car been convicted of driving offences?' He answered: 'No' – which he believed to be true. But he did not know that his son had several motoring convictions. As a result his insurance policy was invalid.*

*A Glasgow firm took out insurance for a lorry. The firm's address was given on the proposal form, and there was a question asking where the lorry was garaged – they replied: 'As above'. In fact this was a mistake. The lorry was normally kept in a garage elsewhere. As a result the policy was invalid and the company could not get compensation when the lorry was destroyed in a fire.*

The moral is clear. You should read the questions carefully before you answer them, and you should make sure that your answers are 100 per cent accurate. If in doubt about whether to mention something – include it (if necessary in a covering letter)!

Further complications can arise when you renew your insurance policy at the end of the year. You will automatically be assumed to confirm that the answers given in your original proposal form are still correct. So if anything has happened to alter the position you should tell the insurance company before you renew. It is for you to write to them – and tell them of *anything* – even if they do not ask you. For instance, if you have since been convicted of a motoring offence you should tell your insurance company before you renew the policy. If you do not you will be in breach of the policy. Your insurers would then be able to avoid paying out under the policy. Obviously it can be difficult to decide what matters are serious enough to bother telling the insurance company about. Unfortunately, the way the law is worded, the only sensible advice is to tell them of everything. Any motoring offence, however trivial, should ideally be notified to the insurance company. So should any other matter that might affect their decision whether to insure you and the amount of the premium (e.g. if you have been convicted of an offence of dishonesty, even if it does not involve motor vehicles). The point to bear in mind is that it is for you to offer this information to the insurance company – even if you are not asked for it.

In practice, of course, reputable insurance companies do not enforce the strict letter of the law. For instance, if you do not tell the insurance company about convictions for less serious motoring offences (e.g. an offence that does not carry penalty points) it is almost inconceivable that the insurance company would hold this against you. But the fact remains that they could!

Most people do not realize that the law is weighted so strongly in favour of insurance companies. It is about time the law was changed. There is no reason why there should be special laws for insurance companies. Why not simply say that the insurance remains valid unless there has been deliberate fraud or deception by the motorist?

### What happens if my insurance is invalidated?

If you have filled in the proposal form wrongly (or not told them about something relevant), the insurance company may be able to avoid paying out under your policy. The same would apply if you broke the terms of the policy (e.g. you used it for business use, when only social and domestic use was covered – see below). In this situation the insurance company still has to pay out to anyone injured in the accident. What the law says is that the insurance company must meet the liabilities under the Road Traffic Act only part of your policy – refer to p. 112, from which you will see that the Road Traffic Act simply requires cover for injury to other people (e.g. pedestrians, drivers, cyclists, your passengers, etc.). So your insurance company will have to pay out compensation on those claims. The insurance company will not have to meet claims for damage to cars, motorbikes and other property damaged in the crash.

But the insurance company will then be able to sue you for reimbursement. If you have any money the insurance company can try to recover sums it has paid out to the various claimants. In addition – if you have enough money – the various claimants can also sue you for the damage to their cars, bikes, property, etc. The end result is that the victims get compensation for their injuries, but you will eventually have to meet the bill if you have any money.

### What is a cover note?

A cover note is a certificate giving you temporary motor insurance. Typically a cover note will be for thirty days. It will usually cover the period between an insurance company agreeing to give cover and the time that it sends out the actual policy and insurance certificate.

A broker who fixes up insurance for you may be able to issue a cover note on the spot. Alternatively, if you make the arrangements by phone the broker will probably agree to send you a cover note. The cover note will say the time of day from which it is effective – it cannot be back-dated by even a few hours.

The cover note only comes into effect when it is delivered to you. Suppose you phone the broker at 2.00 p.m., who promises to arrange cover for you immediately. You arrange to pick up the cover note at 3.00 p.m. But on the way there – at 2.30 p.m. – you have an accident. Strictly speaking you will be uninsured at that time, since you have not collected the cover note. Complications arise if the cover note is to be posted to you. The law says that it is only delivered to you when it is posted by the broker into a post box (i.e. it does not come into effect when the broker says it will be posted to you, or when it is delivered to you by the postman – the important time is when the broker puts it in the post box!). So it is vital that your broker should keep to any promise to put your cover note in the post. If you begin driving before it is put in the post box, technically you will be uninsured!

If you should be unlucky enough to be uninsured in these circumstances you would – strictly speaking – be committing a criminal offence (i.e. no insurance). But in practice the police would be very unlikely to prosecute. Incidentally, although you might – in the eyes of criminal law – have no insurance, the insurance company would still meet any claim that you might have as a result of the accident.

When you receive a cover note you should check it carefully. Check that the dates and times are correct. In addition look to see what cover you have been given. You may find that your temporary cover under the cover note is less extensive than that under the final policy (i.e. it may not be as comprehensive).

### What is the difference between an insurance certificate and an insurance policy?

The *insurance certificate* is a summary of the terms of the *insurance policy*. The insurance certificate is in a standard form, laid out in the Road Traffic Act. It must set out the details of the vehicle, the policy holder, the date the insurance begins, the date it ends, the people entitled to drive, and so on. All this will be set out, in order, on one sheet of paper. The insurance policy, on the other hand, will usually be a lengthy document and will often be written in legalese. It is the insurance certificate (not the policy) that has to be produced to the police (see p. 15), or after an accident (see p. 11), or when renewing road tax (see p. 261). In those situations it is not sufficient to produce the policy.

If the insurance certificate and the insurance policy contradict each other (e.g. one says that you are covered for business use, the other that you are covered only for social use), it is the insurance policy that prevails. In cases of doubt look at the wording in the insurance policy, not the insurance certificate.

### Does a car policy automatically cover a caravan or trailer?

Almost certainly your insurance policy will cover a trailer and a caravan. The only exception would be if you had the minimal Road Traffic Act only policy (see p. 112). In practice very few people have such limited cover. All other policies will normally give third-party cover if an accident is caused by a trailer or caravan. In other words, the policy will compensate people who were injured by your trailer or caravan, but will not normally give you compensation if your trailer or caravan is damaged in an accident. If you want that additional cover you should specifically tell your insurance company and they will arrange it for you. If you do not want to be covered for the value of the trailer or caravan there is no need for you to notify your insurance company. Provided you have third-party or comprehensive insurance you will be legally insured under your existing car policy.

### Can I use my private car for business use?

It all depends on the wording of your insurance policy. The typical policy will limit the use to 'social, domestic and pleasure purposes'. So if you intend to use the car for business purposes you will not be covered. You will want to make sure the policy is extended by having the words 'and by the Policy holder in person in connection with his business or profession'. If your use is limited to social and domestic use, in practice it is legitimate to use the vehicle for driving to and from work – but not while at work. If you have any doubt as to whether you will be using your vehicle for business purposes you should query the position with your insurance company. You should not run the risk of being uninsured:

*A car was insured for 'social, domestic and pleasure purposes'. The insured was a garage proprietor. He drove the car to a meeting with the owner of another business, with whom he was intending to make a deal. It was held that this was business use, so he was not covered under the terms of his policy.* Wood *(1948)*

*A policy covered 'social and domestic' use. The vehicle was used for carrying hay (for cows to eat). It was held that the insurance was invalidated by this use, and thus the motorist was convicted of not having insurance.* Whitehead *(1962)*

It is easy to fall foul of this rule. If your employer asks you to use your car at work you should specifically check the position with your insurance company (and ask the employer to pay any increased premium!). If you do not take this precaution you may find you have no insurance – not only will you be guilty of a criminal offence, but you may find yourself uninsured if there is an accident.

The Motorist and the Law

### *Who else can use the car?*

It all depends on the wording of the insurance policy. Check it carefully.
Often the policy will simply say that you (the policy holder) are the only
person authorized to drive. Alternatively it may name a specific driver as
also being entitled to drive. Note that your husband or wife will not
automatically be entitled to drive under your policy – so check whether
they are covered. Or the policy may say that it covers 'any other person
who is driving on the Policy holder's order or with his permission'.
Check which applies in your case.

The policy will also make it a condition that anyone who drives 'holds
a licence to drive the vehicle or has held and is not disqualified from
holding or obtaining such a licence'. This will cover someone who only
has a provisional licence, and who has not yet qualified for a full licence.
So you can take a learner driver for lessons in your car, provided they are
otherwise covered under the terms of your policy. You will need to
check that the certificate covers them. You should also check what you
said on the proposal form – for instance, did you state that the car would
not be used by anyone who did not have a full driving licence, or who was
under a particular age?

### *Will I be covered if I charge people for lifts?*

Probably. It used to be unlawful for motorists to share the cost of travel
with their passengers. However, non-profit car-sharing is allowed if
there are not more than eight people in the vehicle, and if the charges are
agreed before the journey starts. The aim is to make sure that motorists
are not in effect taxis, but are merely sharing expenses. You can charge a
bit more than the cost of the petrol (e.g. you could include something to
cover the cost of servicing, insurance, road tax, etc.). The aim is to make
sure you charge a reasonable sum without making a profit. As long as
you come within these guidelines you will not invalidate your insurance.

On the other hand, you will probably be breaking the terms of your
insurance if you do part-time mini cab driving, or charge for fares. If you
do this you should contact your insurance company and make sure that
the policy specifically covers this commercial use of your vehicle. If it
does not you will be uninsured – not only will you be committing a
criminal offence (i.e. having no insurance), but you will not have
insurance cover if there is an accident.

### *What if I lend my car to someone else?*

You should be very careful. It may be that other drivers will be covered by your insurance policy (e.g. if they are a named driver, or if your policy covers anyone else who is driving with your permission). If that is the case there should be no problems.

But if the other driver is not covered by your insurance policy you should be very careful. You cannot simply lend the car and assume it is for the other driver to fix up the insurance. You cannot say: 'It is nothing to do with me.' As far as the law is concerned you will be committing an offence if you 'permit' anyone else to drive your car without insurance. This is so even if you did not know they had no insurance!

Even if you genuinely and sincerely believe that someone you are lending your car to has insurance you will still be guilty of an offence if it turns out that they do not have insurance. This may seem unfair, but it is the law. The law is applied strictly – if someone uses your car without insurance you will be committing an offence. The only exception would be if you lent the car to someone on the specific agreement that they would *first* take out their own insurance cover. If this was a specific term of your lending the car you could not be prosecuted if it turned out that they did not have insurance. But note that this is a strict requirement – you must specifically require them to take out insurance first. This is not the same as simply relying upon their assurance that they are insured. If a friend asks to borrow your car you should say: "Yes, you can borrow it, provided you first arrange your own insurance policy. When you tell me you have done this, you can borrow it.'

If you acted honestly and reasonably (e.g. you relied upon your friend's assurance) it might be that the police would decide not to prosecute you. Even if they did there is no doubt that the court would take your honesty and reasonableness into account when deciding what penalty to impose. Although you would be guilty of having no insurance, the court might decide that there was a special reason (see p. 226 for what this means) for not giving you an endorsement and penalty points.

### *What if my employer does not insure me when I am driving his/her vehicle?*

The normal rule is that you should check whether you are insured before you drive. If you borrow a car from someone, and they tell you that you are covered by their insurance, you will be guilty of a criminal offence if it turns out that they were mistaken. The fact that you were acting honestly, and were not intending to break the law, does not prevent you being guilty of the offence (see above). But if you were using your employer's vehicle you might be able to use a special defence. This defence would allow you to escape conviction for no insurance if:

● the vehicle neither belonged to you, nor had been hired out or lent to you and

● you were using it in the course of your employment (e.g. delivery duties) and

● you did not know, and had no reason to know, that there was no insurance.

If, as an employee, you came within these three rules you would not be convicted. Note that the exception only covers employees who are driving in the course of their employer's business. If you are a van driver, and your employer lends you the van for use over the weekend, you would not be able to use this defence – because the van had been lent to you, and also because you were not using it in the course of your job.

---

## WHAT'S THE PENALTY?

*For no insurance*

MAXIMUM PENALTY: four to eight penalty points (plus an endorsement) and a maximum fine of £1,000. You could be disqualified

LIKELY PENALTY: much will depend upon circumstances. A typical case will merit a £100 fine and four penalty points. The punishment will be more severe if the attempt was deliberate (e.g. seven points and a substantial fine). Young offenders may get a short disqualification period, as a short sharp shock

*For failure to produce an insurance certificate to the police see p. 242*

*(For more on penalties see p. 216)*

---

### What insurance do I need if I take my car abroad?

Your insurance policy will give you third-party cover in all EEC countries, and in a number of others, but if you want additional cover (e.g. comprehensive cover) you will have to arrange to be issued with an international motor insurance certificate (i.e. a Green Card). A Green Card is compulsory in some non-EEC countries.

If you are staying within the EEC, and you do not want more than third-party cover, you can simply rely upon your existing insurance certificate.

It is advisable to check with one of the motoring organizations before taking your car abroad. They will be able to tell you the rules in detail. As regards your driving licence you will probably find that this covers you in most countries. However, in some countries (e.g. Hungary, Poland, Spain and the Soviet Union) you will need an international driving permit (see p. 95). You should make sure that you carry the vehicle registration document with you when you go abroad – it is not good enough to take your own photocopy. If the vehicle is not in your name you will probably need a letter from the registered keeper confirming that you are authorized to take the vehicle outside Britain. Once again the motoring organizations can give you the details. Finally, you will probably find that you must also have valid British road tax while you are abroad.

### What is an excess?

If you have an insurance policy the chances are that you have to pay the first few pounds of any claim yourself – this is called the excess. Often this will be £50 or £100 (if you are under twenty-five, or have only recently passed your test, the amount can be fairly substantial).

The idea of the excess is to discourage small claims, which cost insurance companies a disproportionately large amount in administrative expenses.

Even if you have comprehensive insurance you are likely to have to pay the excess. You will be covered for all your losses and expenses except the excess. You will then have to decide whether or not it is worth claiming the excess from the other motorist (i.e. from his or her insurance company). Much will depend on who was to blame for the accident – if another motorist was solely to blame they should be liable to reimburse you for the amount of your excess. See p. 178 for how blame is apportioned in road accidents.

If you have a comprehensive policy, and recover the excess from the other motorist (or the motorist's insurance company), you will probably not lose your no-claims bonus.

### Are there any special rules for insuring motorbikes?

No. The same rules apply to motorbikes as to cars.

However, one point to notice is that most motorbike insurance policies are by reference to a particular motorbike. So if you change motorbikes it is vital that you tell the insurance company – otherwise you will probably be uninsured.

Problems can arise when accessories are stolen from a bike (e.g. a spare crash helmet or radio equipment). Generally this equipment will not be covered by the insurance policy unless the bike is stolen at the same time. If the accessory alone is stolen, the chances are that the policy will not cover it. However, the practice does vary from one insurance company to another – so you should check with your own company. If there are particular accessories of value that you wish to have insured you should check that you are covered under your policy.

With any insurance policy the policy holder (whether a motorcyclist or a motorist) agrees to keep the vehicle in a roadworthy condition. If you allow the vehicle to be unsafe (e.g. to have defective brakes) the insurance company could avoid liability under the terms of the policy. In practice insurance companies rarely press this point – unless the defects are obvious, and serious. But it is often the case that young motorcyclists ride bikes that are not safe – which are, legally, in an unsafe condition. Apart from the obvious dangers of riding an unsafe motorbike these motorcyclists should realize that they may be invalidating their insurance.

If you are a motorcycle despatch rider (whether full-time or part-time) you should take out special insurance. This is because most insurance companies specifically exclude despatch riders from their policies. It is estimated that there are about 15,000 despatch riders in London, and most are between the ages of seventeen and twenty-two. Of these a large proportion have not passed the motorcycle test, and do not have insurance. Special comprehensive cover for an eighteen- or nineteen-year-old despatch rider in London can cost £1,000 per year!

### What is a no-claims bonus?

You may well find that the amount of your insurance premium depends on the amount of your no-claims bonus. Most insurance companies give a discount for each claim-free year of insurance; this is on a percentage basis, and increases each year – usually up to a maximum of 60 or 65 per cent.

Usually a no-claims bonus can be transferred from one insurer to another. If you change insurance companies you will probably find that you can take your no-claims bonus with you – although you may have to negotiate on this point. You will probably not be allowed to take the no-claims bonus with you if you are a motorcyclist, or if you earned your no-claims bonus in cars you did not own (e.g. in company cars), but it is worth trying to negotiate this point as well.

The important thing to realize is that it is a no-claims bonus – not a 'no-fault' bonus. In other words, if there is a *claim* on your insurance policy you will lose your no-claims bonus. Whether or not you caused the accident (i.e. were you to blame?) will probably be irrelevant. As far as the insurance company is concerned they will make you forfeit some of your no-claims bonus if a claim is made under your policy – irrespective of why the claim is made.

Remember that you will have to tell the insurance company if you are involved in an accident (see p. 19). You should immediately fill in a form, or send a letter, to the insurance company giving them details of how the accident occurred. By doing this you will not be risking your no-claims bonus – merely telling them of the accident is not the same as making a claim. If you want to you can avoid any doubts on this score by writing 'for information only' on the form or letter. This will make it clear to the insurance company that you are simply notifying them of the incident, and that you are not – as yet – making a claim. However, if the insurance company pays out money to you (e.g. if you have a comprehensive policy), or to other people (because you are liable under your policy), a claim will have been made, and you will lose your no-claims bonus. If the claim being made by the other people is small, it may be to your advantage to settle it privately – without involving the insurance company. If you do this there will have been no claim under your policy, and so you will not lose your no-claims bonus. See p. 22 for how to do this.

If you are involved in an accident, and both you and the other motorist have comprehensive insurance, it is probable that the two insurance companies will settle the claims under a 'knock-for-knock' agreement.

The Motorist and the Law

### *What is a knock-for-knock agreement?*

The major insurance companies have knock-for-knock agreements. If two motorists are comprehensively insured their respective insurance companies will agree to meet their own motorist's insurance claim. This will save the insurance companies the expense and inconvenience of claiming compensation off each other. What happens is that each insurance company bears its own bill, irrespective of who was to blame.

This is fine from the insurance companies' point of view. After all, they save costs since they do not have to make a claim against each other, but it may not be so good for the individual motorist. For instance, suppose you are involved in an accident and you have comprehensive cover. If the other motorist has comprehensive cover your respective insurance companies will meet your individual claims. In other words, your insurance company will pay for the cost of repairs to your vehicle. Since a claim has been made under your policy you will lose your no-claims bonus. But you may feel this is most unfair – because you were in no way to blame for the accident. You will feel that you were the innocent party, yet you have suffered because you have lost (1.) the amount of your excess, and (2.) your no-claims bonus. In this situation what you must do is make a claim against the other driver for the amount of the excess. This may be a relatively small sum, but it is important that you claim it. If you recover the excess (by suing the other motorist in court, or if it is paid to you voluntarily by the other insurance company), your insurance company will accept that you were not to blame and will give you your no-claims bonus back. However, if you do not recover the excess you will lose your no-claims bonus.

### *What do I do after an accident?*

Refer to p. 16 and follow the checklist there.

### *How do I make a claim against another motorist?*

Refer to p. 21. Bear in mind that you will only win your claim if you can show that the other motorist was to blame for the accident (see p. 178).

### How soon after an accident can I get my car repaired?

You must be careful not to have the repairs done too speedily. This is especially important if the repairs will be expensive.

However inconvenient it may be you must make sure that you obtain a proper estimate for those repairs from a garage. Having done that get the insurance company to approve the estimate. You should not simply take your damaged car to a garage and tell them to get on with the work. If you do you may find that you have great difficulty recovering all the costs from the insurance company. This is because insurance companies can be extremely difficult about paying out compensation – after all, insurance companies are in business to collect premiums, not pay out on policies!

If the damage to your car is major the insurance company may well send a vehicle examiner to look at it.

If the engineer thinks the car cannot be repaired economically it will be declared a write-off. You will then be paid the market value of the vehicle, and the wreckage will probably go to the insurance company (exceptionally, you may be left with the wreckage, and they will deduct its scrap value from the sum they are paying you). Also, if the car is less than one year old, and the cost of repairs is likely to exceed 50–60 per cent of its new list price, the chances are that the insurers will declare such a car a write-off as well. When this happens they will offer you a new vehicle. However, you can generally insist upon having your old vehicle repaired – even if the repair costs will exceed 60 per cent of the list price. Provided the cost of repairs will not exceed the list price you can insist on repairs instead of a replacement vehicle.

If the car was more than twelve months old it is usually the insurance company that can choose between providing a replacement vehicle or carrying out repairs.

If you are offered the value of the vehicle this will probably be on the basis of its value at the time you bought it. In other words, if list prices have gone up since you bought the vehicle, the chances are that you will be offered the lower (old) price. This may seem unfair, but insurers can legally do this. Needless to say, they do not offer you the list (old) price if prices have gone down in the meantime!

If your car was on HP, and is declared a write-off, the insurance monies will go to the HP company. The money will be used to pay off the debt to the HP company, and you will merely get the balance.

### What is betterment?

Legally the insurance company simply has to put the car back in the condition it was before the accident. In other words, they have to repair it. But it will often be the case that the repaired vehicle is in better condition than it was before the accident. For instance, if you have a car with a rusty wing, and are then involved in an accident which damages that wing, the replacement wing will be better than the wing that you had before the accident. When this happens you can expect the insurance company to try and pass part of the cost of the new wing on to you. They will say that your car is now 'better' than it was, and that you should pay 'betterment' – a contribution towards the costs. Legally they are entitled to this payment.

Not unnaturally you may reply that you were perfectly happy with the old, rusty, wing and that this would have proved perfectly satisfactory if the other motorist had not driven into it. However, that argument will not succeed. If the repairs end up improving your car you must expect to pay betterment. Needless to say, these betterment claims are often a source of great dispute between motorists and their insurance companies. It is always worth arguing over a betterment claim – it is the sort of thing that can be negotiated. But, at the end of the day, if your vehicle has been improved you have to accept the fact that you should make a contribution towards the repair costs.

### What if my car is stolen?

You must report the theft as soon as possible, to the police and to the insurance company. If you do not report it to the police, the insurance company may refuse to pay out on your claim.

The insurance company will not immediately pay you the value of your car. They will normally wait several weeks (usually four or six weeks) before agreeing to pay out. This is because most stolen cars are recovered within a few days – they are simply taken by joy-riders who borrow them for a short time.

Once the four-week or six-week waiting period is passed the insurance company should settle your claim in full. Often there will be arguments between the motorist and the insurance company over the value of the vehicle. In practice you will probably have to accept the list price, and you will find it extremely difficult to argue for more (e.g. because your car was particularly well-maintained, etc.). You will need firm evidence if you are to be able to claim more (e.g. a certificate from a garage confirming that they regularly serviced the vehicle and that in their opinion it was worth £x).

If the insurance company pays you the value of the car, and the car is then found, it will be the insurance company's property, not yours. In practice the insurance company may be quite happy to return it to you (if you agree to return their money), but they cannot normally force you to take the vehicle back.

If you have third-party fire and theft cover, this theft cover will be only for the value of the car. It will include items that are part of the car (e.g. a stereo stystem) but not any personal items that you left in the car (e.g. rugs, cameras, suitcases, etc.). However, if you have a comprehensive insurance policy it may well be that those items are covered (up to a maximum limit). You will have to check the terms of your policy.

Often, stolen cars are recovered after a relatively short time, but are found to be damaged. If this happens the insurance company will have to pay the cost of the repairs – whether you have a comprehensive or a third-party fire and theft policy. You would not be covered if you merely had Road Traffic Act cover only, or merely third-party cover. The normal excess rules do not apply for thefts, so you would not have to pay the first (say) £50 of the cost of repairs, as would be the case if you were claiming after an accident.

### What can I do if I do not agree with my insurance company's figures?

You may well find that you have to negotiate hard with your insurance company. Most people who deal with insurance companies find that the companies are always trying to knock a few pounds off a claim, and that they also try to delay payment. If you think a company is undervaluing your claim (e.g. charging you too much betterment or refusing to pay your reasonable repair costs) do not be afraid to argue the point with them. If in doubt as to your legal position take legal advice (see p. 142).

If negotiation gets you nowhere you will have to decide whether to take the matter further. You have two choices:

1. *You can take the matter to court.* You can take your claim to the county court (assuming you were not claiming more than £5,000), which will decide which figure was correct. In practice this would be very much a last resort.

2. *You can go to the Insurance Ombudsman.* Most insurance com-

panies are members of the Insurance Ombudsman scheme. The Ombudsman is an independent adviser, whose salary is paid by the insurance companies. He is supposed to look at the papers, and decide who is right. Although he is linked to the insurance companies he is independent – and in practice he is. The advantage of using the Ombudsman service is that it is free – you do not have to pay any fee. All you have to do is make your complaint to him within six months of the date when the insurance company gives its final decision on your claim. When the Ombudsman reaches his decision, that decision will be binding on the insurance company – but not on you. In other words, if he decides that you should be awarded money you can accept that decision and the insurance company will have to pay you. On the other hand, you can reject it – and then sue. You will have lost nothing by going to the Ombudsman, since you can still go to court if you do not like his decision. The insurance company, on the other hand, will be bound by the Ombudsman's decision (if you want to accept it) and will not be able to opt for court. Further details from the Insurance Ombudsman Bureau, 32 Southampton Row, London WC1B 5HJ (01-242 8613).

### What if I am involved in an accident with an uninsured motorist?

Every motorist should be insured, but many are not. To deal with this situation the Motor Insurers Bureau was set up (address below). It will pay compensation to the victim of an uninsured motorist – but only for injuries suffered. This is because the Bureau only pays out on Road Traffic Act liability (i.e. injury claims only – see p. 112).

Suppose you were parked at traffic lights, and another car drives into the back of your car. It turns out that the car is stolen, and the motorist does not have insurance. You would make your claim against the motorist in the usual way – who, of course, would probably not have the money to meet your claim. The MIB would, however, meet your claim – insofar as it relates to your injuries. So you would be able to claim compensation for your injuries (e.g. a whiplash neck injury) together with wages lost while you are off work. But the Bureau would not have to compensate you for your other losses – in particular, the damage to your car. Therefore you would probably have to pay for the car repairs yourself. Only if the uninsured driver had enough money to make suing him or her worth your while would you get that extra compensation. In practice most uninsured drivers have no money, and are not worth suing.

*What happens if I am in an accident with a hit-and-run driver?*

Similar rules apply as with an uninsured driver. Once again the Motor Insurers Bureau would meet the claim, so you would not go uncompensated. But, as with uninsured motorists, the Bureau would only compensate you for your injuries (not for the damage to your car, etc.).

As with all accident claims the general rule is that claims against the Motor Insurance Bureau should be brought within three years of the date of the accident. The Bureau's address is Aldermary House, Queen St, London EC4.

# Learners

### What do I need before I can start learning to drive?

Firstly, you must have a driving licence. Usually this will be a provisional licence, but if you already have a full licence for one type of vehicle that might count as a provisional licence for a different group of vehicles (e.g. a full driving licence for a car will count as a provisional licence for a motorbike – you would not therefore have to get a separate one). See p. 134 for information about driving licences. Secondly, you must have valid insurance. You must either take out separate insurance cover in your own name, or make sure that the person whose car you are driving has a valid certificate of insurance that does cover learner drivers.

### What restrictions are there on learners?

Firstly, you must display L-plates (of a regulation size – 4 × 3½ × 1½ inches) on the front and back of the vehicle. Secondly, you must be accompanied by a person who holds a full driving licence for that category of vehicle. For instance, it would not be sufficient if your passenger had passed the test but had not yet bothered to upgrade the provisional licence to a full licence; nor would it be sufficient if your passenger had a foreign driving licence or an international driving permit. Finally, as a learner you cannot go on the motorway or tow a trailer.

If you are learning to ride a motorbike you must display L-plates at both the front and the back. You will only be able to carry a passenger if that passenger holds a full motorbike licence (a full car licence would not be good enough). You cannot go on the motorway or tow a trailer. There are also restrictions on the type of bike you can ride (see p. 135).

132

## Who can act as a driving instructor?

Anyone who holds a full, valid British driving licence is qualified to be a front passenger with a learner. However, you must not accept money or gifts in payment – there are restrictions on who can set up as a professional driving instructor; if you want to charge for your driving lesson you must be registered with the Department of Transport.

## How do I pass a motorcycle test?

Motorbike driving tests are different from car tests in that the test is in two parts. The first test (fee £15.60) is on an off-the-road circuit, when you have to show that you can control your vehicle properly (e.g. in slow riding, figure of eight, emergency stop tests). If you pass you are given a certificate which must be produced before you can apply to take the second part of the test – but you must apply within five years of taking the first test. This part (fee £14.40) is an on-the-road test, similar to the car driving test.

Because of practical difficulties motorcyclists who are resident on some islands do not have to pass the first part of the test. In fact this only applies to a few remote islands (note that it does *not* apply to the Isle of Wight, Lewis and Harris, North Uist, Benbecula and South Uist, mainland Orkney, mainland Shetland and Skye).

## How long does a provisional motorbike licence last for?

Two years. At the end of those two years it will not be renewed for a further one year. The idea behind this is to encourage motorcyclists to take the test (and so increase the general standard of safety amongst motorcyclists).

So there are two time periods:

• the provisional licence lasts for only two years. Ideally, therefore, both parts of the driving test should be passed within that time
• you must apply for the second test within five years of passing the first test. After that time the first test will have to be taken again.

*How can I avoid the two-year period?*

The obvious way to avoid being debarred from riding a motorbike after two years is to take and pass the driving test (this is in two parts – see above). Otherwise you will have to give up motorbikes for at least a year, and change to either a moped or a car (including a three-wheeler). If you drive a car or three-wheeler you will, of course, need an accompanying qualified driver when you drive the vehicle (which you would not need on a moped or motorbike). In fact the best solution would be to go on and pass a test in a car or moped. This is because the holder of any full driving licence is automatically given a provisional licence for all other categories of motor vehicle – including motorbikes. So you can continue to have a provisional licence simply by passing a test on a moped or car. If you have a provisional licence in this way it is not limited to the two years and instead will carry on until your full driving licence expires (i.e. normally until at least the age of seventy). In short, a motorcyclist can dodge the two-year rule by passing the test on a car or moped.

Finally, if you want to stop the two-year period running (e.g. perhaps you are going abroad and will not be able to use the bike) you can give up your right to ride a motorbike by notifying the DVLC – and you will then be able to claim the balance of the two-year period later on. To do this use the usual licence application form (D1 – obtainable from most post offices). Tick the 'exchange' section and write 'motorcycle surrender' next to the box. Enclose your licence, and a fee of £3. You will eventually be sent your licence back, with Group D (i.e. motorbikes) deleted from it. You can later reclaim the Group D entitlement for the balance of the two-year period (provided at least one month was left of the original two-year period when you gave it up). If more than one year has elapsed since you gave up the licence you can now claim a whole new two-year period. To reclaim your entitlement or to claim a new one you must apply for an exchange licence (use form D1 – ask for 'provisional motorcycle', in section 2(b) of the form). One point to watch is that if you do give up your Group D entitlement you cannot reclaim it in this way for at least two months.

*What happens if I simply carry on riding my motorbike after the two-year period has run out?*

You will be committing an offence, since you will be driving without a licence. The normal penalty is an endorsement and two penalty points, plus a fine (see p. 94). However, this is the penalty that applies during the one-year period during which you cannot obtain a new provisional licence (i.e. the one year after expiry of your two-year provisional licence). After that one year you can apply again for another provisional licence. For some strange reason, if you do not bother to apply for another provisional licence a lesser penalty applies – you will not get an endorsement, or penalty points, provided you display your L-plates! In other words, if you are driving without a licence more than one year after your two-year period ran out you will not normally get an endorsement or penalty points provided you are otherwise legal (i.e. L-plates, etc.). On the other hand, if you are caught in the one-year period following expiry of your two-year provisional licence you will get an endorsement and penalty points.

### What happens if I ride a bike of over 125 cc while a learner?

Your provisional licence entitles you to drive a motorbike of only up to 125 cc. If you drive a more powerful bike you will be guilty of the offence of driving without a licence (even if you do have a provisional licence). In addition you would almost certainly be guilty of driving without insurance, since you would have broken a term of your insurance policy by driving such a powerful machine – see p. 122 for invalidating insurance. In practice the police might well not prosecute for no insurance, provided you had taken out an insurance policy.

Apart from restrictions on engine size there are also restrictions on engine power. A learner must not ride a bike with a maximum engine power of over 9 kilowatts, or with a power-to-weight ratio of over 100 kilowatts per tonne (there should be a plate on the bike giving these power figures). But these power restrictions only apply to 1982 and later bikes.

### Practical motoring: Can I choose where I want to take the driving test?

Yes. You do not have to take the driving test at your local centre. There are centres throughout the country, and you can choose whichever one you wish. In theory it should make little difference whether you take the test in one place as opposed to another – a lot of research goes into making the test routes as similar as possible (e.g. so that they contain the same number of right-hand turns, etc.). However, in practice it can often be difficult to do this – clearly a test taken in Central London can never be similar to one taken in rural mid-Wales. So, if you think there is some advantage to be gained, you can choose to take your test at a centre which is not local to you. In fact you may be able to cut down on the delay in waiting for a test by shopping around at different centres. The delay in London for an appointment is roughly four months; outside London it is more like three months.

You apply by sending your application, with the fee, to the Traffic Area Office covering the centre where you want to take the test. If you are prepared to take a late cancellation appointment you may be able to get an earlier date. If you cannot keep the appointment you are sent you should let the centre know straight away – if you do not give them three clear days' notice (Saturdays, Sundays and Public Holidays do not count) you may lose your fee and have to pay another fee for your next test.

### How do I apply for my driving test?

You apply for an appointment on form DL26 (from post offices). You should have received a booklet, *Your Driving Test* (reference number DL68), when you first received your provisional licence; you can obtain a further copy from the Driver Enquiry Unit, DVLC, Swansea SA6 7JL.

You may be able to get a test more quickly if you make it clear that you are prepared to accept a cancellation at short notice. You will also be given an early date if you are disabled.

If you are a motorbike or scooter rider you will probably have to take the driving test in two parts; you will not be able to apply for the second part until you have passed the first (see p. 133).

### Practical motoring: What will happen when I go for my driving test?

The first thing is to make sure you arrive on time. The examiners have to keep to a strict timetable, so if you are late you will probably not be able to take the test.

The examiner will meet you in the waiting-room, where you will be asked to sign a form. The examiner will then go with you to your car, and on the way will check your eyesight by asking you to read a numberplate on a car parked in the street. In practice you are likely to be asked to read the numberplate from a distance far in excess of that required by the law. If you cannot read it from that distance the examiner will check the distance precisely (using a tape measure if necessary) to see whether or not you comply with the legal minimum. The rule is that you must be able to read a numberplate from 67 feet away (75 feet in the case of the older-style 3½ inch high numbers).

Then comes the driving part of the test. This lasts about half an hour. You may think the examiner is a bit unfriendly by not chatting and making light conversation. Do not misinterpret this – the job of examiners is merely to tell you when to turn left, turn right, slow down, etc. As a policy rule they do not enter into general conversation.

Do not worry if you are nervous – everyone is! The examiner will know that most candidates are nervous, and will probably allow you a few minutes driving to settle in. Also do not be worried if you make minor mistakes; everyone makes some mistakes, and the examiner will be more concerned with your overall performance.

Most of the test will comprise ordinary everyday driving – the examiner will want to see how you cope with normal road conditions. However, in the course of the test you will be asked to carry out three particular manoeuvres – the emergency stop, reversing into a side turning and turning round in the road. Incidentally, although turning round in the road is usually called 'the three point turn', do not worry if you take more than three turns – the examiner will make allowances if you have a large car or if the road is narrow. The important point is that you should be able to turn round safely, and show that you can use the controls smoothly.

At the end of the driving part of the test there is a question-and-answer session. You will be expected to know the Highway Code, and you will also be asked general driving questions (e.g. about skidding). You will probably have to identify some road signs. Once again do not worry if you are not able to give a 100 per cent perfect answer – the examiner does not want you to be able to recite the Highway Code by heart, but is more concerned that you have a common-sense attitude to driving and that you will be a safe road user. So the question-and-answer session is not a memory test, but a test of your attitude to practical driving.

Next you will be told whether you have passed or failed! If the examiner is satisfied that you are 'competent to drive without danger to and with due consideration for other users of the road' you will pass. To prove that you have passed you will be given a Certificate of Competence, which you will have to sign. This is the form that you produce to get your full driving licence (see p. 91). On the other hand, if you fail you will be given a Statement of Failure. This will set out the mistakes that you made – but do not expect the examiner to sit in the car and discuss your faults in detail. Experience shows that this may lead to arguments! Hopefully, this won't arise – and you will pass!

Before going to the test read the little booklet called *Your Driving Test* that will have been sent to you with your provisional driving licence. This will explain the procedure, and what the examiner is looking for.

### What if I fail the test?

If you fail the test you can immediately reapply – although you cannot sit it again for at least a month. There is no limit to the number of tests you can take. You have no legal redress if you fail the test, unless you think the examiner did not conduct the test properly (if so, you can apply to the magistrates' court, but it is not worth doing since the most you can hope to receive is another, free test appointment – the court cannot exempt you from having to take a further test).

### What happens if I pass the test in an automatic car?

You will be limited to driving automatic vehicles. Thus you will not be qualified to drive a car with a manual gearbox unless you have a qualified driver with you (i.e. under the normal rules for learners). If you do pass the test on an automatic vehicle your licence will be marked as Group B; you need a Group A licence to drive both manual and automatic vehicles (see p. 93).

### A friend has asked me to teach him/her how to drive. What are my responsibilities?

You could be legally liable for mistakes made by the learner – although this would only happen exceptionally. The law requires that you stop the learner from driving 'unskilfully or carelessly or in a manner likely to cause danger to others', so if you persistently allow the learner to drive carelessly, or dangerously, you could be prosecuted. On the other hand, if you take the normal precautions, and do all you can to control the learner driver, you have nothing to fear. It all depends on the facts of the case. For instance, in one case a driver allowed a learner to drive home after they had been to the pub together; the drunk learner was swerving all over the road, and the qualified driver was convicted of 'aiding and abetting' the learner to drive with excess alcohol. There is also the question of who can claim compensation if there is an accident; exceptionally you might be liable if you did not control the learner properly (see p. 140).

It would be sensible to check that the learner has valid insurance. If this is not the case, and the learner is driving under your insurance policy, check that it does specifically cover the use of the vehicle by a learner. If in doubt check with your insurance company.

As the accompanying driver you must sit in the front passenger seat (i.e. not in the back).

---

## WHAT'S THE PENALTY?

*For not showing L-plates*

MAXIMUM PENALTY: a £400 fine and an endorsement (and perhaps disqualification), plus two penalty points

LIKELY PENALTY: a fine of £20–£30 plus two penalty points. Young offenders are sometimes disqualified for a short period as a warning

*For driving without an accompanying driver*

MAXIMUM PENALTY: a £400 fine and an endorsement (and perhaps disqualification), plus two penalty points

LIKELY PENALTY: a £50–£60 fine plus two penalty points. Young offenders are sometimes disqualified for a short period as a warning

*For a motorcyclist with an unqualified passenger*

MAXIMUM PENALTY: a £400 fine and an endorsement (and perhaps disqualification), plus two penalty points

LIKELY PENALTY: a £40–£45 fine plus two penalty points. Young offenders are sometimes disqualified for a short period as a warning

*For driving without a driving licence see p. 94*

For all these offences you may get a £24 fixed penalty ticket (plus penalty points) instead (see p. 217)

*(For more on penalties see p. 216)*

---

### Who is to blame if a learner is involved in a crash?

The normal rules apply. The fact that a learner is involved will make no difference.

When we talk about blame we are not concerned with criminal

liability (e.g. can someone be prosecuted by the police for careless driving?), but with the question of who is to pay for the damage caused. This is a *civil* claim – suing for damages caused by the negligence of a motorist – completely separate from the question of prosecution. A motorist – or, more likely, the motorist's insurance company – will have to pay compensation (i.e. for the damage and injury caused) only if he or she was negligent. See p. 177 for more information on the negligence laws.

Learners are not treated differently from any other drivers:

*Ms Weston was learning to drive. She asked her friend Mr Nettleship to teach her. He was not a professional driving instructor but said he would help her. On their third lesson disaster struck – Ms Weston went round a left-hand bend, but didn't straighten up the steering-wheel. As a result the car collided with a lamp post, and Mr Nettleship was injured. He then sued Ms Weston (in effect her insurance company) for compensation for his injuries, and the loss of wages while he had been off work. The judge who heard the case dismissed the claim for damages; he said that Ms Weston had done all that could reasonably have been expected of her as a learner driver. He felt that Ms Weston had done her best (incompetent though it might be!) and no more could be expected of her. However, the Court of Appeal would have none of this. It overturned the judge's decision and made it clear that the standard of care expected from a learner driver is identical to that of a fully qualified driver. In other words, learner drivers cannot get away with a lower standard. However, in the particular circumstances they felt that Mr Nettleship should have exercised greater care and so he was also partly to blame. In the end the Court of Appeal held that they were both 50/50 to blame – thus Mr Nettleship got 50 per cent of his normal damages from Ms Weston's insurance company.* Nettleship *(1971)*

*A woman of fifty-one was learning to drive. She had eighteen lessons in the driving school's car (which had dual controls). She then went driving in her husband's car (which did not have dual controls) with the driving instructor. While turning left she went too quickly, failed to straighten up, and they crashed into a tree. The whole incident only took about five seconds. She then sued the instructor for negligence – in allowing her to go on the road in a car without dual controls! So this was not a case of an injured instructor suing the negligent learner, but of a learner suing her instructor. Held: the instructor was not to blame, so the learner driver got no compensation. However, the court did make it clear that it is possible for the accompanying driver to be liable – not exercising proper control or acting irresponsibly will incur blame. In this particular case it could not be said that it was negligent to let a woman of her experience drive a car without dual controls; nor was there anything the accompanying driver could have done to avoid the crash.* Gibbons *(1979)*

Thus, the accompanying driver can be to blame for an accident, but only, as we have seen, by having acted negligently (e.g. by having allowed the learner to go too quickly, or to act irresponsibly, or by not having taken steps to avoid the accident, when this could have been done). In practice this happens relatively rarely – but it does emphasize the point that a motorist who is asked to help someone learn to drive should think carefully before agreeing. It is not something to be undertaken lightly – after all, if a court decides that you are to blame for any accident you could end up having to pay compensation yourself! All in all, it underlines the point that the best practical advice to give a learner is to have a few lessons with a qualified instructor before having lessons from family and friends.

# Legal Aid

*What is legal aid?*

Legal aid is when the State pays some (or all) of a person's legal costs. There are different types of legal-aid scheme – covering criminal cases (i.e. prosecutions brought by the police), civil cases (i.e. compensation claims following road accidents) and general legal advice (see below).

*Where can I get general advice on the law?*

1. *The AA or RAC.* The major motoring organizations offer free legal advice (and sometimes court representation) to their members (see p. 143).

2. *CAB.* Your local Citizens Advice Bureau can give you general advice on motoring law. It can only offer a general service, but it may be able to play an important role in referring you to a suitable local solicitor, or someone else who can help.

3. *A solicitor.* Most solicitors' firms contain someone who knows motoring law in some detail. You will have to pay for this advice unless you come within one of the various legal-aid schemes. See p. 29 for more on solicitors; see below for legal aid.

4. *Your insurance company.* If you have been involved in an accident your insurance company may well end up having to pay out some money (e.g. to other people who were injured, or whose cars were damaged, etc.), so they will not want you to admit liability for any accident until you have spoken to them. If you are being prosecuted for a motoring offence (e.g. careless driving) they may be able to give you general advice. If they could end up having to pay a lot of money out in compensation they might be prepared to pay for lawyers to represent you when you are prosecuted. If you are being sued for compensation following an accident your insurance company will deal with this for you. For more information on insurance see pp. 112–31.

5. *Your local library.* You may want to read up on the law for

yourself. A book such as this is no more than a starting-point. You will need to look at more detailed books for particular motoring offences; Anthony and Berryman's *Magistrates' Court Guide* (published annually; Butterworths) is well worth looking at. The book that criminal solicitors look at for advice on motoring prosecutions is very expensive, and is called *Wilkinson's Road Traffic Offences* (1985; Longman). For a general book on compensation claims arising from motor accidents (i.e. deciding who was negligent) lawyers use *Bingham's Motor Claims Cases* (by J. A. Taylor; 1986; Butterworths). But do bear in mind that law books are written for lawyers – and they assume a familiarity with legal jargon that most lay persons do not have. So by all means look up your own law, but take specialist advice if there is any doubt.

### What advice can the AA and RAC offer?

Both the AA and the RAC provide an excellent legal-advice service for their members. It is free and comprehensive. Any AA or RAC member who is involved in a motoring prosecution should initially seek advice from the motoring organization. Not only will the advice be free – it is likely to be particularly specialized and knowledgeable.

There are slight differences between the two schemes run by the AA and the RAC. Both exclude prosecutions for theft of cars, etc., and (perhaps more importantly) the RAC excludes drunk-driving charges.

It cannot be emphasized too strongly that the AA and RAC are the obvious starting-point for any person (who is a member) who needs advice on motoring law. They will give much more detailed advice than can be found in this book.

Because of the importance of the schemes offered by the AA and RAC full details are set out at the end of this book (see pp. 299–304).

### I am being prosecuted for a motoring offence. Can I get legal aid?

Perhaps – though probably not.

There are various types of legal-aid scheme. There is one specifically designed for criminal cases – called (not surprisingly) criminal legal aid. To get criminal legal aid you must show that:

1. *You are financially eligible* – in other words, you must be sufficiently poor. The means test is fairly strict – the figures are roughly the

same as those for civil legal aid (see p. 146). If you are eligible you may well have to pay a contribution towards the legal costs (which you pay in instalments over twenty-six weeks).

2. *Your case is serious enough to justify legal aid.* Legal aid is not available for every criminal prosecution – it is only for those cases that are serious, or which could have serious consequences. Bear in mind that what you may regard as serious may not be particularly serious in the eyes of the court (which is, after all, used to dealing with people going to prison for substantial periods of time!). The courts have detailed guidelines as to when they should grant legal aid but they only rarely apply in motoring cases. Generally they would be where motorists could show that they faced a 'grave charge' in the sense that they stood a serious chance of going to prison or suffering serious damage to their reputation.

The end result, therefore, is that criminal legal aid is only rarely available to a motorist. Obviously if you are facing a very serious charge (e.g. causing death by dangerous driving – which must be heard in the Crown Court), and perhaps a substantial prison sentence, you will get legal aid. Otherwise you will have an uphill struggle persuading the magistrates to grant legal aid.

Bear in mind that the vast majority of motoring offences are for relatively trivial matters – trivial, at least, in the eyes of the court! – so the vast bulk of prosecuted motorists cannot hope to get legal aid. Even someone up on a breathalyser (drunk-driving) charge cannot automatically expect to get legal aid. Only if they can show that they have a genuine legal defence (e.g. their lawyer has thought of some clever loophole), or if they face particularly grave consequences through being disqualified (e.g. they would lose their job if disqualified), can they hope to get legal aid.

Having said this, there is nothing to be lost by applying for legal aid. The worst that can happen is that it will be refused. But you would be unwise to rely upon getting it.

One alternative that may be available is the 'Green Form' Legal Advice Scheme. This is entirely separate from criminal legal aid. What it offers is general advice and assistance (but, generally, not appearance in court) from a solicitor for those without much money. With the Green Form there is no need to show that the case is serious – you are automatically entitled to help under the Green Form if you come within the financial limits. So someone of limited means can see a solicitor and have a general discussion about their motoring offence under the Green Form scheme. The solicitor will not be able to represent them in court, but will be able to advise generally (e.g. is it worth pleading not guilty; what is the level of the likely fine; what can be said to the court in mitigation; whether it is worth applying for criminal legal aid).

If you cannot get legal aid, and you are not eligible for general advice under the Green Form scheme, you will have to pay a lawyer privately. This means that you will end up paying the lawyer's legal fees yourself. It is difficult to say how much a lawyer charges. Most solicitors work on the basis of £25–£30 per hour. A typical appearance in the magistrates' court for a minor motoring charge is likely to cost a total of £125–£150. These are only guideline figures – solicitors' charges can vary enormously, depending on the solicitor concerned, where the solicitor's practice is, and the amount of work involved in the case. As always, it is advisable to get quotes from solicitors before instructing them.

The ideal solution is to be a member of the AA or RAC. If you are a member they will probably be able to give you free legal advice and appoint a solicitor to represent you (free of charge) – see p. 143.

### Can I get legal aid to claim compensation after a road accident?

Here we are dealing with the question of whether you can get compensation because someone else caused a road accident. In other words, you have got to show that they were to blame. When we talk about blame we are not concerned with criminal liability (e.g. can someone be prosecuted by the police for careless driving), but with the question of who is to pay for the damage caused. This is a *civil* claim – suing for damages caused by the negligence of a motorist – completely separate from the question of prosecution. A motorist – or, more likely, the motorist's insurance company – will have to pay compensation (i.e. for the damage and injury caused) if he or she was negligent. See p. 177 for more information on the negligence laws.

There is a separate legal-aid system for civil claims of this sort. This is simply called legal aid (to distinguish it from criminal legal aid).

To get legal aid you must show:

1. *You are financially eligible* – in other words, you must be sufficiently poor. The means test is fairly strict; see below for details.
2. *Your case justifies legal aid*. Basically you have to show that your claim is sufficiently serious – which generally means that it must be worth £500 or more. If it is not worth that much (i.e. your injuries, loss of

*Legal Aid: Are You Eligible?*

|  | Income from all sources (including child benefit) before deduction of income tax, national insurance contributions and rent | |
| --- | --- | --- |
|  | Maximum gross income permitting free legal aid | Minimum gross income which makes applicant ineligible for legal aid |
| *Type of applicant* | | |
| 1. Single person | £4,181 (£80 p.w.) | £9,500 (£183 p.w.) |
| 2. Married couple | £6,153 (£118 p.w.) | £11,335 (£218 p.w.) |
| 3. Married couple one child aged six | £6,998 (£135 p.w.) | £12,179 (£234 p.w.) |
| 4. Married couple two children aged four and eight | £7,841 (£151 p.w.) | £13,024 (£250 p.w.) |
| 5. Married couple three children aged four, eight and thirteen | £9,219 (£177 p.w.) | £14,402 (£277 p.w.) |
| 6. Married couple four children aged four, eight, thirteen and fifteen | £10,926 (£210 p.w.) | £16,108 (£310 p.w.) |
| 7. Married man apart from wife paying court order of £1,200 per annum | £5,694 (£110 p.w.) | £10,876 (£209 p.w.) |
| 8. Single parent with two children aged four and eight | £5,240 (£101 p.w.) | £10,422 (£200 p.w.) |
| 9. Single parent with three children aged four, eight and thirteen | £6,617 (£127 p.w.) | £11,798 (£227 p.w.) |

*Note.* These figures are for rough guidance only. They assume that rent or mortgage payments are about £20 per week. If they were more, then the figures would have to be increased (the gross earnings figures would go up by approximately £145 for each extra £100 of housing costs). The figures are for 1986.

earnings, damage to car, etc. do not add up to £500) you will probably not get legal aid. This is because claims of £500 or less come within the county court small-claims procedure – in which lawyers are discouraged and no legal costs are awarded. So you could handle the court case yourself using the small-claims procedure. Phone your local county court (look under 'Courts' in the phone directory). Obviously many motoring compensation claims exceed £500 and there will then be no argument that the claim is worth pursuing – and that legal aid should be granted.

Thus with most compensation claims you are likely to get legal aid – provided you come within the financial limits.

See the table on p. 146 for an indication of legal-aid financial limits.

### Will I get a worse service on legal aid than if I pay a solicitor privately?

No (or at least you certainly shouldn't!). If you get legal aid your solicitor will be paid in full by the legal-aid authorities. Solicitors should give legal-aid clients exactly the same service as they would to private clients who are paying their solicitor themselves.

The only disadvantage of being on legal aid comes if there is a problem with your case. If, quite simply, it looks as if your case is becoming quite hopeless your legal aid may be withdrawn – legal aid will not pay for hopeless cases, or for cases where a reasonable offer in settlement has already been made. If you were not receiving legal aid you would not have this problem – you could simply pay to carry on with the case, irrespective of your lawyer's advice.

### How do I apply for legal aid?

You fill in an application form. Most solicitors have stocks (as do most CABs). It is advisable to ask a solicitor, who will know how best to answer the questions and so increase the chances of your being given legal aid, to fill in the form for you, though it is possible that you would be charged for this service. However, the Green Form scheme may well cover the costs (if you are financially eligible – see above), or some solicitors may agree to do this for free – in the hope that you will get legal aid, and they will then be able to act for you.

It can often take some time for legal aid to be granted – sometimes two to three months (it depends which part of the country you are in). Your solicitor will not do anything for you in that interim period – you will simply have to wait for the legal aid to be granted. This is because solicitors will not be paid any money for the work they do unless legal aid has actually been granted (i.e. they cannot do the work in advance of legal aid being granted – unless you are prepared to pay, privately, for the work).

### What if I lose my claim for compensation? Does legal aid pay all the costs?

Yes. If you go to court to claim compensation, but lose your case (i.e. the court decides that the other motorist was not to blame), you will probably find that legal aid meets all the costs involved. In practice the most you will be asked to pay is any contribution that you originally made towards the legal-aid costs. Otherwise the chances are that your legal aid will be free and you will not have to pay anything further in legal costs. To this extent you are better off than someone who is not on legal aid – who, if they lose their case, will normally have to pay all the costs of the other side (i.e. the person they were suing). They will, of course, have to pay their own legal costs as well. This can be a hefty sum! So someone on legal aid has an advantage over someone else who isn't, in that their liability for costs, should they lose, is likely to be much less.

### If I win my claim for compensation, will the legal-aid authorities take any of my money?

Possibly. If you did win you would almost certainly expect your legal costs to be paid by the other motorist (or at least by the motorist's insurance company), because the general rule is that the loser pays the winner's costs. So virtually all your legal costs are likely to be paid by the other, losing, side. If that happens legal aid will not need to take any of your damages. On the other hand, if the other side do not pay all your costs the balance of your solicitor's and barrister's costs will come out of your damages – the legal-aid authorities will take the money from your damages before giving you the balance. Generally one is only talking about a relatively small sum.

If you turned down a realistic settlement offer from the other side, before trial, there is a possibility that you might have to pay more legal costs. If the other side paid some compensation into court, and you then chose not to accept it, you would probably have to pay some of the legal costs if the judge did not eventually award you more than the money paid into court by the other side (in particular the costs of the trial – always the most expensive part of any case). These costs would come out of your compensation.

Legal aid – and suing – can be complicated. For further information refer to the *Penguin Guide to the Law*.

# Lights

*What lights must a car have?*

It is compulsory to have two headlights and two sidelights at the front, plus two rear lights and two rear reflectors. In addition there must be rear brake lights (i.e. lights that come on automatically when the brake pedal is pressed) and a numberplate light. The sidelights and rear lights must be usable without the headlights having to be turned on. Dim-dip lights (i.e. intermediate-strength headlights that come on when a vehicle is about to start) will probably have to be fitted to a car made after October 1986, and first used after April 1987. Note that these dim-dip lights do not count as headlights (so they cannot be used instead of headlights at night).

General principles are that:

- there must be no red light at the front
- rear lights must be red (except reversing lights, numberplate lights and direction indicators)
- lights must not dazzle or discomfort other road users.

There are detailed rules on the obligatory lights. These apply to virtually all vehicles (except those registered before 1 January 1936, and some vehicles with a maximum speed of 15 m.p.h. – occasionally, 25 m.p.h.). What follows is merely a summary of the detailed regulations – ask the police (or one of the motoring organizations) for the up-to-date details:

*Front sidelights.* There must be two of these, one on each side, and they must be white. However, if the sidelights are integral with the headlights, and the headlights are yellow, the sidelights can also be yellow. For a post-1972 vehicle only an approved form of sidelight can be used. Any sidelight must be at least 0·51 metres from the ground, but no more than 1·5 metres (2·3 metres for a pre-April 1986 vehicle). Also it must not be more than 0·4 metres from the side of the vehicle (0·51 metres for pre-April 1986 vehicles).

*Headlights*. There must be two headlights (except on three-wheeled vehicles, on which generally only one headlight is needed). The headlights can be yellow or white (see below). The headlights must be dipping (i.e. they go from main beam to dip, or alternatively they go off and another dipped light comes on). The minimum dipped wattage is 30 watts (24 for a three-wheeled vehicle). The headlights must be at least 0.5 metres from the ground; the maximum height is 1·2 metres from the ground. No headlight may be more than 0·4 metres from the side of the vehicle (unless it is a pre-1972 vehicle).

*Direction indicators (i.e. flashers)*. There must be two indicators at front and rear; there must also be an indicator on each side of the car. One extra indicator can be fitted to each side, and there can also be an extra indicator on each side at the rear. Bulbs must be of 15–36 watts; for post-August 1965 vehicles the lights must be amber. The indicators should flash at between 60 and 120 flashes per minute (unless semaphore arms are used); there must be some form of internal warning in the car so the driver knows the lights are flashing (e.g. a clicking noise or a warning light). Flashers must be at least 0·35 metres above the ground; they must be at least 40 millimetres away from any dipped-beam headlight or front fog light.

*Rear sidelights*. There must be two of these; for post-1973 cars they must be of an approved type. The lights must not be more than 2·1 metres from the ground; they must not be further than 0·8 metres from the side of the car.

*Stoplights (i.e. brake lights)*. For post-1970 vehicles two stoplights are needed (earlier vehicles need only one – which must be at either the centre or the offside). The stoplights must be of an approved design if the vehicle is post-January 1974; otherwise bulbs must be 15–36 watts. The lights must come on automatically when the brakes are applied. The stoplights must be at least 0·35 metres, but not more than 1·5 metres, above the ground. They must be at least 0·4 metres apart.

*Rear reflectors*. There must be two reflectors (vertical and facing squarely to the rear). Post-June 1970 vehicles need an approved form of reflector. The reflectors cannot be more than 1·525 metres above the ground; they must not be more than 0·61 metres from the side of the car.

*Rear numberplate light*. There are no specific power requirements: all that is required is that there be at least one light which is capable of adequately illuminating the rear numberplate. The light can be white.

*Rear foglights* are compulsory for post-March 1980 vehicles. A single rear foglight is acceptable. The light must be of an approved type, and it must not be wired in such a way that it comes on when the brakes are applied. There must be a visual indicator to the driver, warning that the light is on (i.e. a warning light). Rear foglights must not be less than 0·25 metres and not more than one metre above the ground. Also they must be at least 0·1 metres away from any stoplight (brake light).

*Hazard warning lights* are compulsory for post-March 1986 vehicles.

### Are yellow headlamps legal?

Yes – provided it is the bulbs that are yellow. Strictly speaking it is illegal to use a clip-on cover (or masking) as is often used on continental journeys. If the headlamp bulbs are yellow the sidelights can also be yellow.

### I want to fit some extra lights to my car. Are there any rules to be followed?

It depends on the type of light:

*Headlights, front foglights and front spotlights* must be no less than 0·4 metres and not more than 1·2 metres above the ground. Extra main-beam headlights must be dippable (i.e. they must dip or operate so that when they are turned off another light goes on to dip).

*Rear foglight.* For post-March 1980 vehicles a maximum of two rear foglights is allowed. For the rules see above. For pre-April 1980 vehicles there is no limit on the number of rear foglights that is allowed – but they must not come on with the brakes, and they must be at least 0·1 metres away from any brake light.

*Hazard warning lights* are not compulsory. If fitted they must work even if the engine is off. All the direction indicators must flash at the same time. There must be a flashing warning light in the car.

*Reversing lights* are not compulsory. A maximum of two reversing lights is allowed, and they must be white. Maximum power is 24 watts (unless of an approved type). For post-June 1954 vehicles either there must be a warning light in the vehicle (i.e. indicating that the reversing lights are on), or the lights must come on only where reverse gear is engaged.

*Stoplights (i.e. brake lights).* There is no maximum number of lights that can be fitted; check that they comply with the height restrictions (see above).

*What about rear foglights?*

Since April 1980 all new vehicles must have at least one rear foglight. The foglight must not be connected to the brake light (i.e. it must not come on with the brake lights). See above for the detailed rules.

Rear foglights can be used only during bad road conditions – the law says that the visibility must be so bad as to 'seriously reduce the ability of the driver' to see or be seen. In any event these rear foglights can be used only when the car is moving or when it has to be stationary (e.g. in a traffic jam or at traffic lights) – but never as parking lights.

*What happens if my lights are broken; can I drive in the daytime?*

Certain lights are compulsory (i.e. headlights, sidelights, rear lights, rear numberplate light and perhaps a rear foglight – see above). If any of these – or any stoplights or flashers – are broken you should have them mended straight away. You will be committing an offence if they are not 'clean and in good working order'.

*Between what hours are lights compulsory?*

Lights must be used in the 'hours of darkness' – half an hour after sunset and half an hour before sunrise. Between those times your front and rear sidelights, and your rear numberplate light, must be on. You must also put your headlights on, unless the road has street lamps which are lit up and which are less than 200 metres apart. In practice, of course, people take the view that it is safer to use dipped headlights even in built-up areas. During fog or snow, instead of the headlights you can use either two foglights or a foglight and a spotlight together. Dim-dip lights do not count as headlights.

It may also be necessary to put your lights on during daylight hours. If visibility is seriously reduced, lights must be used as though it is dark.

*Are lights needed in the day time?*

Yes – if visibility is seriously reduced. If so, you must use your lights (in particular your headlights) as though it is dark.

The law does not say exactly what is meant by 'seriously reduced visibility' – it is all a matter of the circumstances. For instance, the term would cover fog, mist, a snow storm, heavy rain, road spray thrown up by other vehicles and badly overcast weather, but it does not only apply when the weather is bad – it could be applicable if you were travelling through a poorly lit tunnel, or through smoke blowing from burning stubble. In short, you must use your lights if ever there is seriously reduced visibility. You must use your sidelights and your headlights (although you can opt to use foglights instead of your headlights – provided each foglight is no more than 0.4 metres from the edge of your car).

### What happens if a bulb blows during my journey?

Strictly speaking you should not drive any further. The law says you must have the obligatory lights (see above), and it is no defence to say that the bulb has just gone. However, the police would be most unlikely to prosecute in these circumstances, if you explained what had happened. If they did prosecute, the chances are that a magistrates' court would give you an absolute discharge and not impose any other penalty (see p. 157). Obviously this assumes that you behaved reasonably in driving on (which would not be the case in heavy fog, or if you were driving at speed down a motorway). But, strictly speaking, the light must be in 'good working order' at all times.

### Must I leave lights on when I park the car at night?

It depends where you are. You need not leave lights on if you are within a 30 m.p.h. area (see p. 277 for what this means), and provided you are parked with the nearside of your car next to the pavement (i.e. you must not be parked against the flow of traffic: this would be dangerous, because oncoming vehicles would not see your car's reflectors). In addition the car must not be within ten metres of a road junction (even if that road junction is on the other side of the road). To summarize, provided you park in a 30 m.p.h. area, on the correct side of the road, and not near to a junction, you do not need lights.

Otherwise you do need lights – unless you are parking in a recognized parking bay (e.g. a lay-by, meter bay or marked parking area).

If lights have to be shown you must leave on your front and rear sidelights and numberplate light. It is not legal simply to leave the offside lights on. The law says you must never park with your headlights on – even at night.

### *How is the ten-metre rule worked out?*

We have seen that, at night, you may not need to park with your lights on if you are more than ten metres from a junction. Since most junctions have curved corners it is important to know where the ten metres runs from. The answer is that it runs from the beginning of the curve (i.e. not from the start of the junction), as this illustration shows:

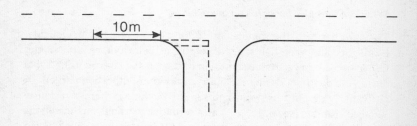

### *What about parking a trailer at night?*

If a vehicle is towing a trailer the obligatory lights (i.e. front and rear sidelights, plus the numberplate light) must be left on when the vehicle is parked at night on a road. This is so even if the vehicle is within a 30 m.p.h. area (if the vehicle was not towing a trailer, lights might not be needed – see above). The trailer's lights must also be left on. The car's headlights and foglights must be turned off.

If the trailer is unhitched from a vehicle, and is left parked on the road, it must have its rear lights on, together with a pair of white front sidelights.

There are detailed regulations on the location of lights, reflectors, etc. on trailers.

### Are movable spotlights allowed?

At one time there was a fashion for movable lights; usually they were fixed to the inside of the windscreen, so the driver or passenger could move the light as the car was being driven. Such lights are illegal. There must be no moving lights on a car (the only exceptions are for front headlamps that adjust with the load, or which move in synchronization with the wheels).

### What are the rules for lights on motorbikes?

They are basically the same as those for cars – except that sidelights, headlights and rear lights need not be in pairs but can be single. Otherwise the rules are the same – in particular the laws on using lights during the daytime, during the hours of darkness and when parked. In particular, you must use your lights in the daytime if there is seriously reduced visibility (see p. 153). As an alternative to using your headlights when visibility is poor, you can use a foglight (one foglight will do, even if you have two headlights).

There are detailed rules on the fitting of compulsory lights on motor-bikes. Summarized, these are as follows:

- *dipped headlight:* compulsory for post-1970 bikes
- *main beam headlight:* compulsory, except for pre-1972 motorbikes of under 50 cc
- *front (position) light:* not needed if the bike has a headlight
- *flashers:* compulsory for post-March 1986 bikes (except for single-seaters)
- *rear light:* always compulsory
- *rear reflector:* always compulsory
- *stoplight:* compulsory for post-March 1986 vehicles (unless under 50 cc)
- *rear numberplate light:* compulsory (assuming there has to be a rear numberplate!).

### Is it illegal to have dirty lights?

Yes. Lights must be 'clean and in good working order' at all times.

### What lights must a pedal cycle have?

There must be a light at the front, and at the rear, and also a rear reflector. Bikes made after September 1985 must also have reflectors on the pedals.

### What is the legal effect of flashing your headlights?

Legally the answer is that it has no meaning. In practice, of course, it has two meanings – which are totally contradictory! People use it to mean either 'You can come on now' or 'Watch out, I am coming'! As far as the

---

## WHAT'S THE PENALTY?

*For having broken or dirty lights*

*For not using lights at night*

*For not using dipped headlights at night or in seriously reduced visibility*

*For having a headlight, or a front or rear foglight that dazzles, or causes discomfort to other people*

*For lighting a headlight, or a front or rear foglight when the vehicle is parked (except for a rear foglight used as an emergency light when the vehicle is parked)*

*For using a foglight (front or rear) when visibility is not seriously reduced*

*For using a reversing lamp when not reversing*

*For misuse of hazard warning lights (i.e. they are only to be used when the vehicle is stationary and is a temporary obstruction)*

*For using a flashing yellow beacon*

*For using a flashing green beacon (unless you are a doctor)*

*For using a blue or amber flashing light other than in an emergency (or as a warning to people)*

MAXIMUM PENALTY: for all these offences the maximum penalty is a £1,000 fine. The maximum fine for an unlit number-plate is £400. No endorsements or penalty points are possible

LIKELY PENALTY: a fine of between £30 and £50. It is likely to be towards the lower figure if the road was lit; and towards the higher figure if the road was unlit. But you may get away with a £12 fixed penalty ticket instead (see p. 217)

*(For more on penalties see p. 216)*

---

Highway Code is concerned: 'The flashing of headlamps has only one meaning – like sounding your horn it lets another road user know you are there. Do not flash your headlamps for any other reason.' So, legally, you would be unwise to rely on flashing headlamps from another motorist as a legitimate reason for you to proceed in a dangerous situation. See p. 182 for a case history of a motorist who relied on flashing headlights.

*Practical motoring:* **How often should I check my lights?**

If you are sensible you will check your lights every day – and certainly before you go on any major journey. Bear in mind that properly working lights are essential to your safety – and to the safety of other road users. As the Highway Code says: 'make sure that all your lamps are clean, that they work and that your headlamps are properly adjusted – badly adjusted headlamps can dazzle road users and lead to accidents'. Do not forget that dirt can seriously reduce the visibility of lights; so make sure that you regularly clean all the lights on your car (even if you don't bother to clean the rest of the car!). In any event it is an offence not to keep compulsory lights in a clean condition; it is also an offence to have lights that dazzle.

*Practical motoring:* **What lights should I use in fog?**

If fog seriously reduces your visibility you should use your rear foglights (if fitted). As regards your front lights remember that your sidelights will not be sufficient by themselves. The main thing is to make sure that you can be seen: in daylight you will probably find that headlights on main beam do not dazzle oncoming drivers (because the fog disperses the light). At dusk it is better to use dipped beams rather than headlights.

Always take extreme care when driving in fog. Probably the most important thing to do is to leave sufficient room between you and the vehicle in front – do not simply follow the rear lights of the car ahead, otherwise you will probably not have enough time in which to stop if there is an emergency!

If you are following another vehicle you may feel that the fog is less thick than it really is – because the car in front will be moving through the fog, and so 'thinning it out' for you. As a result you may think that road conditions are not as bad as they really are. This could be particularly serious if you began to overtake, only to find that visibility was worse than expected. Another point to watch is not to project too much light on to the back of the vehicle in front – the danger is that you will make driving even more difficult for the other motorist, who will have to contend with the shadow thrown on the road ahead by your lights. Your lights should allow you to see – and be seen – but they should not be so bright that they cause danger and inconvenience to other road users.

Take great care when crossing a road junction in fog. If necessary wind down your windows so that you get a better view and can hear oncoming vehicles. Move extremely carefully and make sure you are as visible as possible. If you do not have special rear foglights a good idea is to keep your foot on the brake pedal when you are stationary (the bright brake lights will be more easily seen by motorists behind you than your normal rear lights).

One final point about rear foglights: use them only when visibility is seriously reduced (for instance, by fog, smoke, heavy rain, snow, etc.). They should not be used if conditions are merely a little difficult (e.g. in the dusk or in normal rain) – apart from committing an offence you will be driving badly. The excessive brightness of rear foglights can cause glare and dazzle to motorists behind you. Show consideration to other road users and do not use these bright lights unless visibility is *seriously* reduced.

### What should I do if my lights fail at night?

There are two separate points to be considered. Firstly, there is the question of whether or not you will be committing a criminal offence. Almost certainly you will – if one of your compulsory lights fails you will be committing an offence by continuing your journey (see above).

Secondly, and more importantly, you must consider the question of whether your unlit vehicle will be a danger to other road users. If there is an accident you will almost certainly be found to blame. So, if it is dark, you should try and park the car in a safe place (where no one else can run into it) and turn on the hazard flashing lights. If you have a warning triangle erect it. However, the general view is that warning triangles are not as effective as hazard lights – so always use the hazard lights, if fitted. If you don't park safely you can be partly to blame if there is an accident:

*A motorbike was following a car. The car indicated right, and the motorcyclist assumed that the car was going to turn right. In fact the car was only signalling that it was pulling out slightly, to overtake a parked car. Assuming that the car was going to turn right, the motorcyclist passed it on the inside and crashed into the parked car that was being overtaken. The motorcyclist sued the owner of the parked car, claiming damages. In reply the owner of the parked car said that the accident was the motorcyclist's own fault – after all, the street was well lit, and he should have been looking where he was going. Held: the owner of the parked car was 25 per cent to blame. The motorcyclist was 75 per cent to blame. So the motorcyclist got 25 per cent of his normal damages from the owner of the parked car. Hannam (1984)*

That was probably a borderline case. Provided you take all reasonable steps to minimize the danger you may not be liable if there is an accident:

*A lorry's lights failed on an open country road – despite the fact that the driver and his mate had checked them when starting the journey, and again at lighting-up time. The driver parked the lorry by the nearside verge and tried to fix them. While he did this his mate stood down the road, to warn oncoming vehicles. Unfortunately another lorry was approaching, and didn't see the mate; it ran straight into the back of the unlit lorry. Were the owners of the unlit lorry responsible for the accident? Held: no. The lorry driver and his mate had not been negligent. They had done all that could be expected of them: they had checked the lights several times, and nobody could be blamed for the lights failing. They had tried to warn oncoming vehicles as best they could; they could not have driven the lorry on to the grass verge because of its weight. So, in the absence of negligence by the driver or his mate, the lorry's owners were not liable. Moore (1968)*

In practice the courts are reluctant to find that there is no negligence on the part of drivers of unlit vehicles. Often, therefore, the courts will try and find some way to say that drivers or owners were to blame (e.g. they should have checked the lights before starting their journey; they should have checked them at lighting-up time; they should have pulled off into a side road, or on to the verge; they should have tried to warn other traffic, etc.). However, in the exceptional case, when no blame can be attached to the unlit vehicle, a motorist who crashes into it will go uncompensated – although, fortunately, such cases are extremely rare.

# Minibuses

### What is a minibus?

Basically a minibus is a small vehicle which carries eight or more passengers (excluding the driver). There are two categories of minibus: those that carry eight to sixteen passengers (small), and those that carry over sixteen (large).

### When is a licence needed?

The normal rule is that if passengers are carried 'for hire or reward' a public service vehicle (PSV) licence is needed. But non-commercial groups can get a permit which exempts them from the normal PSV licensing rules. Any group can apply for a permit provided they do not intend to use the minibus for carrying members of the general public, and provided they do not intend to make a profit. Strictly speaking the organization must be concerned with education, religion, social welfare or any other activity which is for the benefit of the community – in practice this covers virtually every voluntary and social organization.

Most permits are for small (i.e. eight to sixteen passengers) minibuses. Permits for large (i.e. over sixteen passengers) minibuses are generally only granted to umbrella-type organizations which co-ordinate the activities of several community groups within a particular area. In effect it is more difficult to get a permit for a large minibus.

The permit will specify the particular organization it covers; it will also identify the individual vehicle. However, the organization need not own the vehicle (so an organization that hires a minibus occasionally could take out a permit for a particular minibus and then arrange with the hire company that they always hire that individual vehicle). Alternatively several organizations may club together to buy a minibus, in which case each organization could have its own permit to operate the shared minibus.

The application can be made by a named individual on behalf of the group. Once the permit is granted it will not normally have a time limit: it will simply continue in operation until the organization or group no longer uses the vehicle. Conditions can be laid down on the granting of the permit (e.g. that it only covers the transportation of disabled people, etc.). Do not forget that if a different minibus is to be used a new permit will be needed.

Finally, it should not be thought that the granting of a permit means that the organization or group is exempt from all the PSV rules. All it means is that the normal licence rules (for both the vehicle and the driver) do not apply – but all the other safety rules (e.g. construction and design of the vehicle) still do.

### What other legal requirements must be followed?

Any minibus driver must be at least twenty-one years old with a full licence (i.e. a provisional licence is not sufficient). Any minibus with more than eight passenger seats must have an annual MOT test (there is no exemption during the first two years). Normally road tax will be paid at the same rate as for a private car (unless the minibus is used as a goods vehicle or as a taxi).

If a permit has been issued the driver's hours rules (i.e. if there are more than fourteen seats – see p. 71) will not apply. Similarly the rules on recording the hours of driving, and on tachographs, will almost certainly not apply.

### Our club wants to take a minibus abroad. Are there any special points to watch?

Special rules apply if the minibus can carry nine or more people (excluding the driver). When the vehicle is used outside the UK the driver's hours and tachograph rules will normally apply. In addition different rules apply to what are called 'occasional closed-door tours' (e.g. when a group of people do a round trip on the Continent). If you are thinking of taking a minibus abroad apply for the leaflet *Taking a Minibus Abroad* from the Department of Transport.

### What are the speed limits for minibuses?

The maximum speeds are: on a motorway, 70 m.p.h.; on a dual carriageway, 60 m.p.h.; otherwise, 50 m.p.h.

## What is a public service vehicle (PSV)?

A public service vehicle (PSV) is a vehicle that is hired out to passengers. Any vehicle that is hired out for 'hire or reward' will be a PSV – and so be subject to the PSV rules – if:

● it carries passengers who have each paid their own fares (e.g. a bus or coach service), whatever the size of the vehicle

● it has eight or more passenger seats (e.g. a minibus or coach) and is used for passengers who do not pay separate fares. Thus, if the vehicle is hired out to one person who then pays the fare for everybody (e.g. a club outing), the rules apply. Note that the PSV rules apply only if the vehicle has eight or more passenger seats – otherwise every taxi would count as a PSV.

Any commercial bus or coach service (and even a minibus service) will come within the PSV rules. More importantly, minibus outings by voluntary groups and clubs will also come within the PSV rules (but see p. 161).

## What special rules apply to PSVs?

The vehicle operator must have a PSV licence, and there are special laws as to the safety and fitness of the type of vehicle used. The idea is to ensure that bus and coach travel is safe and that high standards are imposed on all operators.

In the past these rules caused difficulties to groups and organizations who wished to organize minibus outings and coach trips for their members. However, the rules have now been changed so that many of these groups can operate PSVs without the need to apply for a licence. Instead they can apply for permits – for which fewer formalities are required and a simpler procedure operates (see p. 161).

# Motorways

*Do the usual motoring laws apply to motorways?*

All the normal motoring laws apply, but there are also extra laws to be observed on a motorway. For instance, bad driving on the motorway will still be punishable as careless driving (see p. 59). The only difference will be that, if it happens on a motorway, the chances are that the court will regard it more seriously, and so impose a stiffer penalty. Overtaking on the inside would probably be regarded as careless driving.

*What other rules are there for motorways?*

There are numerous detailed rules. The most obvious are: you cannot reverse down a motorway; you must go in the right direction; you must not park on the verge or hard shoulder. In addition some vehicles are banned: any vehicle that cannot reach 25 m.p.h. on the level, invalid carriages and motorcycles under 50 cc. Also, learners are banned.

*When is it legal to stop on the motorway?*

Generally the only time you can stop on the motorway is if you are in a traffic jam! Otherwise you can stop if the car breaks down (e.g. you have run out of petrol); if there is an accident; if someone becomes ill or there is another emergency; or if you are stopping so that something lying on the motorway can be moved. You can also stop to help someone dealing with one of these categories of emergency. But you must immediately drive on to the hard shoulder, if at all possible. If you do not you will be committing an offence. What is more, you can only remain on the hard shoulder for as long as is necessary to fix the problem that has arisen.

Stopping for other reasons is not allowed. For instance, the motorist who stopped his car, parked on the hard shoulder, and then got out of the car to pray towards Mecca was convicted!

### What if I feel drowsy when driving on the motorway?

You are allowed to stop on the hard shoulder in case of 'illness or other emergency'. So, if you begin to feel drowsy while driving on the motorway, it is permissible for you to stop for a short time. In practice, of course, the police are very strict about cars that park on the hard shoulder and they will probably not be convinced if you merely said that you felt tired. In any event, if you felt tired before you got on to the motorway, they would rightly say that you should never have gone on the motorway in the first place – and so it cannot be said that an emergency arose.

From the safety point of view you should get off the motorway as soon as possible if you are feeling drowsy or at all unwell. Obviously if you feel really ill you must stop and park on the hard shoulder. Make sure your car is parked as far over towards the verge as possible; put your hazard lights on. Do not get out of the car unless you have to.

### Can I use the verge?

No. It may seem safer to park your car on the grass verge than on the hard shoulder (in case of emergency). But you should not do so – if you do you will be committing an offence.

### What vehicles are banned from the outside lane?

When there are three lanes (not two) some vehicles are banned from the outside lane. This covers lorries and other goods vehicles (over 7·5 tonnes), coaches (over 12 metres) and any vehicle drawing a trailer (e.g. a caravan). There is a total prohibition on these vehicles using the outside lane – even for overtaking – unless, most exceptionally, it is the only way they can overtake an abnormally wide vehicle that is blocking the two other lanes!

### What are the motorway speed limits?

For most cars the maximum speed is 70 m.p.h. Coaches over twelve metres long have a limit of 60 m.p.h. Vehicles drawing a trailer (e.g. a caravan) have a 60 m.p.h. maximum (40 m.p.h. if more than one trailer is being drawn).

For goods vehicles under 7·5 tonnes the speed limit is 70 m.p.h.;

vehicles heavier than that have a maximum of 60 m.p.h. (as do articulated vehicles – unless they are towing more than one trailer, in which case the maximum is 40 m.p.h.).

These are the maximum speed limits. If there are roadworks lower speed limits can be imposed. Despite what some motorists think those temporary speed limits are legally binding. The limits that are not legally enforceable are the guideline speeds that the police often put up in motorways during bad weather. These have no legal effect. So motorists who drive at 70 m.p.h. through fog when there is a suggested speed restriction of 30 m.p.h. will not be guilty of speeding (although the police might be able to get them for careless driving).

---

## WHAT'S THE PENALTY?

*For reversing on a motorway*

MAXIMUM PENALTY: a £1,000 fine, plus three penalty points (and an endorsement) and perhaps disqualification

LIKELY PENALTY: three penalty points, plus a fine – perhaps £150 for reversing on the main motorway, or £75 if on a slip road. If on the main motorway, you may also get a disqualification (e.g. three months)*

*For driving in the wrong direction on a motorway*

MAXIMUM PENALTY: a £1,000 fine, plus three penalty points (and an endorsement) and perhaps disqualification

LIKELY PENALTY: three penalty points (plus an endorsement), and a fine of perhaps £200 for driving on the main motorway, or £100 on a slip road. If on the main motorway, perhaps disqualification (e.g. three months) will result*

*For driving on the central reservation, hard shoulder or verge*

MAXIMUM PENALTY: a £1,000 fine, plus three penalty points (and an endorsement) and perhaps disqualification

LIKELY PENALTY: three penalty points (plus an endorsement), and a fine – perhaps £130 for the central reservation and £60 for the hard shoulder or verge*

*For going the wrong way down a slip road*

MAXIMUM PENALTY: a £1,000 fine, plus three penalty points (and an endorsement) and perhaps disqualification

LIKELY PENALTY: three penalty points (plus an endorsement), and a fine of £75*

*For making a U-turn on a motorway*

MAXIMUM PENALTY: a £1,000 fine, plus three penalty points (and an endorsement) and perhaps disqualification

LIKELY PENALTY: three penalty points (plus an endorsement). Also a fine (e.g. £140), and perhaps three months' disqualification*

*For a learner driver on a motorway*

MAXIMUM PENALTY: a £1,000 fine, plus three penalty points (and an endorsement) and perhaps disqualification

LIKELY PENALTY: three penalty points (plus an endorsement) and a £75 fine*

*For driving a prohibited vehicle (e.g. a moped)*

MAXIMUM PENALTY: a £1,000 fine, plus three penalty points (and an endorsement) and perhaps disqualification

LIKELY PENALTY: three penalty points (plus an endorsement) and a £75 fine*

*For speeding on a motorway*

MAXIMUM PENALTY: a £1,000 fine, plus three penalty points (and an endorsement) and perhaps disqualification

LIKELY PENALTY: three penalty points (plus an endorsement). The fine will vary with speed – say £2.50 per m.p.h. over the speed limit (perhaps double for a heavy vehicle). There might be a short disqualification if the limit is exceeded by more than 30 m.p.h.*

*For stopping on the hard shoulder*

MAXIMUM PENALTY: a £1,000 fine

LIKELY PENALTY: a £50 fine (£25 if on a slip road)

*For driving a heavy vehicle (or driving with a trailer) in the outside (third) lane*

MAXIMUM PENALTY: a £1,000 fine, plus three penalty points (and an endorsement) and perhaps disqualification

LIKELY PENALTY: three penalty points (plus an endorsement) and a fine of £100*

*For walking on a motorway*

MAXIMUM PENALTY: a £1,000 fine

LIKELY PENALTY: a £50 fine (for walking on the hard shoulder or verge, say £30)

* Note that for all these offences you may get a fixed penalty ticket (£12 or £24) instead (see p. 217)

(For more on penalties see p. 216)

The Motorist and the Law

*Practical motoring:* **What is the proper way of joining a motorway?**

You will normally join the motorway via a slip road, on the left-hand side of the motorway. The slip road becomes an extra lane of the motorway (an acceleration lane) which gives you sufficient time to judge the speed at which vehicles in the inside lane of the motorway are travelling, and to adjust your speed to their speed. So the normal procedure is that you will accelerate in the acceleration lane and wait for a suitable gap in the inside lane of the motorway. If the motorway is crowded do not try and force your way into the inside lane – wait in the acceleration lane until a gap appears. It is extremely dangerous to try and push your way in. Once you are on the motorway it is usually a good idea to stay in the inside lane for a short while. This gives you an opportunity to adjust to motorway driving (with its extra speed, extra distance required between vehicles, extra lanes, and so on).

As a general point bear in mind that motorway driving puts extra stresses on you – and on your vehicle. Both should be in tip-top condition. In particular check that your lights and indicators are clean (so they can easily be seen) and do not go on a motorway if you are feeling at all drowsy or tired. Everything happens at speed on motorways – your reactions will have to be sharper than they would be on an ordinary road. Remember that your horn will probably be of little use on a motorway – other drivers will simply not hear it. So it is usually better to flash your headlights rather than use the horn. Finally, do not forget to leave a sufficient gap between you and the vehicle in front, so that you can stop if there is an emergency. At 70 m.p.h. – in the dry – you need at least twenty-three car lengths between you and the vehicle in front (see p. 38).

*Practical motoring:*
**What is the proper way of using the three lanes of a motorway?**

Put simply, the three lanes are: the slow lane, the fast lane and the overtaking lane. As on any road the normal rule is that you should drive on the left-hand side, so you should keep in the left-hand lane. But, because vehicles travel at different speeds on motorways, it may be unrealistic – and unsafe – for you to remain in the nearside left lane all the time. When overtaking vehicles that are in the left-hand lane move out into the middle lane. You can stay in the middle lane if there are slower vehicles in the left-hand lane. On the other hand, if there are no vehicles in the left-hand lane you should move back into that left-hand lane – even if you are travelling relatively quickly. However, you should not chop and change from the left-hand lane to the middle lane and then back again. If there are vehicles in the left-hand lane it is safer for you to remain in the middle lane – rather than keep swapping lanes. Remember, it is changing from one lane to another that is the most dangerous manoeuvre on a motorway – which is why it is safer to remain in the middle lane if you would otherwise be moving back and forth between the middle and left-hand lanes.

The most fundamental point to note is that the outside (i.e. right-hand) lane is *not* the fast lane. It is the overtaking lane. In other words, you only use it to overtake vehicles that are in the middle lane. Once you have overtaken those vehicles you should move back in to the middle lane (and then to the left-hand lane if that lane is also empty).

Remember that drivers of heavy vehicles and coaches (and cars with trailers) cannot use the overtaking (right-hand) lane (see p. 165). So do not be one of those inconsiderate drivers who stays in the middle lane and prevents a faster, heavy, vehicle from overtaking. You should pull into the left-hand (slow) lane and let the faster vehicle overtake you.

Take special care when overtaking. When you look in your mirror remember that the vehicles behind you are probably travelling at high speed. Check your mirrors carefully; then signal clearly, and move out – but only if you are sure that there is sufficient room for you to do so. Never – *never* – overtake on the inside (left). Even if the overtaking (right-hand) lane is blocked by a foolish motorist who has not pulled over, you should resist the temptation to overtake on the inside. Flash your headlights to give warning of your presence, and then wait until – hopefully – the other driver eventually moves over. Resist the temptation to drive up close behind the other vehicle so as to exaggerate your presence – that is how accidents are caused.

*Practical motoring:* **What is the correct way of leaving a motorway?**

Plan ahead. Normally there will be an exit sign one mile from the exit junction, together with a second sign half a mile from it. Begin to plan your exit at this stage. Nearer the exit there are count-down markers one hundred yards, two hundred yards and three hundred yards from it. Make sure you are in the inside (slow) lane well in time and make your change of speed gradual. Change one lane at a time – never change from the outside (overtaking) lane to the inside (slow) lane in one manoeuvre. When you join the deceleration lane (i.e. the extra piece of carriageway between the motorway and the slip road) begin to slow down – not through heavy braking, but by reducing speed. Bear in mind that you will be used to driving at high speeds – and you will probably underestimate the speed at which you are travelling. Make sure you are not going too quickly when you reach the intersection at the end of the slip road. Then, when you continue on non-motorway roads, remind yourself that you will need to slow down since all the traffic will be going more slowly than that on the motorway.

## Practical motoring: **Can I stop on the hard shoulder?**

There are strict laws on when you can stop on the motorway and on the hard shoulder (see p. 164). If you have to stop on the hard shoulder switch on any hazard flashers since this will increase the chances of other motorists seeing your vehicle. Pull over to the left-hand side of the hard shoulder and take great care when getting out of the driver's door. In fact it is usually more sensible not to use the offside doors, but the nearside doors instead. This reduces the chances of your being struck by a passing vehicle. Neither you – nor your passengers – should get out to stretch your legs. Unless there is a pressing reason for you to get out, you should stay in the vehicle.

If you need to use one, the emergency phones are usually about a mile apart. If you look carefully on the hard shoulder you will find a marker post (these are 110 yards apart). The post has a telephone symbol, and a red arrow showing the direction of the nearest phone. If you walk to that phone take great care to keep to the inside of the hard shoulder and well away from the carriageway. Incidentally, if you see that something dangerous has fallen on to the motorway (e.g. it might have fallen off a passing vehicle) do not be tempted to remove it from the road. In this situation the Highway Code advises you to use the telephone to tell the police. Let them remove it – not you.

# MOT Test

## When is an MOT certificate needed?

Once a vehicle is three years old, the chances are that it needs an MOT certificate.

The law says that an MOT certificate is needed once a vehicle is three years old if it is:

- a car
- a motorbike (including a moped or scooter)
- a van (up to 1,525 kilograms unladen weight)
- a motor caravan.

But minibuses (i.e. more than eight passenger seats), public service vehicles and taxis need an MOT certificate as soon as they are one year old (i.e. not three years old).

If a certificate is needed it is an offence to *use* the vehicle on a public road – thus an untested vehicle can be kept parked on a private road or in a garden. Once the vehicle is used on the public highway an offence will be committed. The main exception is when the vehicle is being taken to a prearranged MOT test. But this is a limited exemption: it does not cover motorists who take their untested car out looking for a garage who will give them a test – you must have arranged the appointment beforehand. Also it will not be a defence to say that you were driving the car to a garage so that the necessary repairs could be carried out. The only solution for motorists faced with that problem is to have their untested car towed to the garage. Some motorists have tried to exploit the rule that allows the vehicle to be driven without an MOT to a prearranged MOT test. When prosecuted for failing to have an MOT certificate they have argued they were driving to an MOT station, but had not fixed up a previous appointment because the MOT station clearly advertised itself as being able to give MOT tests on the spot. Not surprisingly most courts take a very cynical view of such claims – the general view is that the word 'prearranged' means that the test must have been fixed up in advance, and it is not good enough simply to turn up in the hope that a test can be given on the spot. Thus this particular dodge is usually doomed to failure.

The only other occasions when an MOT certificate is not needed are:

• if the vehicle has failed an MOT test, and is being taken to or from a garage for repair (or is being taken to a breakers)

• for an imported vehicle being driven from the UK entry port to the owner's or driver's home

• for vehicles used on certain small islands.

Goods vehicles have to be tested each year (there is no three-year exemption). These tests are not done at MOT garages but at government testing stations.

Certain vehicles are exempted from the MOT test rules: the most important exemption is for invalid vehicles weighing less than 306 kilograms (510 kilograms if supplied by the DHSS, etc.).

### *What about foreign vehicles?*

If a car is imported from abroad it should be registered in this country. If it is a secondhand car, and is three years old, it should have a valid MOT certificate as soon as it arrives in the country. The three-year period does not run from the date of importation, but from the date when the vehicle was made. However, if the vehicle is more than three years old, whoever is importing it can drive it from the port of entry to their home without an MOT certificate. Apart from that limited exception foreign cars are treated in exactly the same way as British cars. Once the importer has got the vehicle home it can of course be driven to an MOT test station without a certificate, provided it has previously been booked in for a test.

As far as foreign visitors to the UK are concerned, they can bring their cars with them for a period of up to twelve months. At the end of that time the vehicle should be registered in this country, and an MOT certificate will then be needed if the vehicle is three years old. Once again the three-year period runs from the date the vehicle was made – not the date when it was first brought into the UK.

## How comprehensive is an MOT test?

An MOT certificate does not guarantee that a vehicle is sound and in good condition. All it amounts to is confirmation that – at the time of the inspection – all the items that had to be checked were in sound condition. Theoretically, therefore, you could drive home from an MOT test and find yourself prosecuted for having defective brakes – the mere fact that you had just obtained an MOT certificate would not be a defence if, in fact, the brakes were defective. In practice such a prosecution would be extremely unlikely since the police would normally simply tell you to get the defect fixed. If a prosecution did result the court would probably have sympathy on you – you would have to be convicted, but would probably be given an absolute discharge (see p. 237). The point to grasp is that an MOT certificate is not a guarantee that the car is in good condition.

The MOT test is not a test of all parts of the car. The examiner only looks at the following: brakes; steering; headlamps, reflectors, obligatory side- and rear lights; tyres; wheels; brake lights; seat belts; indicators; windscreen wipers and windscreen washers; exhaust (including the silencer); horn; and bodywork and suspension.

So, as not all items are tested, a car might, for instance, have a broken reversing light, and yet it could not legitimately be refused an MOT certificate (because the reversing light is not an obligatory light and so is not covered by the test).

In practice the examiner has a considerable discretion and it is extremely difficult for the individual motorist to argue against the examiner's decision. There is a procedure for appealing (form VT 17 must be sent to the Traffic Area Office within fourteen days; a fee equal to the amount of the MOT fee is also payable), but it is virtually unheard of for a private motorist to appeal.

If an appointment has been made beforehand the garage is legally obliged to carry out the test. They cannot change their mind and refuse to carry out the test, except in a few circumstances (e.g. if you do not produce the registration book or some other evidence of when the vehicle was made; if the vehicle is so dirty that it would be 'unreasonably difficult' to examine it – for instance, if there is so much mud underneath it that the steering cannot be properly seen; if there is not enough petrol, fuel or oil in the vehicle; if goods on the vehicle are not removed or secured as the examiner directs). Also, if the garage discovers that the condition of the vehicle is so bad that a braking test would be dangerous (because they might crash!), they can refuse to carry out the brake test. They must however carry out the rest of the test and check all the other items, but of course a test certificate will be refused.

### *What are the fees?*

At the present time the standard fee is £10 (£6 for motorbikes without a sidecar).

Different fees apply when a vehicle that has already failed the test is retested. There are three possibilities here:

If the vehicle is *left at that MOT garage*, and repaired by them, no fee has to be paid for the retest. This is because the failed items would have been checked during the repair, and the garage knows that the condition of the other items has not changed since the original test. So no fee is payable.

If the vehicle is *taken away from that MOT garage*, and then taken to *another MOT garage* for repair and a second test, only half the full MOT test fee is payable (provided the second test is within fourteen days of the failed test). Only a half-fee is payable because the second garage should have tested the failed items when it was carrying out the repairs, and is thus being paid a reduced fee to test the items that originally passed (i.e. at the time of the first MOT examination).

*Otherwise* the full MOT fee must be paid again on a retest. If you take the vehicle away from the MOT station, and then have the repairs done other than at an MOT garage (or you do them yourself), you have to pay the full test fee again. This is so even if there is only a small time-lag between the vehicle failing the test and the defect being fixed. Suppose the car fails the test because an indicator bulb has gone. You go outside and replace the bulb, and come back five minutes later – you would have to pay a full test fee again. It would obviously have been better to ask the garage to replace the light bulb since that would probably be cheaper than the full test fee!

### *What happens if I lose the MOT certificate?*

It is usually possible to obtain a duplicate MOT certificate. If you apply to the garage that carried out the test they should be able to go through their records and – having checked that the vehicle did pass the test – issue you with a replacement certificate (£1 fee). Alternatively you can apply to the Traffic Area Office (you will find their address in the phone book). They will need the name and address of the garage that issued the certificate, or alternatively the number of the MOT certificate. Once again a £1 fee is payable.

If you cannot remember where the test was carried out there is no way you can obtain a duplicate certificate. This is because there is no central index or register of MOT certificates. If this happens you will simply have to arrange for another test to be carried out.

### Can the police demand to see the MOT certificate?

An MOT certificate is one of the documents that any police constable can require a motorist to produce. See p. 15 for the rules on this and other documents. Also see p. 238 for police checks on vehicles.

---

## WHAT'S THE PENALTY?

*For not having an MOT certificate*

MAXIMUM PENALTY: a £400 fine (£1,000 if the vehicle can carry more than eight passengers). No endorsement or penalty points can be imposed

LIKELY PENALTY: a £15 to £20 fine. It might be a bit more if the test is considerably overdue (e.g. three months). There would probably be a separate prosecution for any defects that would have resulted in the vehicle failing an MOT test (e.g. defective brakes)

Note: you cannot get a fixed penalty ticket for an MOT offence

*(For more on penalties see p. 216)*

---

### Should I insist on an MOT certificate when I buy a secondhand vehicle?

Usually. If it is a private car, of course, an MOT certificate will not be needed unless the car is three years old (see p. 171). Otherwise it is a good idea to ask for an MOT certificate. If you do not have the MOT certificate you will be committing an offence if you use the vehicle (see above). But you should not rely on the MOT certificate as being a guarantee of the good condition or roadworthiness of the vehicle – it is not (see p. 173). On the other hand, if an MOT certificate was issued recently you have some evidence that it was roadworthy at that date.

It is possible that you will buy a car with a new MOT and then discover shortly afterwards that you have made a bad buy. When this happens you may occasionally feel that the garage that issued the MOT certificate must have been connected in some way to the garage or person from whom you bought the vehicle. If you think this is the case (and therefore think that the MOT certificate was improperly issued) you should immediately complain to the Traffic Area Office. They may not be able to help you with your immediate problem (i.e. getting compensation), but they may take action against the MOT garage. Also see 'Buying and Selling a Car', p. 44.

# Negligence

## What is negligence?

Motorists are negligent if they are so careless that the law says they should pay compensation for the damage they cause.

So, if someone is negligent and causes an accident, they will have to pay compensation to the people they injure, and to the people whose property they have damaged. But if they were not negligent (i.e. the accident was not their 'fault') they will not have to pay compensation.

Bear in mind that when we talk about blame we are not concerned with liability (e.g. can someone be prosecuted for careless driving?), but with who is to pay for the damage caused. This is a *civil* claim – suing for damages caused by the negligence of the other driver. It is not to be confused with a criminal prosecution brought by the police.

There is no criminal offence of negligent driving. There are, however, other offences that may be brought (e.g. careless driving or reckless driving), but these are entirely separate from the question of negligence. So it is possible for a motorist to be convicted of a criminal motoring offence and yet not be found to have been negligent! For example, suppose a pedestrian steps off the pavement on to a pedestrian crossing just before your car reaches it, and is knocked over. You will almost certainly be guilty of the criminal offence of not giving precedence to a pedestrian (see p. 205 for the strict rules that apply on pedestrian crossing cases). However, another court might find that you were not negligent – in that there was no way that you could have avoided the accident – and so you would not have to pay compensation to the injured pedestrian.

To summarize: Negligent motorists will have to pay compensation for the damage and injury they cause. In deciding whether or not someone has been negligent the court will look at what a 'reasonable motorist' would have done.

The Motorist and the Law

### *How do the courts apportion blame for an accident?*

They look for who is negligent. Sometimes this will be easy – a drunk motorist who drives into a row of parked cars is obviously solely to blame for the accident and is negligent. The drunk (or the drunk's insurance company) will have to pay for all the damage caused.

However, it is rarely so straightforward. Sometimes one motorist is partly to blame along with another motorist. When this happens the courts have to divide liability between the two of them. For instance, suppose a cyclist is pedalling along, at night, without lights, and is hit by your car from behind. The court might decide that the cyclist was partly to blame for the accident – by not having had lights. On the other hand, the court might also feel that you were partly to blame – you should have seen the cyclist earlier, and taken avoiding action. So the court might apportion blame between the two of you – deciding perhaps that you were 75 per cent to blame, but the cyclist must bear 25 per cent of the responsibility for the accident. The lawyers call this contributory negligence – in other words, the *victim* was, to some extent, also to blame.

You will find that in many of the case histories in this book liability is divided between the parties. In those cases the courts have decided that there was contributory negligence.

### *Does it matter if there was contributory negligence?*

If you were guilty of contributory negligence the value of any claim you make for damages will be reduced:

*You were involved in a car crash. You were driving along a main road when your car was hit by an oncoming lorry, which had been overtaking other vehicles. As a result of the accident your car needed repairs costing £1,500; you were off work for two weeks and lost £400 worth of wages; and you also received a few cuts and bruises. The value of your claim might be:*

| | |
|---|---|
| *damage to car* | *£1,500* |
| *loss of wages* | *£400* |
| *compensation for cuts and bruises* | *£500* |
| | *£2,400* |

*That is the amount of compensation that you could expect to receive if you went to court. But your lawyers tell you that you could also be partly to blame for the accident. They point out that the lorry was clearly visible to you, and that you could, perhaps, have taken more avoiding action to prevent a collision. They say*

178

*that you might be found 25 per cent to blame for the accident. If that were to happen your compensation would be:*

| | |
|---|---|
| normal level of compensation | £2,400 |
| less 25 per cent | £600 |
| you would get | £1,800 |

So you pay for your own contributory negligence through a reduced claim against the other motorist. The importance of this is that it gives a lot of scope for arguments and negotiations between motorists (and, more realistically, their insurance companies) as to who was to blame for an accident. Because negligence is such a vague concept there is always scope for arguments as to how much contributory negligence – if any – there was.

In fact a finding of contributory negligence can have surprising consequences:

*In the example above, you – the motorist – were told that you were 25 per cent to blame for the accident. Your claim of £2,400 was therefore reduced to £1,800. But, if the advice you were given was correct, it follows that the lorry driver also had a claim against you (but with the driver being 75 per cent to blame). Now, suppose the lorry had crashed and had been a write-off with the driver being killed. It is not difficult to see how that claim would run into many thousands of pounds – probably well over £50,000. Thus, if you were one quarter to blame, you would still be liable for a sizeable amount. For instance, even if the claim was only £50,000 you would still be liable for £12,500! In practice – thankfully – your insurance company would meet that claim. But it does explain why your insurance company might be extremely reluctant to settle your claim (i.e. for £2,400) on a 25 per cent contributory negligence basis with the lorry driver's insurance company, although, for your part, you might be happy to accept the £1,800 offered (i.e. 25 per cent contributory negligence), in order to settle the matter. This explains why insurance companies often refuse to settle when their customers want them to.*

### Can you have 100 per cent contributory negligence?

Perhaps in theory, but certainly not in practice. If a court feels that you were to blame they might well make a deduction for your contributory negligence, but that would never be as much as 100 per cent. In practice a motorist is not likely to be found more than 80 per cent to blame – in other words, blame will be apportioned 80/20 between the two motorists. Bear in mind that the apportionment of blame is a fairly rough-and-ready process – after all, the whole idea of negligence (i.e. what would the reasonable motorist have done in the circumstances?) is very vague.

The point to grasp is that insurance companies are always arguing that there is contributory negligence by other motorists. Thus, you may be involved in an accident and think you were not to blame at all, but may well find that the other motorist's insurance company will make all sorts of suggestions about your negligence. Their reason for doing this is to try and achieve a finding of contributory negligence and so reduce the amount they have to pay.

### Am I negligent if I do not follow all the advice in the Highway Code?

Probably – but not definitely. The Highway Code lays down the standard of driving that we should all aspire to. It is full of sensible advice, although we all know that we do not drive to that standard all the time. But, if you are in clear breach of a provision in the Highway Code, the chances are that a court will find you to blame (at least partly, if not totally) for an accident. Certainly you would have an extremely uphill struggle to avoid liability!

Similar principles apply when motorists are convicted of the criminal offence of careless driving (see p. 59). Once they are convicted it is extremely difficult, and in practice quite exceptional for them to avoid being liable (through their insurance company) to pay compensation.

### How can I work out whether I was to blame for an accident?

We have told you the theory (see above): now for the real world! You may be looking at this book because you have been involved in an accident and you want to try and work out whether you – or the other motorist – were to blame. All we can do is give you some general hints and indications. You must bear in mind that no two road accidents are ever identical – visibility, road conditions, the amount of other traffic, weather and the other circumstances all play a part. However, throughout this book you will find case histories of court decisions following actual accidents. All you can do is go through these and try and extract a general impression of how the courts approach road accident cases. You must not rely upon particular case histories as cast-iron proof that another motorist was to blame for your accident – or that you were not to blame!

In the following pages we look at some of the more common accident situations – such as overtaking, failing to give a signal, crossroads accidents. And numerous other case histories can be found in other chapters of this book; in particular see: 'Animals'; 'Brakes'; 'Children'; 'Commercial Vehicles'; 'Learners'; 'Lights'; 'Parking'; 'Pedestrians'; 'Seat Belts'; 'Speeding'; 'Tyres'; and 'Unsafe Vehicles'.

### The door of a parked car is opened, knocking over a cyclist. Who is to blame?

The car driver is solely to blame. Such accidents are all too common, and a court would have no hesitation in deciding that the car driver (or passenger) was negligent in not checking that the road was clear before opening the door. Normally there would not be any fault on the part of the injured cyclist, who would get full compensation from the driver's insurance company.

Incidentally, there is also a specific criminal offence of opening a vehicle door 'so as to cause injury or danger to any person' (under the Construction and Use Regulations). The penalty is a fine of up to £1,000.

### Who is to blame if there is an accident when a motorcyclist overtakes a stationary row of cars?

Here we are dealing with queue-jumping. The Highway Code is quite clear: 'in a traffic hold-up, do not try to "jump the queue" by cutting into another lane or by overtaking the vehicles waiting in front of you.' Not surprisingly, therefore, motorists who queue-jump do so at their own risk.

Often it is a motorcycle that is overtaking the stationary line of traffic. Not unnaturally the motorcyclist feels that it is pointless to wait in the traffic jam when there is room to overtake the parked vehicles. The difficulty comes when another vehicle is edging out of a side turning, and the cars waiting in the traffic jam allow that vehicle to pull out. But the motorcyclist does not see that vehicle, and so there is an accident. Who is to blame? The courts feel, strongly, that the overtaking motorcyclist is largely to blame:

*There was a traffic jam, with cars two abreast. Mr Moody's car was in a side turning, and he was trying to get across the stationary cars and turn right. There was a gap in the line of cars, and the driver of a milk tanker in the queue waved Mr Moody on. He inched out extremely slowly until he came to the edge of the line of cars. As he did so he collided with a motorcyclist, who had been overtaking the stationary traffic jam. The motorcyclist was injured, and sued Mr Moody for compensation (i.e. for the injuries he had received, his loss of earnings and the damage done to his bike). However, Mr Moody (or at least his insurance company) argued that the accident was the motorcyclist's own fault. Held: the motorcyclist was 80 per cent to blame. Thus, Mr Moody, the car driver, was 20 per cent to blame and the motorcyclist only received 20 per cent of his normal damages.* Powell *(1966)*

*The driver of a parked car wanted to pull across a line of heavy traffic, to get to the other side of the road. A bus slowed down, to let him pull out, and the bus driver flashed his headlights. The car driver pulled out extremely slowly. But a moped had begun to overtake the bus and collided with the car. The injured moped driver sued the car driver, and he also sued the bus driver (for negligently flashing his lights to tell the car driver to 'come on'). Held: the accident was solely the moped driver's fault. The car driver could not have pulled out more carefully, and so was not negligent. Nor was the bus driver negligent – by flashing his headlights he had merely told the car driver: 'You can come on as far as I am concerned.' The moped driver was to blame – he should have realized there was danger when the bus stopped. He should have stopped himself.* Clarke *(1969)*

So we see that the courts take a tough line with motorcyclists who overtake stationary vehicles. The same applies when it is another car that is doing the queue-jumping – although then it is perhaps more understandable that the courts should find the overtaking motorist solely to blame:

*A car was waiting at a side turning, wanting to turn right across the busy main road. Two cars stopped, to let him cross; one of the drivers waved him on. As he pulled out slowly, he collided with another car – which was overtaking the two stationary cars. Held: the driver of the overtaking car was solely to blame for the accident. There was no way in which the car coming from the side turning was to blame – after all, what else could the driver do, except edge out slowly?* H. L. Motorworks *(1977)*

**Who is to blame if there is an accident when a motorist turns out of a side road into a main road?**

Normally the motorist coming from the side road would be liable – for not having kept a look-out for vehicles in the main road and made sure that it was safe before pulling out:

*A car was waiting in a side road until it was safe to cross the main road and turn right. A bus was approaching, and signalled left, to turn into the side road. The car driver watched it coming for about 150 yards, and then saw the left-hand indicator. He could not see any other vehicles, and so pulled across, in front of the bus, to turn*

182

*right. As he did so he struck a motorcyclist who was overtaking the bus. The motorcyclist sued. Held: the car driver was solely to blame. It is obviously a dangerous manoeuvre coming out of a side road into a main road, and the motorist should have taken extra care. He should have waited a bit longer, to check that there was nothing behind the bus. He had to pay full compensation to the motorcyclist – who was not to blame in any way.* Harding *(1964)*

What would have happened if the bus had not turned left (as it was indicating) but had gone straight on – who would have been to blame if the car and bus had collided? The answer is that the court would probably have found both drivers partially to blame:

*A car was in a side road, waiting to cross a main road. The driver looked carefully and saw a motorcycle approaching – but it had its left-hand indicator flashing. Assuming that the motorcyclist was going to turn left the driver pulled out. The motorcyclist did not turn left – he had not realized that the indicator was on – and there was a crash. Held: the car driver was two thirds to blame, and the motorcyclist one third to blame.* Wadsworth *(1978)*

Incidentally, the Highway Code is quite clear on this point. It says: 'when waiting to emerge at a junction do not assume that a vehicle approaching from the right which is signalling with its left-hand direction indicator *will* turn left. Wait to make sure.' In view of this clear wording you might have expected the court to find that the car driver was 100 per cent to blame, and the motorcyclist to blame not at all. However, the court took a more robust view – and the case shows that the courts take a more rough-and-ready approach to the realities of everyday driving than is allowed for in the Highway Code.

### How is blame decided in crossroads accidents?

The cases above give an indication of the courts' approach. The normal rule is that motorists pull out of a side turning into a major turning at their own risk. In other words, they are likely to be to blame if there is an accident. However – as with all negligence cases – this is not a hard-and-fast rule. It may be that the driver in the main road should have been more careful, and may therefore be found partly to blame:

*A car drove out a side turning, straight into a main road. It collided with a lorry that was on the main road. However, the lorry driver had not looked at the side turning, and had not slowed down in any way. If he had looked he would probably have seen the car and have been able to take some avoiding action. Held: the lorry driver was 25 per cent to blame. So the car driver got 75 per cent of his normal level of compensation (which would, of course, have been paid by the lorry driver's insurance company).* Butters (1967)

Not surprisingly cases of this sort attract a lot of criticism. In recent years the courts have been much more reluctant to find main-road drivers guilty of any negligence in accidents such as this. Only if it is obvious that main-road drivers could have taken evading action will the courts find them negligent. The courts now prefer to say that it is totally unrealistic to expect drivers on a main road to take their foot off the accelerator, or look carefully, every time they pass a side turning. This is particularly so in a busy town. A less sympathetic approach might be taken in the country – where there are relatively few side turnings, and cars might be travelling at higher speeds.

### What about an accident on a country lane?

It is all too common for two vehicles to meet, head on, on a relatively narrow country lane. Who is to blame when this happens? Often there will be no independent evidence to show that one of the motorists was solely to blame (e.g. by being on the wrong side of the road). Generally the courts take a rough-and-ready approach – and find both drivers half to blame. This is on the basis that they were both careless. Thus both will recover 50 per cent of the normal value of their claim from the other. Naturally this will not apply if there is clear evidence that one or other of the motorists was more than half to blame.

### What is wrong with the negligence laws?

A lot! Anyone who reads all the cases in this book will realize what a confused approach the law takes to road accident claims. Everything depends upon showing that someone else was negligent. This has to be argued out in the calm and peace of the court room, where there is a tendency for the everyday realities of motoring life to be replaced with a counsel of perfection. The end result is that findings of negligence do not always accord with what the man-or-woman in the street would think as being fair and reasonable. In addition, of course, there is the considerable delay and expense in taking a compensation claim to court. We have seen that there are often arguments about contributory negligence – when it is said that the victim was also, in some way, to blame. These arguments are often no more than legal red herrings, and cause delay and frustration to everyone involved. Bear in mind that, whenever there is a finding of contributory negligence, the end result is a reduction in the victim's compensation. What the insurance company saves from its damages bill, the victim loses in compensation.

There is also the problem of a person who is injured in an accident for which no one else is to blame. Quite simply, the accident was no one's fault – the victim was not to blame, and nor was anyone else. In such circumstances the victim does not get any compensation – after all, the law only gives compensation when there was clear blame by someone else:

> *A doctor agreed to act as a first-aid official during a motor race. A car crashed, and the doctor was killed. Could his family bring any claim for compensation? Held: no. The car had crashed because of a latent defect in the brakes – which no one could have found out about. Also the organizers of the race had not been negligent. In other words, the accident did not happen through anyone else's negligence, so there was no legal entitlement to compensation.* O'Dowd (1951)

In addition, of course, there are numerous cases where the victims themselves were to blame for the accident (particularly in the case of a young child who is run down by a car – see the case history on p. 68). If we accept the everyday realities of motoring life – after all, we all make mistakes at some time – it does seem unduly harsh to punish the victim by not awarding any compensation. It is easy to forget that road accidents can cripple, maim, and kill – they can deprive a family of the breadwinner, and cause untold misery and distress. To impose a system of fault and negligence into this situation seems unnecessarily harsh. The solution lies in abandoning the whole idea of negligence and not bothering to find out who was to blame for the accident. Instead, we could follow New Zealand, where they have a no-fault system of compensation. Their State-run scheme pays compensation to the victims of all accidents – irrespective of blame. Quite simply, they take the (seemingly sensible) view that normal people do not deliberately injure themselves and it is therefore wrong for victims to lose their compensation merely because they were negligent themselves. In fact in 1978 a Royal Commission in our country recommended that such a scheme be introduced for road accident compensation claims. To date nothing has been done about this proposal – and its chances of introduction, in the short term, would seem to be zero.

It is only when one becomes the victim of an accident that one realizes how unfair and unkind the present negligence system is.

### *What if I am injured by a hit-and-run driver? Who can I sue?*

Don't worry – you may still be able to get compensation. As we have seen, the normal rule is that you can only get compensation if someone else was negligent. Clearly your worry will be that you cannot trace the person who was negligent – the hit-and-run driver. However, that need not prevent you from getting compensation. If it can be shown that the hit-and-run driver was to blame for the accident (i.e. it was not your fault) you will still be able to get compensation. The compensation will be paid by the Motor Insurers Bureau (see pp. 130–31).

# Noise

### What can I do about motorbikes with noisy exhausts?

A noisy motorbike (or, indeed, a noisy car) is illegal. Firstly, there are specific noise limits (measured in decibels) that apply to any vehicle. In practice, however, expensive noise-measuring equipment is required, so prosecutions are fairly rare. Secondly, it is also an offence to use a motorbike or other vehicle which 'causes any excessive noise' – and there is no need for scientific evidence of how noisy it was. So owners or drivers of noisy motorbikes can be prosecuted – in practice their only defence is likely to be that the noise was due to a temporary mechanical breakdown that they could not reasonably have foreseen (e.g. the engine was very noisy because the bearings had suddenly started to go).

If you are troubled by noisy motorbikes the answer is to take the registration numbers and report them to the police, who, one hopes, will then investigate – in practice an informal warning from the police often has the desired effect and the motorcyclist will fit a proper silencer.

### What if my silencer is not noisy, but it has a hole in the side?

The law says that the silencer must be 'in good and efficient working order'. Therefore it is illegal to have a rusty or broken silencer, even if the silencer is not particularly noisy. Crazily, this rule only applies to the silencer – so, if the tail pipe (i.e. the pipe that comes out of the silencer) is disintegrating, no offence is committed (assuming, of course, it does not cause undue noise)!

### When is use of the horn prohibited?

On two occasions. Firstly, you cannot use your horn when the vehicle is stationary (e.g. parked or in a traffic jam) unless you need to do so to warn other road users of danger. Secondly, you can never use the horn between 11.30 p.m. and 7.00 a.m. on a restricted road (i.e. if there is a 30 m.p.h. speed limit, or if street lamps are no more than 200 metres apart). Surprisingly this ban on using the horn applies even if there is danger! Of course, in practice the police would be most unlikely to prosecute if there was a legitimate reason for blowing the horn – and, if they did, most magistrates would give an absolute discharge (see p. 237 for absolute discharge).

### Can I have a horn that plays a tune?

No. At one time 'Colonel Bogey' horns were popular. They are now banned. Only normal, one-tone horns are allowed. The only exceptions are for emergency vehicles (which can have two-tone horns, or, indeed, any other type of horn) and for ice-cream vehicles, etc. Sales vans, such as ice-cream vans, can have a horn which is 'designed to emit a sound for a purpose of informing members of the public that goods are on the vehicle for sale'. But the goods must be perishable (e.g. fresh fruit, ice-cream), and the chimes or loudspeakers must not be operated so that they 'give reasonable cause for annoyance to persons in the vicinity'. Just what this means is a matter for argument. So ice-cream van owners can play their chimes for a short period, but excessive use of the chimes will be illegal. Basically they are allowed to do enough to make their presence known to the local population – and for that purpose a short burst of chimes should be sufficient. In any event this exception only applies between 12 noon and 7 p.m.

### What about anti-theft alarm bells?

An exception to the normal rules is made for anti-theft devices. Often these are simply fitted to the existing horn; however, a separate horn (making a siren or two-tone type of noise) is allowed. But any anti-theft device must have an automatic cut-out so it will stop after no more than five minutes.

### Practical motoring:
### What does the Highway Code say about use of the horn?

'When your vehicle is moving use your horn when it is necessary as a warning of your presence to other road users – but never use it as a rebuke.' In other words, don't use the horn as a means of telling off other drivers!

---

## WHAT'S THE PENALTY?

*For horn offences*

*For causing excessive noise*

*For exceeding the prescribed noise levels*
MAXIMUM PENALTY: a £100 fine
LIKELY PENALTY: a £15 fine, but you may get away with a £12 fixed penalty ticket instead (see p. 217)

*For using an ice-cream chime (etc.) outside hours or not for business*
MAXIMUM PENALTY: a £2,000 fine
LIKELY PENALTY: a £40 fine

*(For more on penalties see p. 216)*

---

# Parking

## *What do yellow lines on the road mean?*

Yellow lines are no more than a rough guide as to parking and loading restrictions. For the details you must look at the traffic signs (which should be near by). The system is:

- *dotted yellow lines on the road:* no waiting or parking except during the hours given on the traffic sign. Thus some waiting and parking is allowed during the working day
- *single yellow line on the road:* no waiting or parking during the working day
- *double yellow lines on the road:* no waiting or parking during the whole of the working day, and also for some of the rest of the day. In practice most double yellow lines mean that parking is banned twenty-four hours per day.

One point to note is that 'working day' often includes the whole of Saturday. It varies from area to area, but the net effect is that it will often be unlawful to park on a single yellow line on a Saturday afternoon. Indeed, because the regulations are extremely complicated, and there are often local variations, yellow lines on the road should be taken as only a very rough guide. Instead, rely on the yellow signs that set out the parking restrictions. Note that the restriction will be in force every day of the week (including Sundays and Bank Holidays) unless the sign says otherwise.

In addition there may well be yellow marks on the kerbstones. These relate to loading and unloading (i.e. not parking). In practice they mean roughly the same as yellow lines marked on the road:

- *one yellow line on the kerb:* loading and unloading is only allowed during the hours stated on the traffic sign
- *two yellow lines on the kerb:* no loading or unloading throughout the whole of the working day

• *three yellow lines on the kerb:* no loading or unloading throughout the whole of the working day, and also during additional hours.

### Are there any exceptions for loading and unloading?

Perhaps! Whether or not you can load or unload is shown by the markings on the kerb (i.e. not the yellow lines on the road). If you load or unload in breach of the loading restrictions (as shown by the yellow lines on the kerb, and on the traffic sign) you will commit an offence. On the other hand, if you do not break those restrictions you will be allowed to load and unload even though there are parking restrictions (as shown by the yellow lines). In other words, you can load and unload on yellow lines provided you do not break specific restrictions on loading and unloading (as shown by yellow marks on the kerb).

But what is meant by loading and unloading? Plainly a trade delivery by a lorry to a shop will certainly count as unloading. In practice most of the arguments arise with private motorists who argue that they are loading their cars with shopping. Each of these cases has to be decided on its own facts. But it should be borne in mind that simply loading an individual parcel or two into a private car will not amount to loading goods. On the other hand, if the car is being used for loading a large bulky item (e.g. a washing machine or piece of furniture) this probably will count as loading and so be permitted. Certainly what is not covered is parking a car, popping into a shop and buying a relatively small article (or a takeaway meal), and then going back to the car. That will not be a case of loading and unloading and a parking offence will have been committed. Similarly motorists who park their car outside the bank while they pop in to collect cash cannot normally claim to be loading.

Other problems arise with van and lorry drivers who park for an unduly long time. The idea of the exception is that the van or lorry should be used for loading and unloading throughout most of the time it is stationary. Lorry drivers who have some goods to collect but spend, say, twenty minutes filling in the forms and paperwork, and then a mere five minutes loading the van, would be acting unreasonably and so would be guilty of a parking offence. In any event there is frequently a local regulation which gives a maximum time for unloading, often twenty minutes – in which case a lorry driver would be parking illegally even if unloading throughout the whole of a 25-minute period.

Even if loading and unloading is permitted the engine must be turned off. If this is not done the driver will be committing an offence (see p. 200).

Finally, do not forget that the small print of parking restrictions will be found in local regulations and bye-laws. There are slight variations in these throughout the country – so if you are thinking of raising a technical legal defence to a parking charge you should check the local regulations carefully.

### Can disabled drivers ignore yellow lines?

No. But disabled drivers may be able to apply for an orange badge allowing them to park on yellow lines (whether dotted, single or double) for up to two hours (unlimited time in Scotland). A special parking disc must be left on the car, showing the time when it was parked. In addition this exemption does not apply if there is any ban on loading or unloading (e.g. as shown by yellow marks on the kerbstones), or in a bus lane. For the penalties for misusing an orange badge, and for wrongly parking in a disabled person's parking area, see p. 86.

### What if the yellow lines can't be seen?

The general rule is that there must be yellow lines and also traffic signs. In other words, if there is one, but not the other, the motorist usually cannot be prosecuted. So if yellow lines have become faded, and are not visible, the motorist may be able to avoid prosecution. The same will apply if the local authority simply forgot to paint the yellow lines on the road. But there are limits to this argument; for example, you cannot claim to have a defence just because the yellow lines were covered by snow, or by other illegally parked cars! It is all a matter of degree. In one case there was a gap in the yellow lines (just over the length of a car) which had been caused by roadworks. The motorist knew that there should be yellow lines, and there were clearly marked parking restrictions (on yellow signs). When prosecuted for parking he argued that there were no yellow lines on the road. Surprisingly the court accepted this argument – saying that the council could only get away with minor gaps in the yellow lines. However, most courts would not be so sympathetic!

### What do the different types of parking sign mean?

There are three main types of parking sign:

● *small yellow signs* are put up when there are yellow markings on the road (see above). They are not put up in parking controlled zones
● *controlled-zone signs* are white, rectangular signs with 'NO WAITING' markings on them, and the words 'CONTROLLED ZONE'. They are usually put at the entrance to a meter or disc zone, and the sign will set out the parking restrictions (i.e. when you cannot park). There will be no yellow signs within the controlled zone (unless there are localized additional restrictions on parking)
● *blue signs:* these small blue signs often contain waiting restrictions (e.g. limiting waiting to twenty minutes and prohibiting return within one hour). In fact these blue signs do not have as much legal effect as the yellow signs, or the controlled-zone signs. This is because the road will not have been marked as a designated parking place, so any prosecution would not be for parking but for obstruction (see p. 197).

### What about parking meters?

There are several rules to obey:

● you can only park within the meter bay (i.e. the space marked by the white lines). You are not within the meter bay if part of your car is parked over the lines
● it is illegal to feed a meter (i.e. come back and put some more money in). It is also illegal to stay more than four hours on any meter
● you must put the money in the meter as soon as you leave your car. Strictly speaking you cannot go off and look for change (e.g. by going into a nearby shop)
● groups of parking meters are shown by a mark on the road. You cannot move straight from one meter bay into another meter bay in the same zone. You can, however, go from a meter bay in one zone to another in a different zone.

To complicate matters, most local authorities have their own detailed rules on parking meters. For instance, the length of time that must pass before you can return to a meter bay in the same zone usually varies from one local authority to another. Similarly there are often different rules about whether you can park in a parking bay if there is a bag over the meter (i.e. 'METER OUT OF ORDER' or 'METER SUSPENDED'). The general rule is that it is illegal to park in a suspended parking bay, and if you do so you can expect a parking ticket. But, although parking may be suspended, it does not necessarily follow that loading or unloading is suspended – so a driver may be legitimately able to park in a suspended parking area to unload a van. One final point to realize is that local regulations and bye-laws can change these rules slightly. If in doubt you have to check with the local council.

### When can the police wheel-clamp a car?

Wheel clamps are only authorized in some parts of the country (at the moment, some London boroughs only). In those areas the police can wheel-clamp any illegally parked vehicle. One point to note is that the vehicle need not be parked on a double yellow line, or be causing a major obstruction – if it is illegally parked it can be wheel-clamped. For instance, a vehicle wrongly parked in a residents' parking area will be illegally parked and so can be wheel-clamped. The only exceptions are for (1.) vehicles displaying the orange badge (the disabled drivers' sign – see p. 84), and (2.) when a vehicle has stayed in a parking meter bay for up to two hours after its time has expired.

If a vehicle is wheel-clamped there are, in effect, two penalties to pay. Firstly, there will be the usual parking ticket penalty. Secondly, there will be an additional charge for having the wheel clamp removed (currently £25). In practice, of course, for many motorists the real penalty is caused by the inconvenience and time wasted in having the vehicle unclamped. The motorist has to go to the police garage, pay the penalty, and then wait for the police to come back and unclamp the car.

### When can the police tow away a vehicle?

The police have very wide powers to tow away vehicles – they can do so for virtually any parking or obstruction offence. The unlucky motorist has to pay a removal fee (£59 if from a motorway and £55 elsewhere – except in London where it is £57). In addition there is a daily storage charge of £5 per day. And, of course, the motorist will probably have to pay a penalty for the offence that led the police to tow away the vehicle in the first place (e.g. a parking fine). One point to note is that, if not convicted for that motoring offence, the motorist may be able to recover the fees paid for the recovery of the vehicle.

## What is a clearway?

A clearway is a main road on which parking is banned. Generally, stopping on a clearway is only allowed for postal collections and deliveries, to avoid accidents, or with the specific permission of the police obtained beforehand. You cannot stop to let passengers in or out of the car.

If there is a verge you will probably not be breaking the clearway rules by parking on that verge (but see parking on verges, p. 198).

## What rules apply when parking at night?

Firstly, any parked vehicle must 'during the hours of darkness' be parked with its nearside next to the verge (i.e. it must be facing the right way – see p. 154). Secondly, it may be necessary to leave the vehicle's lights on, although, if the vehicle is in a 30 m.p.h. speed limit area (i.e. either there are signs showing this to be the speed limit, or street lights are no more than 200 yards apart), no lights are needed – provided that the vehicle is not within ten metres of a junction. This exception only applies to cars (with no more than seven passenger seats), motorbikes and goods vehicles not exceeding 30 cwt. Otherwise lights must be shown. If lights do have to be turned on, both offside and nearside lights must be on – it is not good enough simply to leave the offside lights on. Generally, see p. 154.

## How do I pay a parking ticket?

Most parking offences result in a parking ticket – which can be paid by a fixed penalty.

The idea is that the motorist can pay a fixed penalty straight away, and so avoid prosecution in court. The fixed penalty is £12 – the fine on a conviction may be much more (although in practice most parking convictions only result in a fine of £25 or so).

If you ignore the parking ticket, and the offer to pay a fixed penalty, you will be prosecuted. It will then be too late to opt to pay the fixed penalty of £12. Instead the case will go to court – although you may decide to plead guilty by post. The end result will be that you will pay a higher penalty, and you may also have to pay some costs to the prosecution.

If you want to pay the fixed-penalty ticket, you should normally do so within twenty-eight days of it being stuck to your windscreen. Simply pay the £12, and that will be the end of the matter.

Alternatively, you can ask for a court hearing – but you must do this within twenty-eight days. You may, for instance, want to do this if you do not think you were guilty of illegal parking, or if you were not the owner of the vehicle. But you must act quickly – fill in the forms, asking for a court hearing, within twenty-eight days.

If you do nothing, and ignore the ticket, the police will serve a formal Notice to Owner of Vehicle on you. Once again, you have a twenty-eight day period in which to respond to this Notice. Firstly, you can opt to pay the £12 ticket within the next twenty-eight days. Secondly, you can ask for a court hearing. Once again, there is a twenty-eight-day period in which to do this. Thirdly, you can fill in the Statement of Ownership (for instance, if you were not the owner at the time). But if you simply ignore the ticket, and do nothing within twenty-eight days, the £12 fine is automatically increased to £18.

The basic point to grasp is that, if you ignore a £12 parking ticket, the fine will automatically be increased to £18.

See below and p. 217 for more details on how the parking ticket and other fixed-penalty systems work.

If you lose the parking ticket contact the Central Ticket Office for your area (or the local council if there is no Central Ticket Office). If you give them the car number, and the date, time and location of the parking offence, they should be able to give you the number of the parking ticket. This will then enable you to pay the fixed penalty.


### How does the fixed-penalty procedure work?

There are three steps:

1. You get a parking ticket (for £12).

2. If you do not pay the ticket you will be sent a Notice to Owner of Vehicle.

3. If you do not fill that in the parking penalty is increased from £12 to £18. The £18 penalty will be registered with your local magistrates' court, which has the same means at its disposal for obtaining the money from you as it has for enforcing a fine (for instance, as a last resort, you could go to prison if you did not pay).

See p. 217 for details of how the fixed-penalty system works.

### *What is an obstruction charge?*

There are two types of obstruction charge, both of which are more serious than ordinary parking offences. Firstly, a motorist can be prosecuted under the Highways Act 1980 for 'wilfully obstructing the free passage of a highway'. Secondly, a prosecution can be brought under the Construction and Use Regulations 1978 for 'causing or permitting a motor vehicle to stand on a road so as to cause any unnecessary obstruction'.

There are two different charges, then. The first is for wilful obstruction, and the second is for unnecessary obstruction.

To confuse matters even further there does not have actually to be an obstruction of the road! What it boils down to is that unreasonable use of the highway is prohibited. Thus a vehicle can be causing an obstruction even if it is not stationary – for instance, driving a lorry at an unnecessarily slow speed down the middle of the road will certainly be causing an obstruction because it is being driven in an unreasonable manner. On the other hand, if a tractor is being driven slowly down the road there will not be an obstruction – even if it is causing even more chaos than the lorry! This is because the driver of the tractor is acting reasonably, and doing merely what has to be done to get down the road. So obstruction charges really come down to a question of reasonableness.

For example, in one case a motorist parked his van up against the bumper of a car. At that time the car driver could easily have removed his vehicle. But in the meantime another car came along and parked in front. The car driver was therefore boxed in. The van driver then refused to remove his van and he was charged with obstruction. In defence he argued that it was not his fault that the car had been boxed in – it had been done by another car. However, the court would have none of this; he had used the road in an unreasonable manner and he was rightly convicted of causing an obstruction. Similarly, in another case an unlucky motorist left his car parked for five hours in a line of other parked cars. He was not prosecuted for parking, but for obstruction – it was held he was guilty of obstruction even though he was merely parked in a line of other cars (and so was not, by himself, causing a physical obstruction of the street). In another case a taxi driver did a U-turn in the road and blocked oncoming traffic; he was guilty of obstruction.

It therefore follows that each obstruction case must depend upon its own facts. What will be an unreasonable use of a main road will not necessarily be an unreasonable use of a side road. Thus parking in a busy road may lead to an obstruction charge, whereas parking in a side road may not.

Problems can often arise with ice-cream and hot-dog vans that are parked while ice-creams, etc. are being sold. The general rule is that the courts will say that the selling of food, etc. is not what the highway was designed for, and so will normally be an unreasonable use of it. This will be so even if the ice-cream van is not causing an obstruction, in terms of causing other traffic to swerve, or blocking the road, etc. In other words, its mere presence on the road may mean that it is legally guilty of obstruction. In one case a mobile snack bar was parked in a lay-by; it was held that this amounted to an obstruction and so the snack bar owner was convicted. The end result is that anyone who operates an ice-cream van or snack bar is wide open to an obstruction charge. In practical terms they are at the mercy of the local police in deciding whether or not to prosecute.

### Can I be prosecuted for illegal parking if my car breaks down?

There are two offences that you would have to watch out for. Firstly, you might be prosecuted for parking (i.e. given a parking ticket). Strictly speaking you would probably be guilty of the offence. However, in practice what you should do is immediately write to the Local Ticket Office explaining the circumstances of the offence; the chances are that (if you can convince them you are telling the truth) they will withdraw the fixed-penalty ticket.

The second possibility is that you might be prosecuted for obstruction. If this happens it is all a matter of reasonableness. Probably, if you can show that you did everything possible to have the car moved as quickly as you could, you would not be guilty of obstruction. On the other hand, if you did not do everything you could you would be guilty. It would all be a matter of what the magistrates decided it was reasonable for you to do in the circumstances.

### Can I park on the verge?

There is a total ban on heavy commercial vehicles parking on verges, footpaths or central reservations. Other vehicles (i.e. not heavy commercial vehicles) cannot park on the verges, footpaths or central reservations of urban roads.

The answer to the question therefore depends upon whether or not your vehicle counts as a heavy commercial vehicle. This is any vehicle with an unladen weight of over 3,050 kilograms. In effect most private motorists can park on verges, footpaths, etc. unless they are on an urban road. The difficulty is that it is not always clear what counts as an urban road. The basic answer is that it covers any road where there is a speed limit of 40 m.p.h. or less. But many local authorities have specifically exempted some of these roads from the rules on parking on verges. In other words, there may well be some roads that have a speed limit of less than 40 m.p.h. where you are legally entitled to park on the verge, footpath or central reservation. There is no easy way of knowing whether or not such parking is allowed – it is a matter of checking with the local authority.

If there is a ban on parking on the verge the only defence to a charge is to show that the vehicle was being used for loading or unloading which could only satisfactorily be done by parking the vehicle in this way.

One other point to watch is that there is a separate offence which often covers parking on footways, or even on private land. The Road Traffic Act makes it an offence to park more than fifteen yards from a road (obviously this does not apply to your own driveway!). So, if you drive on to heathland, or private land, and park within fifteen yards of the road you will probably not be committing a criminal offence. On the other hand, if you go more than fifteen yards you probably will be!

Parking, or driving, on a footpath is always illegal.

### *What other offences can arise from a bad piece of parking?*

There are three other offences to watch out for. The first covers leaving any vehicle in a dangerous position (e.g. on a blind corner). This is regarded as a relatively serious charge; the motorist must be given a warning of intended prosecution within fourteen days of committing the offence (see p. 243).

Another offence to watch out for is that of negligently opening a car door. This is designed to cover motorists who carelessly open their car door and injure a cyclist or pedestrian.

Finally, it is an offence to leave the engine running when the car is parked.

## WHAT'S THE PENALTY?

*For obstruction*
MAXIMUM PENALTY: a £1,000 fine
LIKELY PENALTY: a £25 fine (more for complete disregard of other road users)*

*For parking meter offences*
MAXIMUM PENALTY: a £100 fine (but the fixed penalty may apply)
LIKELY PENALTY: a £15–£20 fine*

*For parking on a verge*
MAXIMUM PENALTY: a £400 fine
LIKELY PENALTY: a £20 fine*

*For driving on a footpath*
MAXIMUM PENALTY: a £400 fine
LIKELY PENALTY: a £20 fine

*For driving on a common*
MAXIMUM PENALTY: a £50 fine
LIKELY PENALTY: a £20 fine

*For negligently opening a car door*
MAXIMUM PENALTY: a £1,000 fine
LIKELY PENALTY: a £15–£25 fine (depending on seriousness)*

*For parking on a clearway*
MAXIMUM PENALTY: a £400 fine
LIKELY PENALTY: a £25 fine*

*For running the engine while parked*
MAXIMUM PENALTY: a £1,000 fine
LIKELY PENALTY: a £5–£10 fine*

*For abandoning a car*
MAXIMUM PENALTY: a £1,000 fine
LIKELY PENALTY: a £35 fine

*For parking in a dangerous position*
MAXIMUM PENALTY: three penalty points (and an endorsement), plus a £400 fine
LIKELY PENALTY: three penalty points (and an endorsement), plus a £30 fine*

*For parking offences connected with disabled drivers, lights and pedestrian crossings see pp. 86, 157 and 209*

\* For these offences you may get a £12 fixed penalty ticket instead (see p. 217)

*(For more on penalties see p. 216)*

---

### How much power do traffic wardens have?

For minor traffic offences they have the same powers as a police officer. Most importantly they can:

- give fixed-penalty tickets for parking offences (see p. 217)
- give fixed-penalty tickets for other non-endorsable offences (see p. 217)
- prosecute for parking without lights (see p. 195)
- prosecute for not displaying a road tax disc (see p. 270)
- direct traffic. If you ignore traffic signals given by a warden (e.g. to turn left or right, or to stop) you can be prosecuted as though it was a signal given by a police officer (and you will commit a further offence if you do not supply the warden with your name and address – see p. 286).

Wardens cannot deal with most other offences. In particular they cannot deal with obstruction charges or tow away vehicles. Since they cannot deal with most obstruction cases it does follow that they will often not be able to take any action if you park on the pavement – whereas they would be able to issue a ticket if you were illegally parking in a no-waiting area! However, it would be dangerous for a motorist to rely upon this. After all, the warden could still report the obstruction to the police, who could then decide to prosecute. Similarly, although wardens cannot arrange for a car to be towed away, they can tell the police – who can then tow it away.

As regards parking tickets bear in mind that wardens cannot (even if they want to) cancel a ticket once they have started writing it out. So there is no point in arguing with a warden who is in the process of writing out a ticket – it is too late. Also, if you are in charge of a car that is illegally parked you are obliged to give the warden your name and address if asked for them. However, the warden cannot ask you to produce your driving licence, insurance, MOT certificate, etc. (see p. 286).

### Can the owner of a parked car be blamed if there is an accident?

Sometimes, yes. In practice, however, this is relatively rare.

When we talk about blame we are not concerned with criminal liability (e.g. can someone be prosecuted by the police for careless driving?), but with the question of who is to pay for the damage caused. This is a *civil* claim – suing for damages caused by the negligence of a motorist – completely separate from the question of prosecution. A motorist – or, more likely, the motorist's insurance company – will have to pay compensation (i.e. for the damage and injury caused) only if he or she was negligent. See p. 177 for more information on the negligence laws.

Someone who parks negligently can sometimes be made to pay compensation, but, though it is all too common for badly parked cars to obstruct visibility, reduce the width of the road, and generally make driving more hazardous, in practice it is only rarely that the person who parked the car will be held liable if an accident happens. Many motorists may feel that these cowboy parkers should be made liable more often, but generally the courts only apportion a small amount of blame to the parker – and take the attitude that the other motorist should have been driving more carefully:

*A motorist was looking for a particular turning. He thought he had missed the turning so he parked his car on a bend and walked back to check a signpost. While he was out of the car a motorcyclist came round the bend and drove into the back of the car. The motorcyclist sued the car driver on the basis that the car should not have parked there. The car driver retaliated by suing the motorcyclist – saying that he should have been driving more carefully, and should not have been going so quickly that he could not stop in time (see p. 38 for the Highway Code on this point). Held: they were both to blame – but not equally. The court said the motorcyclist was 80 per cent to blame, and the owner of the parked car 20 per cent. The motorcyclist should have been travelling more carefully, so that he could slow down in time; the car driver should not have parked on the bend, but should have driven on to a straight piece of road. However, 80/20 was seen as a fair apportionment of blame. So the car driver had to pay for 20 per cent of the cost of repairs to the motorbike; the motorbike owner had to pay for 80 per cent of the cost of repairs to the car (in practice, of course, the insurance companies would have met the costs). Waller (1968)*

*Late at night a van driver parked his van on the inside of a bend. Shortly afterwards a car driver parked his car on the other side of the road (i.e. on the outside of the bend). There was a gap about twenty feet wide between the two vehicles. An accident then happened: a scooter driver collided with an oncoming car. The scooter driver was injured. He claimed compensation from the driver of the oncoming car, and also from the owners of the two parked vehicles (i.e. the parked van and the parked car). Held: the driver of the oncoming car was mainly to blame. But the other two vehicles had been parked negligently, and their drivers were also to blame. The oncoming car driver was 60 per cent to blame, and the drivers of the two parked vehicles were each 20 per cent to blame. Thus the injured moped driver got 60 per cent of his damages from the driver of the oncoming car and 20 per cent each from the owners of the parked van and the parked car (in practice from their insurance companies).* Stevens *(1970)*

If a car is parked at night it may be necessary for the lights to be left on (see p. 195). But a driver may comply with this requirement and still be held liable – if a court feels that it was an unsafe place to park:

*A motorist parked his car, at night, on a busy main road. Lights had to be shown (street lights were more than 200 metres apart, and the speed limit was more than 30 m.p.h. – see p. 195). He did not put on his full parking lights, but simply switched on a parking light on the offside. So he was showing a light – but not all the lights he should have done (see p. 154). Shortly afterwards another car crashed into the back of the parked car. That car driver said he had not seen the parking light – he had been blinded by headlights from oncoming vehicles. He sued the owner of the parked car for negligence – he wanted compensation for the damage to his car and for the injury he had suffered. Held: the owner of the parked car was mainly to blame. But the motorist who had crashed into the parked car was also to blame to an extent – the court said that he should have immediately slowed down once he had been blinded by the other headlights. In the circumstances the owner of the parked car was 70 per cent to blame, and the driver of the crashed car 30 per cent. So the motorist who crashed into the back of the parked car got 70 per cent of his damages from the owner of the parked car, and the owner of the parked car would have got 30 per cent of the cost of repairing his car from the owner of the car that drove into the back of it. (In practice, of course, the motorists' insurance companies would have met these costs.)* Watson *(1971)*

Generally, however, if the car is properly lit, and is in a relatively safe place, its owner cannot be to blame for any accident.

# Pedestrians

### *What are the penalties for jaywalking?*

In some countries there are very strict controls on where pedestrians can cross. In some foreign cities a pedestrian will be committing an offence if he or she crosses anywhere other than at a pedestrian crossing or at traffic lights. There are no such rules in this country – if a pedestrian rushes across a pedestrian crossing at an unsafe time, and causes an accident, the pedestrian will probably not have committed any offence! The same will apply if a pedestrian rushes across a pelican crossing (although there is one small exception here, for there is a specific regulation which prohibits pedestrians from standing on pedestrian crossings for longer than is necessary to cross).

But a pedestrian will be committing an offence by disobeying traffic signs given by a police officer or traffic warden – for instance, by crossing in defiance of a signal given by a police officer on traffic duty. When this happens the pedestrian is obliged to give his or her name to the police officer (or traffic warden); failure to do so will be a second, separate, offence.

One other obvious restriction on pedestrians is that they cannot go on motorways. But, apart from these few exceptions, the fact remains that a pedestrian generally cannot be prosecuted for crossing the road in a dangerous place, or for jaywalking.

### *What is the difference between a zebra crossing and a pelican crossing?*

Both are types of pedestrian crossing, but pelican crossings have traffic lights as well. Similar rules apply to both.

### *What are the rules on zebra crossings?*

For motorists there are three basic points:

1. You must not park within the zigzag lines on either side of the crossing. It will be counted as parking if any part of your vehicle (however small) is on the zigzag lines.

2. You must not overtake when approaching a pedestrian crossing. In addition you must not begin to overtake a vehicle that has already stopped at the crossing (i.e. the front of your car must not protrude beyond the front of the car in front).

3. You must always give precedence to a pedestrian on the crossing. This is an absolute and definite rule. There are no exceptions to it. As soon as a pedestrian puts a foot on to the crossing, the pedestrian is entitled to have precedence over any oncoming vehicle – provided the vehicle is not already on the crossing. Even a pedestrian who has acted in a totally irresponsible and stupid manner by stepping out at the last moment, when a car is a few feet away from the crossing, must, according to the law, have priority. For motorists the moral is to keep a careful watch when approaching a zebra crossing to check that no one is about to step out on to it.

Pedestrians are not on the crossing until they actually set foot on it. Merely standing by the crossing, on the pavement, is not enough. But the moment they step off the kerb on to the crossing, you must give them precedence. If the pedestrian is pushing a pram or pushchair you must stop as soon as any part of that pram is on the crossing – even though the person pushing it may still be on the pavement. In fact the law talks in terms of giving precedence to someone who is crossing 'on foot' – and so it was held in one case that a motorist did not have to give precedence to a person on roller skates since he was not 'on foot'! On the other hand, cyclists pushing their bike across the crossing count as pedestrians – so you must always stop.

When you stop for the pedestrian you must make sure you do not cross the give-way line in front of the crossing. This is a dotted white line which runs one metre outside the black and white crossing. It is not good enough simply to draw up in front of the black and white lines – you must stop before you reach the give-way line.

### *What if the pedestrian steps out without any warning?*

As we have seen, the law says that you, the driver, must always give the
pedestrian precedence. As long as your vehicle is not on the crossing at
the time when the pedestrian first steps on to it you must stop. It is a
hard-and-fast rule – there is no exception based on reasonableness, or
the stupid conduct of the pedestrian. In short it is up to you to make sure
that you are able to stop in time:

> *Mr Hall was driving along at a reasonable speed. He approached a pedestrian
> crossing, and had just gone over the warning studs (i.e. the studs about two metres
> from the crossing) when a woman stepped off the pavement – without looking – and
> walked on to the crossing. Mr Hall did all he could to stop, but was unable to avoid
> an accident. Was he guilty of the criminal offence of failing to give precedence to a
> pedestrian? Held: yes. The fact that he behaved reasonably was not the point. The
> law imposes a strict duty on drivers to give precedence at pedestrian crossings. Only
> if Mr Hall's car had been on the crossing itself (i.e. the striped pedestrian crossing,
> and the sets of studs running a few inches from the stripes) would he have had a
> defence.* Hughes *(1960)*

> *A lorry was travelling at about 15–20 m.p.h. Suddenly two children stepped on
> to the crossing, without looking. At this time the lorry was about ten yards away –
> and the driver couldn't avoid an accident. Was he guilty of failing to give
> precedence to pedestrians? Held: yes. The fact that the lorry driver had done all he
> could, and had driven reasonably, was not a defence. It is up to vehicle drivers to
> make sure they can stop should a pedestrian suddenly walk out.* Scott *(1960)*

Having said that, in practice the courts are sympathetic to drivers who
are put in an impossible position – and such a motorist will probably be
convicted, but merely receive a relatively small penalty (for penalties
see p. 216) or an absolute discharge (see p. 237 for what an absolute
discharge is). In both the cases described above the courts held that,
although the driver had to be found guilty, an absolute discharge was
appropriate.

These cases notwithstanding, remember that the law says quite clearly
that you, the driver, must give precedence – unless your vehicle has
already reached the studs at the edge of the crossing. If your vehicle is
even a few inches from the crossing studs, you must stop! If you are
prosecuted for failing to give precedence to a pedestrian, only in the
most exceptional circumstances will you avoid conviction.

Bear in mind, also, that in the above cases we are dealing with
criminal liability – have you, the driver, committed a criminal offence in
failing to give precedence? This is a separate issue from whether or not

you would have to pay compensation if you knocked down a pedestrian. These questions of blame and negligence are decided by different courts – on different principles. So the carelessness of pedestrians who simply step out on to a crossing, without looking, may be held against them in a damages claim (see p. 214).

One final point to note is that, if there is a central island or refuge in the middle of the road, in the eyes of the law there are two pedestrian crossings. So you need not stop if there is someone on the crossing on the other half of the road – you need stop only if the pedestrian steps off the central reservation on to the crossing on your side of the road.

### What if the zebra crossing is controlled by a police officer?

Sometimes a police officer or traffic warden will control the crossing. In this case pedestrians cannot insist on their right simply to cross the road and have cars and other vehicles stop. If the police officer or traffic warden tells them to wait, they must wait – and if they do not they will have committed an offence (see p. 286).

### Is it illegal to park on the 'far' side of the zebra crossing?

On each side of a zebra crossing are zigzag lines. No parking is allowed within those zigzags. But it used to be the case that the ban on parking applied only to the zigzags on the approach side of the crossing (i.e. it was possible to park on the far side of the crossing – the idea being that by parking there you were not obstructing the view of the pedestrian or of oncoming vehicles). The law has since been changed – it is now illegal to park on either side of the crossing, within the zigzag lines.

There are virtually no defences to a charge of parking within the zigzags. For instance, one motorist ran out of petrol on the zigzags and argued that this was a valid defence – the court held it was not. The court said it was his own fault if he had run out of petrol, so he was guilty.

Similar rules apply as regards overtaking (or beginning to overtake) within the pedestrian crossing area. But you need not completely overtake the car in front to commit an offence – you will be guilty if any part of your car goes past the front of the car ahead. However, this only applies within the zigzag lines on the *approach* side of the crossing, so it would not be an offence to overtake within the zigzag lines on the far side. Incidentally, it is no defence to say that there was no pedestrian anywhere near the crossing at the time – as far as the law is concerned it is an offence to overtake between the zigzags and the crossing.

### What special rules apply to pelican crossings?

The rules are basically the same as for zebra crossings. However, because there are traffic lights involved the rules have had to be altered slightly. Rather than zigzag lines there is a double line of studs at the beginning of the crossing area. Parking within that area is banned, as is overtaking.

Pedestrians should look at the flashing signs. When the little figure is red, pedestrians should wait. If the little figure is green they can cross – with care. Once the little figure starts flashing green they should not begin crossing (if on the crossing already they should carry on crossing). As far as motorists are concerned the lights mean:

- *green:* you can proceed across the crossing
- *amber:* you must stop your car, unless it would be unsafe for you to do so (e.g. there might be a collision)
- *red:* you must stop. This is so even if there are no pedestrians on the crossing
- *flashing amber light:* you can go ahead and drive over the crossing if there is no one on it. However, if there is anyone on the crossing you must give them precedence (i.e. as if it was a zebra crossing).

### Can 'lollipop men/women' order cars to stop?

Yes. School crossing patrols (i.e. lollipop men and women) can control traffic and order cars to stop. But they must be carrying their sign (i.e. 'Stop – Children' in black letters on a yellow and red circular background). They must also be wearing an approved uniform (e.g. a white coat). As with the zebra crossing rules you commit an offence if you do not stop in time – it is no defence to say that you weren't given enough time in which to stop. But in such a case the chances are that the court would give an absolute discharge (see p. 237).

## WHAT'S THE PENALTY?

*For failing to give precedence to a pedestrian on a crossing*

*For parking (or waiting) on a crossing\**

*For overtaking within a crossing area*

*For disobeying a lollipop man or woman's sign\**

MAXIMUM PENALTY: all these offences carry a maximum penalty of a £400 fine, plus three penalty points (and an endorsement) and perhaps disqualification

LIKELY PENALTY: a fine of between £20 and £30 (probably doubled if a pedestrian was injured) and three penalty points (plus an endorsement). For a serious offence of failing to give precedence, or overtaking at a crossing, a short disqualification might be imposed

*For a pedestrian loitering on a crossing*

MAXIMUM PENALTY: a £400 fine

LIKELY PENALTY: a £10 fine\*

*For offences involving pedestrians on motorways, and pedestrians who jaywalk or fail to comply with a constable's instructions, see pp. 167 and 287, respectively*

\* For these offences you may get a £24 fixed penalty ticket (plus penalty points) instead (see p. 217)

*(For more on penalties see p. 216)*

### What does the Highway Code say about the safety of pedestrians?

The Highway Code is quite clear. If you are a motorist you should:

Drive carefully and slowly when pedestrians are about, particularly in crowded shopping streets, when you see a bus stopped, or near a parked milk float or mobile shop. Watch out for pedestrians emerging suddenly, for example from behind parked or stopped vehicles. Remember, pedestrians may have to cross roads when there are no crossings; show them consideration.

Two out of three pedestrians killed or seriously injured are either under 15 or over 60. The young and the elderly may not judge speeds very well and may step into the road when you do not expect them. Watch out for blind people who may be carrying white sticks (white with two red reflectorised bands for deaf/blind people) or using guide dogs and for the disabled or infirm. Give them plenty of time to cross the road. Remember that deaf people may not hear your vehicle approaching.

The Motorist and the Law

Drive slowly near schools and look out for children getting on or off buses. Stop when signalled to do so by a school crossing patrol showing a 'Stop – Children' sign. In places of particular danger, there may be a flashing amber signal below the advance sign which warns of a school crossing patrol operating ahead.

Be careful near a parked ice-cream van – children are more interested in ice-cream than in traffic.

### How is blame worked out when a pedestrian is run over?

It all depends on who was to blame for the accident. When we talk about blame we are not concerned with criminal liability (e.g. can someone be prosecuted by the police for careless driving?), but with the question of who is to pay for the damage caused. This is a *civil* claim – suing for damages caused by the negligence of a motorist – completely separate from the question of prosecution. A motorist – or, more likely, the motorist's insurance company – will have to pay compensation (i.e. for the damage and injury caused) only if he or she was negligent. See p. 177 for more information on the negligence laws.

Although, as a general rule, the courts accept that pedestrians often have to cross the road in less than ideal places, and expect motorists to keep a good look-out for them, pedestrians must expect to bear some of the blame for an accident that occurs in such circumstances:

*Mr Baker was about to cross a main road. The road was about thirty-three feet wide, and in open country. He looked to his left and saw a car a hundred yards away. He walked across the road – and was struck by the car when he was half-way across. He sued the car driver for compensation for the injuries he had received, plus his loss of wages while off work. Was the car driver to blame, or was the accident Mr Baker's own fault? Held: both were to blame, although the major blame was on the car driver. The driver must have seen Mr Baker waiting at the kerbside from at least 200 yards away, and he should then have seen him at 100 yards away when he began to cross the road. There was evidence that the car was going too quickly. In any event the car driver should have been on his guard, and should have taken evasive action. Mr Baker, as a pedestrian, was also careless – he should not have misjudged the speed of the car, and should have kept looking as he crossed the road. An apportionment of blame between the car driver and the pedestrian of 75 per cent to 25 per cent was held to be fair, so Mr Baker got 75 per cent of his normal damages from the car driver (in practice the car driver's insurance company). Baker (1970)*

*Two pedestrians began to cross the road. It was a wide road, and brightly lit. An oncoming car had to slow down slightly, but the pedestrians did not present him with any problem. However, that car was overtaken by another car which collided with the pedestrians. Held: the overtaking car was 80 per cent to blame, and the two pedestrians were 20 per cent to blame. They should have kept an eye open – and realized that the fast-approaching car might not see them in time. So the pedestrians recovered 80 per cent of their normal compensation.* Mulligan *(1971)*

The clear moral for pedestrians is to take care when crossing – they should keep alert for cars coming from both directions, and appreciate that cars may not stop in time:

*Mrs Hurt began to cross the road about a hundred yards from a bend. There were no cars coming, but by the time she got to the centre of the road she was knocked down by a car. That car was driving well over the 30 m.p.h. speed limit. Held: the car driver was mainly to blame. However, Mrs Hurt should have taken more care. She should have kept looking from one side to the other as she crossed the road. She was held to be 20 per cent to blame, so she only got 80 per cent of her normal damages from the car driver.* Hurt *(1971)*

Similarly car drivers must keep an eye out for pedestrians. They must realize that pedestrians need to cross the road sometimes, and that pedestrians move very, very slowly when compared to a car! Motorists should anticipate likely events. For instance, in one case a pavement had been narrowed by building works – a pedestrian put one foot in the gutter as she passed this narrow point, without looking behind her, and was struck by a car. Although the accident was mainly the pedestrian's fault the court held that the car driver was also to blame – he should have realized that it was likely that a pedestrian might walk into the road, without warning, at this point.

But the courts do not expect perfectionist driving! They just require a motorist to drive responsibly and reasonably. In another case, therefore, a motorist who struck two men running across a dual carriageway was held not to be to blame in any way. He had been driving reasonably, his driving could not be faulted – so he was not to blame.

### What about pedestrians walking along unlit roads at night?

The Highway Code is quite clear in the advice it gives:

Where there is no footpath, walk on the right-hand side of the road – it is safer to walk on the side facing oncoming traffic.

Always wear or carry something white or light-coloured or reflective in the dark or in poor light. This is especially important on roads without footpaths.

In view of this, one would expect the courts to take an unsympathetic approach to pedestrians who are run over while walking down country lanes at night when they are not carrying lights and not wearing reflective clothing. However, in practice the courts take – what is for them – a relatively lenient line. In particular the courts have said that the Highway Code is not totally binding – in other words, a person who disobeys the Highway Code is not automatically wholly to blame:

> *It was late at night, and the car driver was driving down a straight, unlit road. He saw two women pedestrians on the nearside of the road, walking in the same direction as he was going. But he did not see two men who were about twenty yards away from the women. He hit both the men. When sued he argued that the two men had been negligent – one had been 4 feet 6 inches in the road, and they had clearly not followed the Highway Code advice (i.e. they had not been walking towards the oncoming traffic and had not gone on the verge). Held: the motorist was solely to blame. Despite the clear breach of the Highway Code the pedestrians were held not to blame at all.* Parkinson (1973)

In practice these compensation claims are paid by motorists' insurance companies, not motorists personally (i.e. from their own bank accounts). Accordingly most people would welcome the courts' sympathetic attitude to pedestrians who are run over – the general view is that it is only right that such people should receive compensation for their injuries. Fair enough, one may say. However, these decisions are clearly out of line with the courts' decisions in other cases involving negligent motorists. In other words, the courts tend to be more sympathetic to pedestrians who are involved in accidents than they are to motorists.

### Does a pedestrian who causes an accident have to pay compensation to the motorist?

Yes, the same principles apply as with any other accident claim. Bear in mind that here we are talking about blame as meaning who has to pay compensation for causing the accident. The law decides this on the basis of who was negligent (see p. 177). So a pedestrian who causes an accident will have to pay compensation to the motorist:

> *Mr MacDonald was walking with his young son. Without any warning, Mr MacDonald stepped out into the road, to cross. Unfortunately a motor scooter was passing by, and there was a collision. The motor scooterist was killed. The widow sued Mr MacDonald for negligence – saying that he was solely to blame for the*

*accident in which her husband had been killed. Held: on the evidence it was clear that Mr MacDonald was totally to blame for the accident, so he had to pay full compensation to the motor scooterist's widow.* Barry *(1966)*

In fact this was a relatively unusual case, because there was a clear admission by Mr MacDonald that he was solely to blame for the accident. Generally the courts tend to feel that a motorist – such as the unfortunate motor scooterist – should keep an eye out for pedestrians and appreciate that they might walk on to the road without warning. In practice, therefore, the courts do tend to find the motorist to blame to some extent (e.g. 20 per cent).

An important point to note is that a pedestrian will not normally be insured. If a court orders compensation to be paid to a motorist the money will generally have to come out of the pedestrian's own pocket, as there will not be an insurance company to pick up the bill – unless the pedestrian has a special Accidents Policy, which few people do. On the other hand, a claim for compensation against a motorist will almost certainly be met by an insurance company. Therefore it is likely to be much more serious for a pedestrian to be found negligent than it is for a motorist – though the fact that the money for damages will have to come out of the pedestrian's own pocket will also be bad news for the motorist who is suing, since most people are simply unable to scrape together enough money to pay substantial damages. If the pedestrian does not have enough money to pay the compensation the motorist will go uncompensated – however severe and serious the injuries caused – whereas a pedestrian who is injured by an uninsured motorist can take advantage of a national compensation scheme that will ensure that an insurance company will meet the claim (see p. 130). The answer to this particular problem would, of course, be for the uninsured motorists' compensation scheme to be extended to include uninsured pedestrians.

### What if a pedestrian does not bother to use a pedestrian crossing?

If there is a pedestrian crossing near by, a pedestrian should use it. Not having used the crossing is a factor that may be held against the pedestrian in a compensation claim. Bear in mind that, here, we are dealing with a claim for compensation – for the injuries received by the pedestrian in an accident. Consequently the court will look at who was to blame – who was negligent:

*Mr Snow was crossing a busy road. He crossed near a junction, and not far from a pedestrian crossing that had a central refuge. He walked between the stationary cars on one side of the road, and then waited in the middle of the road for a gap in the oncoming traffic. As he stood there he was struck by a motorbike that was overtaking the stationary traffic. He claimed damages from the driver of the motorbike for his injuries and also for his loss of wages while off work. Held: the motorcyclist was mainly to blame. He should have been going more carefully, and should have seen Mr Snow. However, Mr Snow should have used the pedestrian crossing, since it was so close to him. The court decided that a pedestrian – such as Mr Snow – who chooses not to use a pedestrian crossing must take extra care to avoid an accident. The court decided that the motorcyclist was 75 per cent to blame, and Mr Snow 25 per cent. So Mr Snow got 75 per cent of his damages from the motorcyclist (in practice, of course, this would have been paid by the motorcyclist's insurance company).* Snow *(1969)*

### Is a pedestrian who is knocked down at a crossing bound to get compensation?

Not necessarily. All compensation claims are dealt with on the basis of who was to blame for the accident – who was negligent.

Remember that the criminal law is very strict about saying that a motorist must give way to a pedestrian who is on a pedestrian crossing. A motorist who does not give way is almost bound to be convicted. For illustrations see the cases on pp. 205–7. But we are not concerned here with the criminal offence of failing to give precedence, but with the issue of whether the driver has to pay compensation to the pedestrian. As we have seen, this is decided on a different principle – negligence.

So a motorist may be convicted by a criminal court for failing to give precedence on a crossing, but at the same time partly absolved from blame by a different court (i.e. a *civil* court hearing a compensation claim). If the pedestrian was careless, or did not keep a proper look-out, it is likely that the court will reduce the level of damages:

*A forty-year-old woman ran on to a pedestrian crossing without looking. At the time a car was about fifteen yards away and travelling at 25 m.p.h. The driver could not avoid an accident, and the woman was injured. Held: the pedestrian had behaved unreasonably, and the driver had done all he could to avoid the accident. But he should have kept a better look-out. The court decided that the driver was 75 per cent to blame and the pedestrian 25 per cent. So the pedestrian only got 75 per cent of her normal damages. (In practice, of course, the motorist's insurance company would have paid these costs.)* Kozimor *(1962)*

Pedestrians who behave really stupidly may not get any compensation:

*A pedestrian walked across a crossing, waited at the central reservation, and then stepped out without warning into the path of a scooter. Did the scooter driver have to pay compensation? Held: no. The accident was totally the pedestrian's fault and the scooter driver was in no way to blame. So the injured pedestrian got no compensation.* Jankovic *(1970)*

In fact this is a fairly extreme decision. In practice pedestrians knocked down on a crossing can expect some compensation – however sillily they acted. For a pedestrian to be found totally to blame for the accident, as in this case, is extremely rare.

# Penalties

*What penalties can be imposed for motoring offences?*

In practice the most likely penalties are:

- a *fixed-penalty ticket* (see p. 217)
- a *fine* (see p. 222)
- an *endorsement and penalty points* (see p. 223)
- *disqualification* (see p. 232).

In addition serious offences can be punished with *prison*, though this only applies in exceptional cases (e.g. bad cases of reckless driving or drunk driving – see p. 110). Also, if a juvenile is being prosecuted (e.g. for joy-riding) the court has numerous other penalties at its disposal (e.g. community service, an attendance centre order, a supervision order, etc.).

*How can I find out the penalties for a particular offence?*

Look at the appropriate penalty chart. This will set out the maximum penalty and also the likely penalty for the offence. Bear in mind that maximum penalties are very rarely imposed, but by comparing the maximum penalties for different offences you can get an idea of the seriousness of the particular charge that is being brought. Of more use is the likely-penalties list. This shows penalties that may typically be imposed on a first offender. However, it is essential to bear in mind that these are no more than guidelines – a 'guesstimate' of what a typical court may impose on a typical offender. It does not follow that your court will impose that sentence on you! Every court behaves slightly differently, and you should not look upon these likely penalties as in any way the 'correct' penalties. Certainly do not make the mistake of telling the justices that they should follow them!

# Fixed penalties

### What is a fixed-penalty ticket?

Many of the less serious motoring offences can be dealt with by a fixed penalty.

There are two levels of fixed penalty. For the trivial offences (e.g. parking) the penalty is £12. For the more serious offences (e.g. speeding) it is £24. But if the motorist does not pay the penalty within twenty-eight days it is increased, by half as much again. Thus, a £12 fixed penalty becomes £18, and a £24 fixed penalty becomes £36.

Before 1986 fixed penalties were mainly for parking offences, but at the end of 1986 this system was changed. Now fixed-penalty tickets can be given for various other motoring offences, including some that carry an endorsement and penalty points.

### What is the difference between a fixed penalty and a fine?

To the motorist they probably seem much the same – they both involve paying money! But there is an important difference between the two. A fine is imposed by a court, following conviction – the guilty motorist can therefore be said to have been convicted of a criminal offence. A fixed penalty does not imply a criminal offence, and no criminal conviction results. It is just a financial penalty.

### When can a fixed penalty ticket be given?

Not all motoring offences can be dealt with by a fixed penalty, but only those given in the list below. However, even if the offence is one that is listed below, it does not follow that the police have to give a fixed-penalty ticket – they can, if they prefer, prosecute instead. If that happens, the case goes to the magistrates' court, in the usual way – and if the motorist is found guilty it will be for the court to decide what penalty to impose.

If the offence does not carry endorsement (or penalty points) the fixed penalty is £12. If it does carry endorsement (and penalty points) the penalty is £24.

| Fixed penalty offences | |
| £12 (not endorsable) | £24 (endorsable and penalty points) |
| --- | --- |
| Disobeying a traffic sign | Motorway offence — 3 |
| One-way street offence | Pedestrian crossing offence (but not if the vehicle was moving) — 3 |
| Residents' parking offences | Play street offence — 2 |
| | Speeding — 3 |
| No road tax | Motorcycle passenger offence — 1 |
| Numberplate offence | Traffic direction or sign offence — 3 |
| Motorcycle helmet offence | Parking in a dangerous position — 3 |
| Seat belt offence | Construction and use offences — 3 |
| Not stopping for a police officer | Driving licence offences — 2 |

### How is a fixed penalty given?

It depends on whether the offence is endorsable (i.e. £24) or not endorsable (i.e. £12). The exact procedure also depends upon whether the driver is present or whether the ticket is fixed to the car.

*Endorsable offences (£24 ticket):*
The more serious offences are endorsable (and carry penalty points) – see the list above. They also carry a fixed penalty of £24.

For one of these offences the police officer can ask you to produce your licence. If you have your licence on you, and show it to the officer, he or she will then check how many points you have already got. Remember that if you have acquired twelve points within three years then you will probably be disqualified for at least six months (see p. 224). If a fixed-penalty ticket (with the points it automatically carries) would bring you up to twelve points in three years, the police officer will not give you the ticket. Instead you will be prosecuted in the usual way – which means that your case will go to court, and you will be able to argue to the magistrates that you should not lose your licence. But if you are not in danger of losing your licence the police officer will give you a fixed-penalty ticket (i.e. £24) and hold on to the licence.

You can then choose between three courses of action, but you must act within twenty-eight days.

1. *You can pay the £24.* If you pay within twenty-eight days your licence will be endorsed (and the penalty points entered) and then returned to you. That will be the end of the matter.

2. *You can ask for a court hearing*. If you do this you will be prosecuted for the offence, and you will be able to argue your case in court. This means that you will have the opportunity of arguing that you are innocent, and so be acquitted. You will also be given the opportunity of arguing for a lower financial penalty, and perhaps avoiding endorsement and penalty points. On the other hand, if you are found guilty there will probably be a stiffer fine, and you may have to pay legal costs as well.

3. *If you do nothing* in the twenty-eight-day period (i.e. you do not pay the £24 or ask for a court hearing) an extra penalty is imposed. You will now have to pay one and a half times the original fixed penalty – a total of £36. Your local magistrates' court will be told about the penalty and can enforce it against you as if it were a fine (for instance, in an extreme case, you could be sent to prison for up to seven days for failing to pay). In addition, your licence will be endorsed and any penalty points entered. The licence will then be posted back to you.

So if you ignore the fixed penalty ticket you will have to pay £36, not £24. You will also have lost the opportunity to fight the case.

If you were not able to produce your driving licence to the police officer (e.g. you were not carrying it with you) a slightly different procedure applies. You can select a police station where you then have seven days to produce your licence. The police officer on duty will look at your licence and decide whether you are in danger of being disqualified (i.e. twelve points in three years – see above). If you are, you will be prosecuted in the usual way, and the fixed penalty will no longer apply; if not, you will be given a fixed-penalty ticket (i.e. £24). You will then have twenty-one days in which to decide whether to pay or ask for a court hearing. Once again, if you do nothing, and ignore the fixed-penalty ticket, the £24 fine will be increased to £36.

All these endorsable offences carry penalty points – see the list above. In these cases you do not just have to pay the fixed penalty (i.e. £24 – or £36 if you default), but get penalty points as well. The only advantage of the fixed-penalty procedure to you, the motorist, is that you avoid having a record for a criminal conviction, and you also avoid the risk of having a higher fine imposed upon you. *The important point is that you still get the penalty points*.

*If the offence is not endorsable (£12 ticket):*
See the list above for which fixed-penalty offences are not endorsable and so carry a £12 penalty. Parking is the main non-endorsable offence.

The usual procedure is for a fixed-penalty ticket to be stuck to the windscreen. However, if the driver was present – and physically given the ticket – a simplified procedure applies.

Normally the driver is not present, and the ticket is stuck to the windscreen of the vehicle. When this happens you have a choice. The important point to note is that you must act quickly – you have only twenty-one days in which to decide what to do. You have three courses to choose from.

1. *You can pay the £12* within twenty-eight days. If you do, that will be the end of the matter.

2. *You can ask for a court hearing*, provided you do this within twenty-eight days. If you ask for a court hearing you will be prosecuted in the usual way. The case will go before the magistrates and you will have an opportunity to argue that you are not guilty, and also to argue for a lower penalty. But you have only twenty-eight days in which to ask for prosecution.

3. *If you do nothing* the police will serve a formal Notice to Owner of Vehicle. You then have a further choice (once again you must act within a twenty-eight-day period):

- *you can pay* the £12 penalty within the twenty-eight days. If you do, that will be the end of the matter
- *you can ask for a court hearing*. Once again, you must do this within twenty-eight days. If you ask for a court hearing the case will go before the magistrates, and you will be able to argue that you are not guilty, and also for a lower penalty
- *you can fill in the Statement of Ownership*. If you were not the owner at the time you will not be liable for the offence and that will be the end of the matter. If you were the owner, but not the driver, whether you have to pay the penalty depends on whether the driver signs the Statement of Facts for you. If you can get the driver to sign the Statement of Facts the police will summons him or her, and not proceed against you. On the other hand, if you cannot get the driver to sign the Statement of Facts you will have to pay the penalty of £12 (£18 if you do nothing – see below)
- *if you ignore the Notice to Owner of Vehicle*, and do nothing, you will have to pay the increased penalty (£18). So if you do nothing within twenty-eight days the fixed penalty will be increased from £12 to £18 and this will be registered with your local magistrates' court, which will be able to recover the £18 from you as though it were a fine (for instance, in

an extreme case, you could be sent to prison for up to seven days if you did not pay).

To summarize: if a ticket is stuck on the windscreen of your vehicle (i.e. you, as the driver, are not present when the ticket is given) there is an initial twenty-eight days in which to pay the £12 fine. If the police do not hear from you within that time they will serve a Notice to Owner of Vehicle on you. You then have another twenty-eight days. If you do nothing the £12 will increase to £18 and you will have to pay. Alternatively, you can ask for the case to go to the magistrates' court, or you can state that you were not the owner or driver.

If you were present when the fixed ticket was given out the procedure is simplified. You have twenty-eight days in which to pay the £12. If you do not it is increased to £18 and registered at the local magistrates' court.

### What if I was not the owner of the vehicle?

If you were no longer the owner of the vehicle when the fixed-penalty ticket was given you should notify the police. For a non-endorsable offence they will ask you to fill in a Statement of Ownership. Give them the name and address of the new owner, and you should hear no more about it.

### What if it was my vehicle, but I was not driving it at the time?

Once again, tell the police. If the offence is not endorsable (e.g. parking) you may have to pay the £12 penalty, even though you were not driving. However, if you can get the person who was driving to countersign the Statement of Facts served on you by the police, the penalty will have to be paid by them – not by you. However, if the driver refuses to sign the Statement then you may find yourself liable for the fixed penalty (i.e. £12). The best way to avoid this happening is to opt for magistrates' court trial – so you can argue your case before the magistrates and convince them that you were not driving. If you can persuade them of this (depending on the offence you were charged with), you will be found not guilty.

### What happens if I ignore a fixed-penalty ticket?

If you ignore it you will end up having to pay a higher penalty. The basic rule is that you have twenty-eight days in which to pay the penalty or to opt for magistrates' court trial. If you do nothing the penalty is increased by half as much again, so the £12 penalty (for a non-endorsable offence) becomes £18 and the £24 penalty (for an endorsable offence) becomes £36. The local magistrates' court will then enforce that penalty against you – you could even be sent to prison if you refuse to pay.

So it is no good ignoring a fixed-penalty ticket! If you do not think you are responsible for the offence it is important that you reply within twenty-eight days.

### Can a traffic warden hand out a fixed-penalty ticket?

It depends. If the offence is endorsable (e.g. speeding) only a uniformed police officer can give a fixed-penalty ticket. For non-endorsable offences (e.g. parking) a police officer or traffic warden can give a ticket.

### Who decides if I get a fixed-penalty ticket or am prosecuted?

The police. It is for them to decide. You, as the motorist, cannot insist that you be given a fixed-penalty ticket. For instance, if you were caught doing 45 m.p.h. in a 30 m.p.h. area you could probably expect a fine of at least £30, plus an endorsement, and three penalty points. On the other hand, if the police agreed to give you a fixed penalty you would only have to pay £24 (although you would still get the three penalty points and the endorsement). It is for the police to decide whether you should be given a fixed-penalty ticket or be prosecuted – you cannot opt for the fixed-penalty ticket. On the other hand, if you are given a fixed-penalty ticket by the police you do have the right to opt for a court hearing (in practice you would only do this if you thought you were not guilty of the offence).

## Fines

### What is the maximum fine that can be imposed?

No magistrates' court can impose a fine of more than £2,000. However, most motoring offences have a lower maximum fine. Refer to the likely-penalties lists in the penalty charts for more realistic guidance as to probable penalties (see above).

*Should a poor person be fined the same amount as a rich person?*

Generally, no. The court must look at the means and finances of the convicted motorist. But it is for you, the motorist, to tell the court about your finances. That is why it is useful to go prepared with wage slips, bank slips, etc. If you think you face a hefty fine it is a good idea to prepare a short financial summary of your income and expenditure (see p. 252). This will help the court, and there will be no danger of the court's thinking that you are richer than you are.

The courts take the view that a fine should be reduced for someone who is poor, but not increased for someone who is rich. So the mere fact that you are well-off will not result in your having to pay an increased fine.

Do not be reluctant to ask for time in which to pay a fine. Usually this will be given if you can show that you do not have enough money. If you are given time to pay, make sure you do not get into arrears with those payments. If your finances change, so you cannot afford the payments, it is important to contact the court and notify them of the problem. The court will probably agree to give further time to pay. If you do not pay the fine (either because you do not pay it on the date stated, or because you default on the instalments), the court has numerous powers that can be used to make you pay (e.g. intercepting earnings from your employer, sending you to prison).

## Endorsement and Penalty Points

*What is an endorsement?*

If you are convicted the magistrates can often order that your driving licence be endorsed. This means that details of the conviction are marked on your licence – and, more importantly, you will be given penalty points.

The important point about an endorsement is that it will normally result in penalty points. If you get twelve penalty points in three years you will usually lose your licence.

*How does the penalty points system work?*

If you look at the penalty charts throughout this book you will see that many of the offences are said to be endorsable and also to carry penalty points. Generally, in such cases, the court has no choice. If it finds you guilty it must order that your licence be endorsed and – more important-ly – that you get penalty points.

The number of penalty points is usually fixed. For instance, not having a driving licence is worth two points; driving while disqualified carries six points; speeding is three points; leaving a car in a dangerous position is three points; reckless driving is ten points. But for a few offences the court has a discretion as to how many penalty points to impose. In particular, a careless-driving conviction can result in between two and five points; failure to stop after an accident can be worth five to nine points; not having insurance can be worth four to eight points. Looking at the likely-penalties list in the penalty charts will give you an indication of the number of points that may be imposed. But bear in mind that these figures are not a definitive guide (see p. 216).

### Does it matter how many points I get?

Yes. The basic rule is that if you get twelve points within three years you will have to lose your licence. Generally the court will have to disqualify you for at least six months (although it could be at least twelve months, or longer – see p. 225). Suppose you already have eight penalty points. You are then convicted of careless driving, which could carry between two and five penalty points. If the court gives you two or three points you will not be disqualified (because you have not reached the total of twelve). But, if the court imposes four or five points you will be disqualified for at least six months. This is because you will have had a total of twelve points within three years.

### How is the number of points worked out?

There are two basic rules to grasp:

1. *Only points imposed within the last three years count.* However, the three years do not run from the date of the court hearing, but from the (earlier) date of the offence. Suppose you commit a careless-driving offence in April 1987, but the case does not go to court until September 1987. The three years will run backwards from April 1987, not from September. The reason for this is that, if the three years ran from the date of the court hearing, defendants would do all they could to

postpone court hearing dates (also try and avoid the effect of some of their old points).

2. *If you are convicted of several offences you only get points for the most serious offence.* Suppose you face several charges as a result of one spell of driving and all are dealt with at the same time. For instance, you may be facing charges for careless driving (two to five points); failing to stop at a stop sign (three points); and driving in a play street (two points). If the court imposes five points for the most serious offence, the careless-driving charge, that is the number of points that will go on your licence. The court will not impose five points for the careless driving, three for the stop sign, two for the play street, and end up with a total of twelve points (in which case you would be disqualified)!

### Does the court have to impose the penalty points – or can it let me off?

If the offence carries penalty points the general rule is that the court *must* impose those points. The only exception is when the motorist can show that there were 'special reasons' that applied in his or her case. If you can show special reasons the court need not impose an endorsement, or impose the penalty points. But special reasons is not as wide-ranging a term as it may sound – it is a legal term that is interpreted very narrowly. In practice very few motorists are able to claim special reasons. See p. 226 for what count as special reasons.

### How long is the disqualification for?

We have seen that if you have twelve points within three years you can expect to be disqualified. The normal rule is that the court must disqualify you for at least six months (it can be longer if the court thinks it appropriate). However, if you have already been disqualified once before within the last three years the court must disqualify you for at least twelve months (not six months). If you have had two previous disqualifications within the last three years the minimum period of disqualification is two years.

Suppose that two years ago you were disqualified for one year for drunk driving. Shortly after you get your licence back you are involved in an accident but fail to stop. As a result you get, say, eight points. Shortly afterwards you are prosecuted for careless driving (two to five points). If the magistrates impose four or five points you will have reached twelve points and will have to be disqualified. But in this case the disqualification will be for at least twelve months – since this will be your second disqualification within the three-year period. Of course, the court may well feel that you should be disqualified for a longer period – and may insist that you take your driving test again, in view of your appalling record.

If you are disqualified under these twelve points in three years rules the slate is then wiped clean. In other words, when you are disqualified all your existing points are cancelled. When you get your licence back, at the end of the period of disqualification, there will be no points on it.

Disqualification under the twelve points in three years rules is sometimes called totting up.

### Can the court decide not to disqualify?

The general rule is that the court must disqualify if the motorist has twelve points in three years. However, exceptionally, the court can decide not to disqualify – or to impose less than six months' disqualification – if there are 'mitigating circumstances'. In practice it is extremely difficult for a motorist to show mitigating circumstances and very few motorists are able to avoid being disqualified. See p. 229 for what can count as mitigating circumstances.

### Can I be disqualified if I have three endorsements in three years?

No. You are thinking about the old endorsement rules that were abolished in 1982. Before that time the rule was that you must lose your licence, for at least six months, if you had three endorsements in a three-year period. The unfairness of that system was that it did not differentiate between the serious and the non-serious offences (i.e. they all carried one endorsement). It was an inflexible and unfair system, so it was replaced with the present penalty points system – which grades the seriousness of the offence by the number of points imposed.

### What are 'special reasons' for not endorsing and imposing penalty points?

The general rule is that it is extremely difficult for motorists to show special reasons and they must expect an uphill struggle in trying to convince the court that there are *special reasons* in their case.

A fundamental point is that the special reasons must apply to the *offence*, not the motorist. In other words, there must be something special about the way in which the offence was committed, and it is not good enough to argue that imposing penalty points would be unfair on that particular motorist or be an excessive penalty – the effects on the motorist are irrelevant at this stage.

This is better explained by pointing out what you will *not* be able to offer as special reasons:

- that it was a trivial offence, or that no damage was caused
- that you have a long driving history and have never had an accident before
- that you are a member of the Institute of Advanced Motorists
- that you are a professional driver or a driving instructor
- that you are disabled and had no way of getting home without using your car (and the fact that you will need your car in the future)
- that losing your licence will cause severe hardship to your family (e.g. you will lose your job)
- that any accident that occurred was not your fault
- that the roads were quiet at the time, and you drove only a short distance.

All these are mitigating factors, but they would not amount to special reasons – because they all relate to the circumstances of you, the individual motorist, and not to the actual offence. Special reasons can be said to apply in only a very few cases. Someone on a breathalyser charge, who can prove that their drinks were laced, and that they did not know that they had been drinking that much alcohol, would be regarded as having a special reason. Or, in the case of someone who had to drive because of a medical emergency (assuming no ambulance or other emergency services were available), the court might decide, reluctantly, that they had no choice but to drive and so find that there were special reasons. But this would not apply to some domestic emergency (e.g. having to deliver the babysitter back home late at night, or driving to pick up an aged relative whose car has broken down).

You will have seen by now that it is only in the most exceptional cases that special reasons can be shown. The vast majority of motorists who face endorsements will not be able to argue special reasons. However unfair they think it may be, the fact remains that they will normally face an endorsement and penalty points.

Remember, if penalty points are imposed, and you will have had twelve points in three years, the court will normally have to disqualify you (see above). But the court can take *mitigating circumstances* into account and decide not to disqualify you (or disqualify you for a shorter period). See p. 229 for what count as *mitigating circumstances* – in practice, virtually all the things that have been listed here as not being special reasons could count as mitigating circumstances.

### Is there any other way of avoiding an endorsement and penalty points?

There is one way. We will see (p. 293) that there are various offences that can be brought under the Construction and Use Regulations. These regulations give details about the design and maintenance of vehicles and also their use. Some of the offences are relatively trivial, but others result in an endorsement (and points). The offences that do result in endorsement and points are those involving brakes, steering, tyres, dangerous condition, dangerous load, danger because of the number of passengers and danger because the vehicle was being used for an unsuitable purpose. But with all those charges there is a special defence available. If motorists can show that they did not know – and had no reasonable cause to suspect – that the offence was being committed no endorsement (or points) can be imposed. They will still be convicted and fined, but will avoid endorsement and points.

Suppose you collect your car from the garage after it has just been serviced. In those circumstances you would be able to show that you had no reasonable grounds for thinking that there was anything wrong with the vehicle (unless, of course, the defect was blatantly obvious). Similarly, suppose you hire a car from a garage, or you are a professional driver and drive for your employer. In those cases, as an innocent driver you may well be able to avoid endorsement and points. It all depends on the facts of the case – you will have to show the court that you could not reasonably have been expected to know about the defect. Obviously the main question that the magistrates will want to know is why you did not notice the defect before you started your journey and while you were going along. If you can provide a satisfactory answer to that question you are likely to avoid an endorsement and points. Note that, if you convince the magistrates that you didn't know about the defect, the magistrates *must* agree not to endorse or impose points. They have no discretion – so they cannot impose points even if they want to!

**Must the magistrates disqualify under the twelve points in three years rule? Or can they agree it would be unfair to disqualify?**

Perhaps. If the motorist can show convincing *mitigating circumstances* the magistrates can disqualify for a shorter period (i.e. less than six months), or not at all.

We have seen that, for motorists to avoid an endorsement, they must show *special reasons* (see p. 226). We have also seen that it is extremely difficult, in practice, for motorists to do this. This is because the courts only accept excuses that are directly linked to the offence, and not the individual motorist. However, different rules apply once the motorist has twelve points in three years, and the court is deciding whether or not to disqualify. The court then has a wider discretion. It can take into account mitigating circumstances.

Mitigating circumstances are different from special reasons. The easiest way of understanding what would amount to mitigating circumstances is to look at the list of excuses that were *not* special reasons (see p. 227), virtually every one of which could be a mitigating circumstance. So, if you were the defendant, excuses such as your long accident free driving history or the fact that you were disabled and would not be able to get around if you lost your licence would both be legitimate mitigating circumstances. However, whether or not the court would decide that they were sufficient to justify not disqualifying is another matter – each case would depend on its own merits.

Showing that you will lose your job if you lose your licence is by far the most effective mitigating circumstance. But even then you will have to produce convincing evidence to show the court that this is not just bluff on your part. Ideally your employer should attend court and tell the magistrates that you will have to be sacked if you lose your licence (or, as a second best measure, you should produce a letter from your employer). Bear in mind that courts do not like the idea of professional drivers thinking that they can flout the law with impunity because they will never be disqualified. Any suggestion of that sort is likely to rebound on the motorist! But the fact remains that professional drivers who would otherwise lose their job have got a good chance of being able to show mitigating circumstances. This assumes, of course, that they do not have an appalling driving record, and that the particular offence was not too serious.

Ill health may also count as a mitigating circumstance. If you can show that you were suffering from a temporary spell of illness, the court can take that into account as a mitigating circumstance, although this is just the sort of circumstance that could not be considered a special reason (i.e. as to why no endorsement or points should be imposed). However, even here you should be careful. The magistrates have a duty to inform the Secretary of State about prosecuted motorists who have a disability that may affect their driving (see p. 92 for the sort of disabilities that apply to driving licences). So you may successfully argue that you should not have your licence taken away because you suffered from a heart attack, only to find it withdrawn by the Secretary of State. If that happened you would only get your driving licence back by proving yourself to be medically fit again, which would probably take more time than the six months or so you would have been disqualified for. It is not wise to exaggerate medical complaints!

### Can old endorsements be taken off a driving licence?

Yes – but not by you. It is possible to have old endorsements, and penalty points, removed from a driving licence, but there are complicated rules as to when this can be done.

Why should anyone want to remove endorsements and penalty points after they have expired? After all, if the points are no longer effective (i.e. more than three years have passed) what harm is there in having those endorsements on a driving licence? The answer is more a practical than a legal one. In theory any penalty points that have expired should be ignored. So if a motorist is asked to show his or her driving licence to a police officer, the officer should not be influenced by previous endorsements and points. In practice, however, it is likely that the police officer will be influenced, if in two minds as to whether to report the motorist. The sight of a heavily endorsed licence (indicating that the motorist may be a perpetual offender) may well tip the balance and make the officer decide to prosecute. Similarly, magistrates should not be influenced by old endorsements and penalty points, but, once again, they are bound to be subconsciously influenced if they see a heavily endorsed licence before passing sentence. Thus there can be an advantage in removing old endorsements and penalty points from a licence. In theory there should be no need to do so – but in practice it can be a sensible precaution!

## When can endorsements and penalty points be removed?

In four years' time is the general answer. But, as always with the law, it is not as straightforward as that:

- *if the motorist was not disqualified when the endorsement (and points) were imposed:* four years from the date the offence was committed
- *if the motorist was disqualified when the endorsement (and points) were imposed:* four years from the date of the court hearing (not the date of the offence)
- *if the motorist has since been disqualified, after the endorsement (and points) were imposed:* the endorsement and points can be removed immediately. Disqualification wipes them out, and there is no need to wait four years
- *if the motorist was convicted (and disqualified) for drunk driving:* eleven years from the date of the court hearing
- *if the endorsement (or points) were imposed for reckless driving:* four years from the date of the court hearing.

For most motorists, therefore, the simple answer is that an endorsement can be removed four years after the offence was committed. The main exceptions are for reckless driving (when it is four years from the date of the court hearing) and for drunk driving (when it is eleven years from the date of the court hearing).

To have the endorsements removed apply to the DVLC on form D1 (obtainable from main post offices). If you do not bother to have the endorsements removed they will remain on your licence until you renew it (e.g. on your sixtieth birthday), when they will automatically be removed.

*A summary of the law on penalty points:*

**The more serious motoring offences carry penalty points. Only very exceptionally can a court decide not to impose those penalty points. If you receive twelve penalty points in three years you will be disqualified for at least six months. However, if you can show strong mitigating circumstances (e.g. you will lose your job), the court need not disqualify you.**

## Disqualification

### *When can a motorist be disqualified?*

There are two main ways in which a motorist can be disqualified: firstly, for committing a very serious motoring offence (e.g. drunk driving) which will entail disqualification as part of the punishment; and secondly, under the twelve points in three years rule (see above).

Confusingly, different rules apply to these two types of disqualification. If you are facing disqualification under the twelve points in three years rule read the section above on 'Endorsement and Penalty Points'. If you are facing disqualification for a serious motoring offence (e.g. drunk driving) read the section below.

### *When can the court disqualify?*

In theory there are numerous occasions when the court can disqualify. In fact, if the court has power to impose an endorsement, it can also disqualify (if it wishes)! If you look at the penalty charts in this book you will see that an enormous number of offences can be endorsable – in which case the magistrates do have power to order a disqualification if they want to. In practice they rarely do so (see below).

However, for the more serious motoring offences the court *must* disqualify. These offences are:

- drunk-driving offences
- causing death by reckless driving
- a second conviction in three years for reckless driving
- manslaughter
- racing on the highway.

In all these cases the court *must* disqualify for at least one year. If a motorist is convicted of a second drunk-driving charge within a ten-year period the court must disqualify for at least three years.

### *What are the chances of being disqualified?*

If you are convicted of an offence for which you *must* be disqualified (see the list above) you can only escape disqualification if you can show *special reasons*. In practice, it is extremely difficult to do this, because special reasons cannot relate to the individual circumstances of a motorist (e.g. it will cause you severe hardship because you will lose your job) but must relate to the way the offence was committed (e.g. you didn't know you were going to be driving over the alcohol limit, because someone laced your drinks). Very few motorists can show special reasons, and so are unable to avoid disqualification when convicted of one of these offences. The rules on special reasons are set out on p. 226. In theory identical rules apply when deciding what are special reasons for not disqualifying as apply for not imposing an endorsement (i.e. p. 226). In practice one detects that the courts are more sympathetic when dealing with a disqualification. In other words, they may be prepared to take into account things that they should, strictly, ignore – such as the fact that disqualification can result in the motorists losing their job.

To some extent this is shown by the statistics on disqualification. Ninety-seven per cent of drunk drivers are disqualified, but only 42 per cent of motorists who commit two reckless-driving offences in three years are disqualified. Theoretically there should be no better grounds for special reasons applying in reckless-driving cases than in those for drunk driving. The practical reality is that magistrates take a much harsher line in drunk-driving cases – and so are more willing to find special reasons in those for reckless driving.

There are also many offences when the magistrates *may* disqualify the motorist. As we have seen, any offence that is endorsable can result in a disqualification. In practice this happens relatively rarely. If you read a legal textbook on motoring law you will probably find that it suggests that disqualification should be considered for many of these offences: failing to stop after an accident; driving while disqualified; crossing double white lines; reckless driving; not having insurance; learner driver offences; not stopping at a pedestrian crossing; speeding at more than 30 m.p.h. over the limit; taking a vehicle without consent; jumping traffic lights; and motorway offences. This is an alarmingly long list. The figures show, however, that it is only rarely that motorists are disqualified for these offences – which will be reassuring to many motorists! The table overleaf shows the approximate percentage of people disqualified for various offences, and illustrates that in practice, therefore, disqualification is extremely rare for all but the most serious offences. For instance, if you are prosecuted for careless driving you have a 2 per cent chance of being disqualified. On the other hand, if you are driving while already disqualified, or while uninsured, your chances increase to 19 per cent and 11 per cent respectively.

| Offence | % disqualified |
| --- | --- |
| Careless driving | 2 |
| Accident offences (failing to stop, report, etc.) | 2 |
| Driving while disqualified | 19 |
| Not having a driving licence | 2 |
| Not having insurance | 11 |
| Speeding | 1 |
| Jumping traffic lights | 1 |
| Crossing a double white line | 1 |
| Not stopping at a crossing | 1 |

### How long will the ban be for?

It all depends. Remember that there are three different ways in which a motorist can end up being disqualified:

1. *Under the twelve points in three years rule.* The normal rule is that the motorist must be disqualified for at least six months (see p. 224).

2. *When the offence is so serious that it carries automatic disqualification.* Disqualification will normally be for at least one year (see p. 232).

3. *When the magistrates decide to disqualify, even though they don't have to.* Here the court has a total discretion. It can impose a short disqualification if it wants to. In fact there is an increasing trend for the courts to impose short disqualifications. In the old days disqualifications tended to be for six months, twelve months, eighteen months – in other words, in six-month steps. Now, short disqualification is preferred. This is because it reduces the chances of a motorist deciding to ignore the ban and carry on driving. For instance, a motorist who was disqualified for two years may well, within a few weeks, decide to ignore the ban. On the other hand, a ban of a few weeks, or a month, is likely to be obeyed – and may well have a salutary warning effect. In particular, bad cases of careless driving, and youngsters charged with provisional-licence offences, are often best dealt with by a one-month disqualification. This is the short, sharp shock approach.

### What is the effect of disqualification?

You are banned from driving. You no longer have a driving licence.

The ban comes into effect immediately. So, if you are banned, you cannot even drive your car home from the magistrates' court. What is more, it is a total ban on using *any* motor vehicle. For instance, suppose a young man has a motorcycle licence and also a provisional car licence. If he is disqualified from driving (e.g. because he drove the car without an accompanying driver) that will also disqualify him from riding his motorcycle. It is a total ban on all motor vehicles. In one case, a farmer had been banned from driving, but in driving his tractor from one field to another he crossed a road, and thereby was guilty of driving while disqualified. So remember that the law is applied strictly.

If you have been disqualified you will have had to hand in your driving licence at the magistrates' court. The licence will then have been sent to the DVLC. About eight weeks before the end of your banned period the DVLC will send you an application form so that you can apply for a new licence. It is important to realize that as a disqualified motorist you no longer have a licence – so you cannot simply start driving at the end of the banned period, but must get another licence. If it was your second disqualification in ten years for drunk driving the DVLC may want medical evidence that you no longer have a drink problem. If so, they will tell you when they send out the driving licence reminder. If you do not hear from the DVLC before the end of the banning period you can simply apply for a licence yourself (send Form D1 – obtainable from any main post office – to the DVLC).

Sometimes the court will impose a ban and also insist that you pass another driving test before you can have a new licence. In practice this happens relatively rarely. However, if such an order is made, you must apply for a provisional licence when your ban ends, and you will have to pass the driving test before you can drive unaccompanied.

If, as a banned motorist, you are irresponsible enough to drive while disqualified you will face severe penalties. Driving while disqualified is regarded as a very serious offence and, although it can be heard by the magistrates, it is often referred to the Crown Court for sentencing. Statistics show that your chances of going to prison are fairly high. If the magistrates sentence you, you stand about an 8 per cent chance of being sent to prison – but if the Crown Court sentences you (which often happens) there is roughly a 50 per cent chance of your going straight to prison!

It follows that no one should be tempted to drive while disqualified. Apart from committing a serious criminal offence they will probably also be driving without insurance (since any insurance policy will be invalidated if the motorist has been disqualified).

### Can a disqualification be appealed against?

Yes. As with any magistrates' court sentence it can be appealed against to the Crown Court (see p. 254). In fact the magistrates can agree to suspend the disqualification until the Crown Court appeal is heard. But the motorist will generally have to ask the magistrates to do this when the disqualification is imposed. In practice relatively few appeals against disqualification are successful. Take legal advice if you are thinking of such an appeal.

Apart from appealing against the disqualification it is possible to go back to the magistrates' court and ask for an existing disqualification to be removed. But this cannot be done for two years. The rule is that a ban of up to four years can be reviewed after two years; a ban of between four and ten years can be reviewed after half the period is gone (e.g. a ban of eight years can be reviewed after four years); a ban of over ten years (e.g. for life) can be reviewed after five years. Very few bans are for more than two years, and thus motorists with up to a two-year ban cannot have their bans reviewed. If a motorist is under a ban of more than two years, and wishes to apply for a review, the application is made to the magistrates' court. But bear in mind that no application can be made for two years – in other words, a three-year ban cannot be reviewed for at least two years.

## Prison

### When can a motorist be sent to prison?

Very few motoring offences are punishable by prison. The main ones are causing death by reckless driving; drunk driving; reckless driving; and driving while disqualified. It is extremely rare for a motoring offence to result in prison. The offence most likely to result in prison is driving while disqualified (see p. 235), with drunk driving and reckless driving the next most likely. Prison is reserved for the most serious cases. Anyone who thinks they may come in that category should take legal advice.

However, courts do have a wide power to send people to prison for up to four days. Sometimes they will do this to drunk drivers in the run-up to Christmas, as also to youngsters who need a short, sharp shock (see p. 110).

## Absolute Discharge

### What is an absolute discharge?

An absolute discharge is when no penalty at all is imposed by the court. But you will still have been convicted of the offence.

For instance, the court may feel that you should never have been prosecuted by the police, or that you were found guilty on the harsh application of a technicality. In that case, the court might have no choice but to convict you – after all, you were guilty of the offence – but it might decide to impose no punishment. It does this by giving you an absolute discharge. So you avoid a fine, endorsement, penalty points or other punishment. Suppose, for example, that you are driving a car when your passenger suddenly suffers a heart attack. You decide it is quicker to drive to the local hospital rather than call an ambulance, and may even exceed the speed limit, as well as drive over some double white lines. The police prosecute you. The court has to find you guilty – after all, you did exceed the speed limit and cross over the white lines, and are therefore guilty of the offence. But, not surprisingly, the court may feel that the police were wrong to prosecute you, and would show this by giving you an absolute discharge, i.e. by imposing no penalty.

One point to note about an absolute discharge is that you have still been convicted of the offence – it is not the same as being found not guilty. That being so, an absolute discharge is not a complete let-off, and so you should tell your insurance company of the conviction when you next renew your insurance policy (see p. 116).

# Police Checks

### Can the police stop me when I'm driving?

Yes. A police officer in uniform (but not a traffic warden) can stop any motorist. This is so even if the motorist has not committed any offence, and even if the police officer is being bloody-minded.

But there are controls on what the police can then do. The officer can ask for particulars (i.e. details of the driver, the registration document, insurance, etc. – see below) and can also carry out a roadside check on the vehicle (see below). But the police cannot search the vehicle, except in certain specialized cases (e.g. they suspect it is being used for carrying drugs or for a serious criminal offence) – see p. 242. The police also have power to set up general road blocks (see p. 242).

### What information can the police ask for?

The police can ask for:

- the name and address of the driver
- the name and address of the owner
- driving licence details
- insurance certificate details
- the MOT certificate
- the registration documents
- the date of birth of the driver (sometimes) – although this is of course on the driving licence anyway (see p. 93).

But this information can only be asked for if:

- you were driving a motor vehicle (e.g. a car or motorbike) on a road, *or*
- the police reasonably believe you were the driver of a motor vehicle when an accident occurred (even if there was no damage to the vehicle), *or*

238

• the police reasonably believe you have committed any motoring offence (however trivial – e.g. a parking offence).

In most circumstances, therefore, the police can ask to see these documents. Only if you were not driving, and it was clear that you had not committed any traffic offence or been involved in any accident, would you be able to refuse them. Of course, few motorists would care to argue, and the end result is that the police can demand to see documents.

If you do not have the documents on you – and most motorists do not – you must produce them at a police station. You will be asked to nominate a police station and you will normally have at least seven days in which to go to that police station with the documents.

### How long do I have in which to produce my documents?

If the police ask to see your documents (see above) you can either produce them on the spot or take them to the police station. See above for when the police can ask to see your documents. The sort of documents we are talking about are:

• driving licence
• insurance certificate
• MOT certificate
• vehicle registration document
• certificate showing you are exempted from wearing a seat belt (e.g. on medical grounds)
• certificate of registration as a driving instructor, or a licence to give driving lessons.

The general rule is that all these documents must be produced within seven days. You can choose which police station you want to go to – but you must name it at the time you are asked to produce the documents. You cannot later change your mind and go to a different police station!

The basic requirement is that you produce these documents within seven days, but this seven-day period is not rigidly enforced. If you can show that it was not reasonably practicable for you to produce the documents within the seven days you cannot be convicted of 'failure to produce'. For instance, suppose you have lost the documents; or they have been stolen; or you have since gone abroad. In such cases you may be able to argue that it was not 'reasonably practicable' to produce them in time, but you should, of course, make sure that you do produce them as soon as possible – do not try and take advantage of this provision by delaying unnecessarily.

This seven-day period does not apply if you have been involved in an accident in which someone was injured. In such a case you have to produce your insurance certificate within five days (see p. 12).

Strictly speaking, there is no seven-day period for producing the vehicle's registration document. But in practice you would be expected to produce it within seven days, with the other documents.

If you are asked to produce your driving licence you will have to go in person to the police station. No one else can go for you. With the other documents it is possible for you to send someone else – although it is usually better if you go yourself.

### Is there any advantage in keeping my motoring documents in the car?

Yes. In practice it is the insurance certificate, MOT certificate and driving licence that the police are usually most keen to inspect. If you keep these in your car you will not be inconvenienced by having to produce them at a police station within seven days (see above).

In fact there is a more important advantage to having the documents in your car. If you are involved in an accident in which someone else is injured you may be able to avoid reporting the accident to the police – provided you produce your insurance certificate at the time of the accident (for instance, to the person injured) and you also give your name and address (see p. 11 for details). The important point to grasp is that if you keep your insurance certificate in the car, and produce it at the time of an accident, you may be able to avoid having to report the accident to the police. That being so, the police may never learn of the accident. If you do not produce your insurance certificate at the time you may well have to report the accident to the police. There is then a danger that, having been told about the accident, they decide to investigate it – with the result that you end up being prosecuted for careless driving! So wise drivers will always keep their documents (in particular their insurance certificates) in the car.

*When can the police do a spot check on a vehicle?*

The police can check any vehicle to see that it meets the legal requirements (i.e. on brakes, silencer, steering, tyres, lights, reflectors, noise,
smoke and fumes). In effect the police officer can check that it complies
with the Construction and Use Regulations as to roadworthiness. In fact
these powers are not just confined to police officers – the Chief Constable can authorize other examiners to inspect vehicles. However, only
a police officer in uniform can stop the vehicle in the first place (see
p. 238).

You can normally opt to have the test deferred until a more convenient time. The only exceptions are when the vehicle has been
involved in an accident, or if the police officer or vehicle examiner thinks
its condition is so bad that a test should be carried out straight away. If
you do opt to have the test delayed to another time you are entitled to
select any seven-day period during the next thirty days during which the
vehicle can be examined (on two days' notice). Not surprisingly the
police do not usually bother to tell motorists that they have the option to
defer the test!

In exceptional cases, if the defects are really bad, you may be told that
you cannot use the vehicle before you have had it fixed – if so, you will
have to arrange for the garage to fetch the vehicle and then tow it away
for repair. In fact this happens very rarely. The usual procedure is that
you (or the owner of the vehicle) will be given twenty-eight days in which
to have the defect remedied (either you must get a certificate from an
MOT station confirming that the defect has been remedied, or you can
simply sign a declaration saying that you have disposed of the vehicle
and will not be using it again). If you do provide a certificate from an
MOT garage the police have a thirty-day period in which to ask to
inspect the vehicle themselves. (These rules already apply in practice,
although the Act making them law has not yet been introduced.)

Apart from requiring that the vehicle defect be fixed, in this way, the
police can of course prosecute for the defect. This will normally be a
prosecution under the Construction and Use Regulations (see 'Unsafe
Vehicles', p. 293).

Foreign goods vehicles are subject to even stricter controls: the police
have additional powers to carry out spot checks.

The Motorist and the Law

### When can the police search my car?

The police can search any vehicle if they have reasonable grounds for thinking they will find stolen goods. Normally the owner of the vehicle will be contacted, but the police do have powers to search unattended vehicles. If this happens the police must leave a note inside the car, stating that the car has been searched and giving the name of their police station. The police can seize stolen or prohibited goods that they do find.

These search powers cannot be exercised if the vehicle is on private property (e.g. a private individual's garden or garage). In that case, the general laws on search warrants apply.

Obviously the police can only search a car if it is stopped. For their power to stop cars see p. 238.

### When can the police set up road blocks?

The police have surprisingly wide powers to set up road blocks. These were given to them by the Police and Criminal Evidence Act 1984. The rules are complicated, but basically a senior police officer can authorize road checks if a serious offence has been committed, and the suspect is in the area.

When the police stop the vehicle they can of course ask the driver for the usual particulars (see p. 238).

This power to set up a general road block and stop all cars is different from the power to stop individual cars (see p. 238).

---

### WHAT'S THE PENALTY?

*For not stopping when ordered to do so by a police officer*

*For obstructing a police spot check examination*
MAXIMUM PENALTY: a £400 fine (£2,000 for a foreign goods vehicle obstructing a roadside test)
LIKELY PENALTY: generally, a fine of £25 (no points or endorsement). If the circumstances were serious (e.g. clear disobedience of a stop signal from a police officer, and then trying to speed away, the fine would be substantially more)

*For failing to produce documents to the police within seven days*
MAXIMUM PENALTY: a £400 fine
LIKELY PENALTY: a £30 fine

*(For more on penalties see p. 216)*

---

# Prosecution

*Must I be warned that I might be prosecuted?*

Sometimes. For some offences the police must give you a Notice of Intended Prosecution. The offences are:

- careless driving (sometimes called driving without due care and attention)
- inconsiderate driving
- most speeding offences
- reckless driving
- reckless or careless pedalling by a cyclist
- parking in a dangerous position
- not following a police officer's traffic directions
- not following certain traffic signs (e.g. stop and give way signs; double white lines; automatic level crossing signs; signs to go left, right or straight on – i.e. a white arrow on a blue circle).

It is only in these cases that the police have to give warning of a possible prosecution. Other offences (e.g. for parking, defective vehicles, no insurance, no licence, no MOT, etc.) do not require a specific warning.

*What warning must be given?*

The idea of giving a warning to motorists is so that they can remember the facts of the accident, and contact any witnesses, etc. before their memories fade. So notice has to be given in the sorts of prosecutions that involve remembering the circumstances of a motoring incident (e.g. careless driving or ignoring a stop sign). If the offence does not come within the list above, warning does not have to be given. However, even if the offence does come within this list there will be no need for a warning to be given if an accident happened. This is because the mere fact that an accident happened will have alerted the motorist to take details of witnesses, etc., and to make a note of what happened. Any further warning is therefore thought unnecessary.

If there was no accident, and the offence was one of those listed above, the motorist must either:

- *have been warned by the police at the time of the accident* of a possible prosecution, or
- *be given written notice within fourteen days* of a possible prosecution.

To summarize: if there was an accident the motorist need not be told of a possible prosecution. If there wasn't an accident the police must give the motorist either a verbal warning at the time or a written warning within fourteen days, provided the offence was one of those listed above – this is called a Notice of Intended Prosecution.

The point to note is that a written Notice of Intended Prosecution (within fourteen days) is only needed if (1.) the offence is one of those listed above; (2.) there was no accident; and (3.) the police did not warn the motorist at the time that a prosecution was possible. In practice, if the police were called it is likely that they will have given a verbal warning to the motorist. This might simply be in the form: 'I must warn you that the facts of this matter will be reported with a view to prosecution.' But there is no strict form of words the police have to use – all they have to do is to give sufficient warning for the motorist to know that a prosecution may follow. Nor does the warning have to be put in writing. A verbal warning given within a few hours of the accident will probably be treated as having been given 'at the time'; the courts do not expect the notice to be given as soon as the police turn up at the scene!

As we have seen, the cases when the motorist has to be given a written notice are relatively few. If written notice must be given, the motorist should receive it within fourteen days (fifteen really – the day of the accident is not counted). Usually this written notice will be no more than a letter from the police stating that the facts are being investigated and that they might lead to a prosecution. There is no need for the police actually to start the prosecution within that period. Therefore the police often decide to keep their options open by sending out a Notice of Intended Prosecution to make sure that they do not fall foul of the fourteen-day rule. It follows that motorists who receive a Notice of Intended Prosecution should not think that they will definitely be prosecuted. Often the police will decide not to prosecute – the motorist will later receive a letter from the police saying that they have decided not to proceed. A Notice of Intended Prosecution is no more than a warning to the motorist – it is not an actual prosecution.

Sometimes motorists claim that they never received the Notice of Intended Prosecution. They say that the police forgot to post it, and therefore that it is too late for the police to prosecute them. This argument gets short shrift from the courts. They are sceptical of such claims and will need firm proof. From the police point of view all they have to do is to send the letter by registered post or recorded delivery to the last known address of either the owner or the registered keeper of the vehicle, so that it will arrive within the fourteen-day period. Alternatively they can personally serve the Notice. But, if the Notice is not received for some reason (e.g. the motorist has moved away or the post office failed to deliver it), the court will probably still say that the police have complied with the requirements.

It follows from this that it is only rarely that a motorist can show that the police have made a mistake and failed to serve the Notice in time.

### Is there any time limit for prosecuting?

The general rule is that a prosecution must be begun within six months of the offence. If it is not brought within that time it is too late for the police to prosecute. But it should be realized that this does not mean that the case has to go to court within six months. In other words, the police can simply ask the magistrates to issue a summons within the six-month period, and then they can sit on it. For instance, if they have difficulty in serving the summons (e.g. the motorist has moved) there could be a delay of several years before the case goes to court!

It follows that when motorists are served with a summons it does not matter if it is served outside the six-month period. However, they should look at the summons to check that the date on it (i.e. the date that it was issued by the court) is not more than six months after the date of the offence. If it is, the whole prosecution (subject to a few exceptions – see below) is too late. Of course, it is rare for the police – and the courts – to make such a fundamental mistake, so a motorist would be extremely lucky to find that the summons had been issued more than six months after the date of the accident. It is a legal technicality that is unlikely to arise.

In any event there are some motoring offences for which the six-month period runs only from the date when the police knew they had grounds for prosecution, not from the date of the accident. But, even in these circumstances, the police can never prosecute more than three years from the date of the offence. The main offences covered by this three-year (not six-month) period are:

● failing to notify the DVLC of a change of particulars on the licence (e.g. change of address)
● driving while uninsured
● forgery and having a false MOT certificate, driving licence or insurance certificate
● a motorist acquitted of reckless driving can then be charged with careless driving, even though more than six months have passed since the date of the incident.

In addition, there are some serious offences (e.g. reckless driving, driving while disqualified) for which there is no time limit – for instance, the police can prosecute even if the offence was committed over three years before.

To summarize: there is normally a six-month time limit within which court proceedings have to be started. But there is no need for the court papers to be served on the motorist within this time – let alone for the court case to be heard! The police and courts rarely miss the six-month period and so very few motorists are able to use it as a technical defence.

### What should I do if I receive a summons?

A summons cannot be ignored. As soon as you receive the summons you should:

1. *Read the summons carefully*. The summons will be written in legalese – you may have great difficulty in understanding it. The first thing to do is to make sure you are clear about the time and date you are supposed to be in court. The next thing is to work out exactly what you are being prosecuted for. Read the summons carefully, to work out the charge against you. You will probably find that the offence is referred to by reference to an Act or Regulation. Do not forget that there may be more than one charge listed on the summons.

You should have been given reasonable warning of the hearing date. If it is in only a few days' time, and you feel that is not sufficient warning, contact the Clerk of the Court straight away, say that you have only just received the documentation, and ask for the case to be adjourned. Though not obliged to do so, the Clerk of the Court may well agree to this. If the Clerk refuses contact the police to see whether they will agree to an adjournment – if they do the court is much more likely to agree. Otherwise you will simply have to turn up on the date of the hearing and ask the magistrates to adjourn the case to another date. Sometimes they will, and sometimes they won't – a lot depends on the seriousness of the charge. If they refuse to adjourn it you will have to go ahead and do the best you can.

2. *Has a Notice of Intended Prosecution been served?* Sometimes the police have to give you warning that you may be prosecuted (see p. 243). It is rare for the police to overlook this formality so you are unlikely to be able to use it as a technical defence. However, if you think the police have not given you proper notice contact them and point this out. If they agree the case will probably be withdrawn. If they dispute your claim you will have to go to court and argue the point – remember that courts are sceptical of people who say they never received the Notice from the police (see p. 245).

3. *Check the penalty for the offence.* The penalty charts in this book set out the penalties for most traffic offences. You will see that two penalties are given in each chart – the maximum penalty and the likely penalty. The maximum penalty is the most that the court can impose. By comparing the different maximum penalties for different offences you can get some indication of the seriousness of the charge against you. However, in practice it is extremely rare for the court to impose the maximum penalty, and you may therefore find it more useful to look at the likely penalty. This sets out rough guideline figures for first offenders. However, it is absolutely essential to realize that these figures are not guaranteed to be accurate – they are no more than a 'guess-timate' of possible penalties. All magistrates' courts are different, and all magistrates have their own individual approaches, so there can be enormous variations up and down the country. However, once again, by comparing the likely penalty for the offence you are charged with and the likely penalties for other offences you can get an indication of the seriousness of the charge against you. Do not rely upon the likely penalty as being a firm guide as to the sentence you will get.

The penalty charts refer to fines, endorsements, points and disqualification. See p. 216 for more information on these. Most motorists will want to know the probable level of a fine and how many penalty points they are likely to get.

4. *Could you lose your licence?* There are two main ways of losing your licence. The first is when you are simply disqualified (e.g. for drunk

driving); automatic disqualification applies only to the serious offences. Secondly, you might lose your licence because you have got too many penalty points. The basic rule is that if you receive twelve points in three years you will lose your licence. This is called 'totting up' (see p. 224).

If there is a real risk of your losing your licence you would be well advised to take legal advice. This is so even if you are clearly guilty of the offence. After all, a good lawyer may be able to make a good speech in mitigation to the court and perhaps (exceptionally) save your licence.

5. *Do you need legal advice?* If the charge against you is serious, and the likely penalty heavy, you should take legal advice. Similarly you should take legal advice if you think you may have a technical defence to the charge (e.g. no Notice of Intended Prosecution was served on you). See p. 142 for the sources of legal advice. Remember that you may be able to get free legal help (through the legal-aid scheme, your insurance company, the RAC or the AA).

If it is obvious that you have no defence to the charge it is pointless to see a solicitor (unless you want a solicitor simply to make a speech in mitigation for you). You will not be able to get free legal aid to defend a hopeless charge, and you would be wasting your money if you decided to pay a solicitor yourself. You should also remember that motorists who plead not guilty when they are obviously guilty can expect to have a heavier fine (or even more points) imposed by the court. The courts do this to discourage other motorists from wasting the courts' time. So, if you do not have a defence, consider seriously whether it is worth paying a lawyer to defend you.

6. *Are you guilty?* You will usually be able to work out for yourself whether or not you committed the offence. If you cannot, take legal advice. One point you should bear in mind is that the court will not be impressed with fanciful theoretical defences. Magistrates' courts take a fairly rough-and-ready approach to cases and are not interested in theoretical flights of fancy as to what possibly could have happened. The conviction rate in magistrates' courts is extremely high.

7. *If you are not guilty.* If you decide to plead not guilty you should let the court know. Return the forms that were sent with the summons, and make it clear that you will be pleading not guilty. Almost certainly the first hearing date will then be cancelled, and you will be sent another date when your case will be heard. This is because the first date (the date on the summons) is usually set on the assumption that you will plead guilty. If in doubt as to whether you have to turn up on that first date (i.e. if you have not had a letter from the court) phone to confirm.

8. *If you are guilty*. If you decide to plead guilty to the charge check whether or not you can plead guilty by post. This will save you the inconvenience and expense of having to attend court. It is easy to tell whether or not you can plead guilty by post – if you can, you will have been sent a Statement of Facts, or Summary of Facts, with the summons. Also, there will be a form for you to sign in which you agree to plead guilty. You may be asked to attach your driving licence as well (if the court can impose an endorsement or penalty points). If you do decide to plead guilty by post send off the form as soon as possible – do not wait until just before the hearing, since you would have to pay attendance costs if the police officer still attended court. If you return the form to the court, pleading guilty by post, you can change your mind – withdraw your plea of guilty and plead not guilty instead – provided you notify the court before the hearing date.

If you want to plead guilty by post, and are supposed to attach your licence but you can't (e.g. because it has been mislaid), do not delay telling the court that you plead guilty. Send off the form pleading guilty, but attach a note saying that the driving licence has been mislaid and that you are applying to the DVLC for another. As soon as you receive it, forward it to the court. Do not wait for the licence to arrive before you return the form to the court. Incidentally, if you have a licence with several old endorsements or points on it (i.e. they were imposed more than four years ago) it may be a good idea to send the licence to the DVLC and ask for them to be removed (see p. 230). In the meantime return the 'guilty' form to the court and explain that your licence is at the DVLC. By doing this you avoid prejudice against you (when it comes to sentencing) due to your previous endorsements or points.

If you plead guilty by post you will not appear before the magistrates, and you will not be able to tell them your side of the case, so it is important that you complete the form carefully – and set out all the mitigating circumstances in your favour (i.e. why you should have a low penalty). The court will read what you say and take it into account when imposing the sentence. But it is important that your mitigating circumstances should not go so far as to amount to a denial of the offence (i.e. a not guilty plea). For instance, if you were being prosecuted for careless driving you might legitimately say that you made only a minor misjudgement, and that no one was injured – but what you cannot say is that you were not guilty of careless driving. If you say that, the court will not accept your plea of guilty, and will adjourn the case so that you can turn up in court to plead not guilty.

If you plead guilty by post the court can impose a fine, an endorsement and penalty points on you. However, it cannot impose a disqualification (i.e. take away your licence) without giving you a chance to be heard. So if the court is thinking in terms of imposing a disqualification (e.g. because you have got more than twelve points in three years) it will fix another hearing date. This will give you a chance to come along and argue why you should not be disqualified (see p. 232). If you do not attend that second hearing the court can simply go ahead and impose disqualification in your absence (if it decides that is the proper penalty). In practice, however, disqualification is unlikely – the court would be more likely to issue a warrant for your arrest. Once you had been arrested and taken to court the motoring charge would then be dealt with.

There is no obligation on motorists to plead guilty by post. If they prefer, they can attend court and plead guilty in person. This has the advantage that they will be able to explain personally to the magistrates why a low penalty should be imposed – in other words, they can set out their own mitigating circumstances in person, rather than through a letter. In practice most motorists prefer to avoid the waste of time and inconvenience caused by going to court and therefore plead guilty by post if offered the chance.

It is only for some offences that the court will offer you the chance of pleading guilty by post. Often you will simply be sent the summons and not given the option of pleading guilty by post. However, even in this case you will frequently find that you can simply write to the court saying that you intend to plead guilty, setting out the mitigating circumstances, and asking that your attendance be excused. Most courts will accept the guilty plea by post, and simply go ahead and sentence. If the court is not prepared to allow you to plead guilty in this way they will probably fix another hearing date (but this would be relatively rare – for instance, if the charges were very serious).

One final point. It is not possible to plead not guilty by post. If you want to argue that you were not guilty you will have to turn up in court (with or without a solicitor) and argue your case. If you do not turn up in court you will almost certainly be found guilty.

9. *Get your documents sorted out.* If the penalty chart shows that the court could impose an endorsement, points or disqualification you will have to produce your licence in court. If you are going to the court (to plead either guilty or not guilty) you should take it with you; if you are pleading guilty by post you should send it to the court. If you do not have

your licence (e.g. you have lost it) apply immediately for a replacement to the DVLC (see p. 229) and tell the court. If you have old, expired endorsements and points on your licence it may be a good idea to have them removed (see p. 230).

You may also be asked to produce your MOT and insurance certificates. If so, make sure that you have these documents to take to court. If you have lost them apply for replacements (see p. 174 for replacement MOT certificates; ask your insurance broker, or the insurance company, for a replacement insurance certificate).

### What penalties can the court impose?

You will have to look at the various penalty charts. These set out the maximum penalties and the likely penalties (see p. 216 for how to interpret the likely penalty).

Virtually every convicted motorist can expect a fine. See p. 222 for more on fines.

Most motoring offences are endorsable. This means that penalty points can be imposed. See p. 223 for more on penalty points and on what can be special reasons for not imposing penalty points.

For the more serious cases the court can disqualify. In fact if you look at the penalty charts you will see that a lot of offences have disqualification listed in the maximum-penalty section. In practice disqualification is reserved for the more serious offences. See p. 232 for more on disqualification.

Finally, for extremely serious offences a prison sentence can be imposed. Generally this will be for an offence such as causing death by reckless driving, a bad case of drunken driving, etc.

### What happens at the court hearing?

Before you go to court you should decide whether you are going to plead guilty or not guilty. If you are going to plead guilty you may well decide that it is easier to plead guilty by post (and so save the expense and inconvenience of going to court).

You should make sure you turn up in good time at court. You may well find that your case is one of several listed for the same time. If that is so you may have a lengthy wait before your case is called. When your case is called you will be asked to go forward, and to stand before the court. You will be asked if you plead guilty or not guilty.

*If you plead guilty* you will have to produce your licence immediately if the offence carries a compulsory endorsement (or a discretionary or compulsory disqualification). A brief summary of the facts of the case will be read out, and you will be asked if you have anything to say. If you have written a letter to the court that will also be read out. The court then may ask for details of any previous convictions. In most motoring cases the courts do not bother to find out about other non-motoring criminal offences (e.g. theft), but the more serious the motoring charge, the more likely it is that the court will be interested in your background and record. You will then be given a chance to address the magistrates so you can set out your mitigating circumstances. If you have employed one, your solicitor will do this for you. The court will then decide what penalty to impose. Before doing this they may well ask about your finances. It is often helpful to have prepared a summary of your finances (i.e. income, net of income tax and national insurance, and expenditure, such as mortgage, rates, rent, HP payments, insurance payments, etc.). The court will want to know how much you can pay by way of fine. Finally, the court will announce the penalty – usually a fine, and perhaps an endorsement plus points, or even exceptionally disqualification. If a fine is imposed you can ask for time to pay. If the court thinks you do need time to pay they will give it to you.

*If you plead not guilty* a different procedure applies. The first thing to realize is that the court date on the summons will probably have been set on the assumption that you will plead guilty. If you turn up at court on that date and suddenly announce that you intend to plead not guilty, almost certainly the case will be adjourned to another date. That is why it is advisable to tell the court beforehand if you intend to plead not guilty – usually they will then simply fix another date. When you do eventually appear before the magistrates you will be asked to plead guilty or not guilty. If you plead not guilty the prosecution (in most cases this will be the police officer in charge of the case) will outline the case against you. The officer will give the court a short summary of the case, and then will call the witnesses and ask them questions. They will give their replies to the court. After the police officer has finished questioning each witness, you can cross-examine (i.e. you can question them yourself). You do not have to question them if you do not want to. Once the police officer's witnesses have been called, it is your chance to present your case. You can give evidence yourself if you wish (although you are not legally obliged to do so). Similarly you can call witnesses to support your case. It is important to arrange that witnesses will attend court and you should sort this out beforehand. You will probably have to pay the costs of the witnesses (e.g. their lost earnings). If a witness refuses to attend court it is possible for you to get a witness order (apply at the court office) – but you should remember that an unwilling witness is often a bad witness.

Once you and your witnesses have given evidence both sides sum up. After that the magistrates (there will probably be three of them) will decide whether you are guilty or not guilty. If you are found not guilty you should immediately ask for costs against the police – but you may not get them (see p. 254).

### Can I ask to be tried in front of a jury?

Almost certainly not. In the magistrates' court your case will be heard by magistrates. In most parts of the country the magistrates' court is made up of three, unpaid, justices of the peace (i.e. amateur judges). In London, and some other big cities, your case may come up before one professional magistrate (called a stipendiary magistrate).

More serious criminal charges are tried at the Crown Court – before a judge and jury. However, very few motoring prosecutions can be heard in the Crown Court. Only if the charge involves dishonesty (e.g. stealing a car), or in a few other cases (e.g. reckless driving or driving while disqualified), can you opt for Crown Court trial. Note in particular that you cannot ask for a Crown Court trial if you are being prosecuted for drunk driving.

### What happens after the court case?

If you have been disqualified you may have problems in getting home! You will not be able to drive. So if you are facing a charge that could well lead to disqualification do not drive your own car to the court. Get a friend to take you, or go by taxi or public transport. Otherwise you will have to leave your car at the court, and arrange for a friend to drive it back.

You should pay any fine on time. If you are allowed to pay the fine by instalments it is important that you stick to those instalments. If your finances change, and you cannot afford to make the payments, tell the court immediately. They will probably agree to give you extra time. If you do not tell them, and get into arrears, you will probably face a further court hearing. In practice courts are sympathetic – provided they are told about financial difficulties.

Do not forget that it will be a term of your insurance policy that you tell the insurance company about any convictions. So when you come to renew your insurance you should tell them about any convictions that you have had since the policy was last renewed. Most insurance companies do not increase premiums because the motorist has been convicted (unless it has had particularly serious results, such as disqualification). The main reason why you should tell the insurance company is so that, if you later have an accident, they cannot argue that your insurance policy is invalid (see p. 116).

If you think you have been wrongly convicted you can appeal. It is possible to appeal to the Crown Court, where the case will be heard before a judge and two (or perhaps four) magistrates. There will be no jury. The case will be heard afresh on the appeal, and all the witnesses will have to give evidence again. Appeals are expensive, and relatively few succeed. If you are thinking of appealing it is essential that you take legal advice. Do not appeal merely because you feel the result was unfair – only appeal if the magistrates got the law wrong, of if their decision was at total variance with the evidence given.

### What about costs?

If you are found guilty you may well have to make a contribution towards the prosecution costs. Because of this it is sensible to plead guilty if you have no real defence to the charge. If you plead not guilty, and are then convicted, you will (apart from paying a higher fine) also have increased legal costs to pay. These will probably be the cost of police time, perhaps the cost of a solicitor who acted on behalf of the police and certainly the witness costs. These can add up to a sizeable sum. So, if you are guilty, it is better to plead guilty rather than risk having to pay extra costs.

Always give the court a lot of warning if you intend to plead guilty. This avoids the risk of witnesses turning up on the assumption that you would be pleading not guilty. If witnesses do come to court, you may well have to pay their loss of earnings and travel expenses, even if you then decide to plead guilty. Often those costs can be more than the fine imposed!

If you are found not guilty you will probably want to claim your costs off the prosecution. Only rarely will full costs be ordered against the police – such as when it is obvious that the prosecution was hopeless and should never have been brought. So, if you do successfully defend your case, you can expect some of your costs (e.g. the expenses and loss of earnings of you and your witnesses) to be paid. You may even get a contribution towards the cost of your solicitor. Whether or not that will be sufficient to pay the whole of your solicitor's bill depends upon the generosity of the court, and the level of fees charged by your solicitor.

# Reckless Driving

### *What is reckless driving?*

Really bad driving. All motorists make mistakes at some time, and in doing so we are guilty of careless driving (see p. 59). Careless driving is the charge which is brought against a motorist who has fallen below the normally high standard expected. Only exceptionally will a reckless-driving charge be brought – when the driving was really so bad that it cannot be described as careless.

For you to be convicted of reckless driving it must be shown that you were driving so badly that you created an 'obvious and serious' risk of injuring someone or causing substantial damage to property. Also it must be shown that you couldn't care less – that either you didn't mind that this would happen, or you didn't bother to think about it.

It is all a matter of degree. For instance, in one case a motorcyclist drove at 77 m.p.h., through a 30 m.p.h. speed limit, in Lowestoft. He hit and killed a pedestrian who couldn't get out of the way. It was held that this was such bad driving that it was reckless driving – it was not merely careless driving. The motorcyclist had been going so quickly that he was obviously creating a risk of injury to other people.

But no one need be injured for there to be reckless driving. It is enough if the bad driving creates a risk of an accident. However, in practice it is very rare for a reckless-driving prosecution to be brought unless there was a fairly serious accident. Examples of bad driving that may lead to a reckless-driving charge are: going through traffic lights at red; overtaking on a bend or on the brow of a hill; going the wrong way down a motorway or dual carriageway; overtaking a long queue of cars; or driving at far too great a speed. In short, anything that is really bad driving – and obviously dangerous – can be reckless driving.

Why should it matter if the motorist faces a reckless-driving as opposed to a careless-driving charge? The answer lies in the stiff penalty for reckless driving – it is always much more serious than that for careless driving. See p. 216 for penalties (and p. 59 for careless driving). The difference in seriousness of the two offences is shown by the fact that careless-driving charges can only be heard in the magistrates' court, while a reckless-driving charge can instead be heard in the Crown Court (before a jury).

### What about causing death through reckless driving?

This is probably the most serious motoring charge that can be brought. If the reckless driving resulted in someone's death the motorist can expect to go to prison.

### What should I do if I am being prosecuted for reckless driving?

Think about the following:

1. *Have the police followed the rules?* The police should have given you warning that you might be prosecuted (see p. 243). If you think they have forgotten to do this you should take legal advice.

2. *Are you guilty?* Read the section on p. 246 to see whether you think you are guilty or not. Bear in mind that a reckless-driving charge is extremely serious. If such a charge is being brought it may well be that you were guilty of careless driving. Often the police will offer a deal – they will prosecute you for both and drop the reckless-driving charge if you plead guilty to the one for careless driving (see p. 62). So you may well be guilty of careless driving, but you should think very carefully about admitting your guilt to a reckless-driving charge. Take legal advice.

3. *What's the penalty?* Look at the chart on p. 259 for details. Penalties are heavy. In any event, if you already have penalty points, bear in mind that twelve points in three years would probably result in your losing your licence (see p. 224). Therefore, if it is particularly important to you that you do not have any more penalty points, you should definitely take legal advice.

4. *Do you need legal advice?* You can probably get legal advice from your local CAB, a solicitor or perhaps from the AA and RAC. See p. 150 for sources of legal advice. A reckless-driving prosecution is serious – always think in terms of taking legal advice.

5. *Check the rules on prosecution and conviction, and also on endorsement, fines and disqualification.* See p. 243 for prosecution; p. 251 for

conviction; p. 223 for endorsement; p. 222 for fines; and p. 232 for disqualification.

### What is the penalty for reckless driving?

The maximum penalties are heavy. You can be fined up to £2,000, and sent to prison for six months. In addition you can be disqualified for an unlimited period and you will get ten penalty points. If it is your second conviction for reckless driving within three years the court *must* disqualify you for at least a year.

As is usually the case, the penalties that are imposed in practice are not as severe as those that could be imposed. But the fact remains that they are still likely to be heavy. It is impossible to give definite guidance on sentences for reckless driving – each case depends on its own facts, and often extremely serious accidents are involved. As a rough-and-ready guide one could say that a typical sentence would be a fine of £250–£300, plus ten penalty points and perhaps six months' disqualification. Since the court has such extensive powers it is wise for the accused motorist to be represented by a lawyer. The lawyer will at least be able to put forward reasoned arguments in mitigation – why the motorist should get a relatively lenient sentence.

Much will depend upon the facts of the particular case. In serious cases you can expect to go to prison. This would be especially so if someone was killed through your driving. On the other hand, the court will take mitigating factors into account (e.g. the offence was a single, momentary lapse; you have an excellent driving record and are of good character; you have shown genuine remorse and shock – especially if the victim was a passenger in your car; the fact that you have pleaded guilty). In such cases you would not expect to go to prison. On the other hand, serious cases could easily lead to an immediate prison sentence (e.g. you had been drinking, or taking drugs; you had been travelling at a vastly excessive speed; you had ignored warnings from your passengers; you had been committing a criminal offence at the time – for instance, stealing the car; you had been driving this badly for several miles; someone was killed).

Having said that, relatively few motorists who are convicted of reckless driving go to prison. The typical case involves the motorist who has a momentary lapse of concentration – resulting in some particularly bad driving and a serious accident. Such a motorist would not normally get a prison sentence – just a heavy fine and ten penalty points (or perhaps a period of disqualification).

---

## WHAT'S THE PENALTY?

*For reckless driving*

MAXIMUM PENALTY: ten penalty points (plus an endorsement). A maximum fine of £2,000, plus prison for six months and disqualification

LIKELY PENALTY: a £250–£300 fine; ten penalty points (and an endorsement). Perhaps disqualification. See above

*For causing death by reckless driving*

MAXIMUM PENALTY: five years in prison plus an unlimited fine

LIKELY PENALTY: four penalty points (and an endorsement) plus disqualification for twelve months. Much will depend upon the circumstances – prison and a longer period of disqualification may well follow in bad cases

*(For more on penalties see p. 216)*

---

# Road Tax

### What is road tax?

Properly speaking it is called vehicle excise duty. Some people call it a road fund licence, or vehicle licence, but most people call it road tax.

### How do I get road tax for a new vehicle?

The chances are that the dealer will have applied for the first road tax on your behalf (when applying for the registration document, or log book). You will probably find it is taxed when you take delivery of it. However, if no application was made, you must ask the dealer for the application form (V55), which you can then take or post to the local vehicle licensing office (not to the DVLC).

### How do I get road tax for a secondhand vehicle?

When you buy a secondhand vehicle you may get some road tax included in the price. In that case, you need not do anything, since the vehicle already has a road tax licence (but you will need to tell the DVLC that you have acquired the vehicle – see p. 267). On the other hand, road tax may not be included. This could be because the seller wants to cash in the existing road tax disc, or because the tax has expired. If so, you must apply for tax straight away, using form V10 (from post offices and local vehicle licensing offices) – you will also need the registration document (with your name and address on it), the tax fee and a current certificate of insurance (or cover note). Also attach your MOT certificate (if the vehicle needs one). You do not have to produce the old (expired) tax disc. Main post offices can issue new tax discs over the counter; you can also obtain them from a local vehicle licensing office. Note that you do not apply for road tax to the DVLC at Swansea.

## How do I renew my road tax?

You should receive a reminder from the DVLC that the road tax is expiring, about two weeks in advance (this will be on a form marked V11). You can renew the tax simply by taking (or posting) the completed form, plus the tax, insurance certificate and MOT certificate (if needed), to a main post office or local vehicle licensing office. There is no need to produce the registration document or old licence. Do not apply to the DVLC at Swansea.

If you are not sent the reminder by the DVLC you must fill in form V10 (from post offices and local vehicle licensing offices). The procedure is then the same as for getting road tax for a new vehicle (see above).

## How far in advance can I renew my road tax?

Normally you cannot apply more than fourteen days before you want the new disc to commence. The only exception is if you are going abroad (e.g. on a holiday or business trip). If the tax will expire when you are abroad you can apply by post to a head post office up to six weeks ahead. You can give a foreign address for the tax disc to be sent to.

## How can I get a refund on a road tax disc?

You can apply for refunds for complete calendar months; you cannot claim for part months. In addition you must make sure that the tax disc is posted or handed in to a local vehicle licensing office no later than the last day of the preceding month. You cannot claim for months that have already expired (i.e. you cannot claim retrospectively and say that you had the vehicle off the road).

Most people apply for a refund either when they take their car off the road (e.g. because it needs major repairs), or if they sell the vehicle and decide not to include the road tax in the price. To claim the refund fill in form V14 (from main post offices and local vehicle licensing offices). Send this, with the tax disc, to the DVLC, Swansea SA99 1AL. If you cannot attach the tax disc (for instance, if it has been lost or stolen) you can still obtain a refund. But you will have to fill in a different form (V33), also obtainable from local vehicle licensing offices and post offices. This is also sent to the DVLC, Swansea SA99 1AL.

The Motorist and the Law

*What if my tax disc is lost or stolen?*

You can apply for a duplicate. Fill in form V20 (from local vehicle licensing offices and main post offices) and post or take this to the local office with the registration document and fee (£2.00). Normally you will be issued with a temporary duplicate on the spot, which will give you temporary cover while the vehicle records are checked. Once that has been done you will be issued with a full duplicate tax disc. If your name is not in the registration book (e.g. you have recently bought it) no temporary tax disc will be issued – you will have to wait until the records have been checked. Finally, it is possible to apply for a duplicate licence to the DVLC, Swansea SA99 1AG (same form and documents, etc.), but they will not issue a temporary tax disc (so do not apply to them if you want to use the vehicle straight away).

*How much is road tax?*

The amount changes frequently. To check the up-to-date figures ask for pamphlet V149 from the post office. This sets out full details of road tax rates.

As an alternative you can buy a disc for six months only (unless the annual duty is £18 or less, in which case you can buy only a twelve-month licence). If you do this you will find that two six-month licences will cost you 10 per cent more than one twelve-month licence. If you want to save up for a licence you can buy saving stamps from post offices (sold in units of £5) which you can later use towards the cost of the licence.

There are different tax rates for different categories of vehicle. If a vehicle is altered, so that it now belongs to a different category (e.g. a private vehicle is now used for trade purposes), the DVLC should be notified. In addition form V70 should be sent to a local vehicle licensing office if the existing tax disc has to be changed.

Also, see 'Commercial Vehicles', pp. 67–76. The numbers of the forms quoted in this section do not apply to heavy goods vehicles (there are different forms for these).

*Will I save any road tax if I have a van (or an estate car with the windows covered over) instead of a car?*

No – though you may save a different type of tax when you purchase the vehicle new (this is because trade vehicles do not pay the same tax). But it will make no difference to your road tax each year. Light goods vehicles (up to 1,525 kilograms) are taxed the same amount as private vehicles. If you do make any alterations to the vehicle you must tell the DVLC. Do this by sending the registration document (give details of the changes on the document) and send it to the DVLC, Swansea SA99 1AR. The DVLC should be told if you change the colour, engine, fuel type, cylinder capacity or weight of a goods vehicle. In addition Customs and Excise have to be told if you do anything that would affect the amount of vehicle tax that would have been paid when the vehicle was bought (i.e. not road tax). For instance, if you add side windows or passenger seats to a van you might have tax problems. To check the position ask for customs notice 672.

### What about the fourteen-day period of grace when applying for a new tax disc?

You are allowed a fourteen-day period in which to apply for your new tax disc, after the old one has expired. Strictly speaking the new tax disc should be received (and displayed on the vehicle) before the fourteen days runs out. In practice the police will usually not prosecute if it can be shown that the licence was applied for within the fourteen-day period.

The fourteen-day period of grace applies only when you are renewing an existing licence. If you have a new car (or you are putting a car back on the road after it has been off the road) you must get the tax before you put the car on the road – you do not have a fourteen-day period in which to apply.

### What about displaying the tax disc?

On a car the tax disc must be on the nearside of the windscreen. Some drivers like to put it in the centre of the windscreen, in front of the mirror, so that it does not obstruct the view; this is illegal. On motorbikes and scooters, etc. the tax disc must be on the nearside of the vehicle, in front of the driving seat and in a weatherproof holder.

Failing to display a tax disc is not the same as being prosecuted for not having tax. Failure to display the licence usually attracts a fixed penalty of £12. If that fixed penalty is not paid prosecution will result, and there is a maximum fine of £400. The only possible defence to a charge of failing to display a tax disc is that the fourteen-day period of grace applies (provided the licence is in fact renewed within that period). In one case a motorist left his car locked, and while he was away the plastic holder containing the licence fell from the windscreen on to the floor of the car. He was convicted for failing to display the licence! In practice, of course, when the motorist is totally blameless – as in that case – the court would normally give an absolute discharge, although the motorist would, strictly speaking, still be guilty. See p. 237 for an explanation of absolute discharge. The same would probably apply if the tax disc was stolen.

On the other hand, if the tax disc is not displayed because there is in fact no tax disc at all (i.e. you have not renewed your tax), the court will take a much stricter line. In addition you will probably be prosecuted for the other offence of not having tax as well.

### What are the penalties for not having road tax?

In practice relatively few tax-dodgers are prosecuted. The offender will probably be sent a letter offering the chance to pay a mitigated penalty instead, within fourteen days, to avoid being prosecuted. This will probably happen if the vehicle has been untaxed for no more than six months (three months in London), and provided that no other prosecution is being brought at the same time. The vast majority of tax-dodgers are offered the chance of paying a mitigated penalty, and do pay it. When this happens the penalty is usually on the basis of: the back duty × 1½ + £10. For instance, if a car had been untaxed for four months (assuming road tax at £90 a year), the penalty would be £30 × 1½ + £10 = £55. When the chance to pay a mitigated penalty is offered it is important that the motorist pays straight away – leaving it for more than fourteen days will almost certainly result in prosecution (and it will then be too late to pay the mitigated penalty instead).

In the rare cases that are prosecuted (because either the offence is too serious, or the motorist does not accept the offer of a mitigated penalty within fourteen days) much severer penalties can apply. In theory the fine can be up to £400 (or up to five times the annual tax due, if that would be greater) plus the amount of the tax due. For instance, if it could be shown that tax had been unpaid for two years (at £90 road tax per year) the maximum penalty could be 5 × £90 + £180 = £630. In practice it is extremely unlikely that the fine would be so high. Normally one would think in terms of having to pay the tax owed plus a fine of twice that amount (i.e. the eventual cost would be three times the amount of the tax unpaid).

It is not easy to put up a defence to such a charge. For example, it would be no defence to argue that the documents were in the post, and that you were simply waiting for the tax disc to arrive (unless, of course, the fourteen days' grace applied). Similarly it would do no good to pop out and get tax a few minutes after you have been spotted by the police! These circumstances merely mitigate the severity of the offence – you might therefore get away with a lesser fine, but you will still be guilty of the offence.

It is calculated that about one in ten motorists dodge road tax. This costs the rest of us about £175 million a year. The obvious solution would be to abolish road tax and recover the money lost by increasing the tax on petrol. It is calculated that this would put up the price of petrol by about 35p per gallon.

### Are there any concessions for the disabled?

If you are disabled you may not have to pay road tax (see p. 86).

### What if my cheque for the road tax bounces?

Any tax disc you pay for with a cheque that bounces is invalid. It is as though no tax disc was ever issued. You can therefore be prosecuted for not having road tax (see above).

### Do I need road tax on private roads?

No. The law says that you must have a tax disc if you drive or park on a public road. The police do not actually have to prove that you own the vehicle for you to be liable; if you are 'in control' of it (e.g. you use it) you must make sure it has a tax disc. The only occasion when you can drive on a public road without a tax disc is if you are going to a prearranged MOT test (but the test *must* have been fixed in advance). It is no defence to say that you were driving to a garage so that the car could be repaired; you should tow it instead. If you do not use the vehicle on public roads you do not need road tax. For instance, if you use a private road, or keep to agricultural land, you do not need road tax. But if ever the vehicle goes on the public road you must have tax. For instance, a farmer with two fields on different sides of the road must have road tax for a tractor that goes from one field to the other.

## WHAT'S THE PENALTY?

*For not displaying a tax disc*
MAXIMUM PENALTY: a £400 fine
LIKELY PENALTY: a £15 fine. You may get a £12 fixed penalty
ticket instead (see p. 217)

*For not having road tax*
MAXIMUM PENALTY: a £400 fine, or five times the annual road
tax plus the tax due (whichever is greater)
LIKELY PENALTY: a fine of twice the road tax avoided plus the
road tax (i.e. three times the total tax dodged)

*(For more on penalties see p. 216)*

## Registration Documents

### What is a registration document?

The registration document shows who is the keeper of a vehicle. But it
need not be the person who is the owner. Often the owner and the
keeper are the same person – but the fact that someone's name is on the
registration book does not prove that they own the vehicle. This is a
point to bear in mind when you buy a secondhand vehicle from someone
you do not know.

The registration document is no more than a current summary of the
keeper's name and address, the registration number of the vehicle and
other information about it (e.g. cubic capacity, colour, etc.). A new
registration document is issued each time the details change.

### What is a log book?

Before all the vehicle registration records were computerized at the
DVLC there was a localized system of issuing registration books. These
were called log books. A log book stayed with a particular vehicle
throughout its life (i.e. it was not replaced whenever the details in it were
changed). Log books are now obsolete, having been replaced by registration documents. So registration documents issued by the DVLC are
not log books – although many people still call them by this name.

*How do I get a registration document for a new vehicle?*

The dealer will normally arrange this for you, by filling in form V55, with your name and address. Some weeks later you will be sent the registration document from the DVLC. You should check that all the particulars are correct – if they are not return it to the DVLC.

If you want to go abroad with the vehicle within three weeks of buying it the DVLC can issue a temporary certificate of registration to cover you while you are abroad. However, if you want such a certificate you should make sure the dealer tells the DVLC of this when registering your car.

*How do I register a secondhand car?*

Whoever is selling you the car should give you the registration document with the car. You should check that their name is in the document as the registered keeper. If it is not – or if they cannot give you the document – you should be very careful and ask for an adequate explanation. You would be unwise to part with your money. Remember that a person can be named in the registration book as the keeper, and yet not be the owner (see 'Buying and Selling a Car', p. 55).

As soon as you buy the vehicle you should tell the DVLC. You can do this simply by completing the back of the registration document. You should not wait until you next need to tax the car.

If, for some reason, you do not have the registration document (e.g. the seller could not give it to you or you have lost it) you must still notify the DVLC. You will have to complete form V62 (obtainable from local vehicle licensing offices and main post offices), which you then send to the DVLC, Swansea SA99 1AR. There is no fee (provided you bought the car from someone who did not give you the registration document).

Why should you bother to tell the DVLC? The answer is that, if you do not, you will be committing an offence. In addition there are more mundane, practical reasons. For instance, you will not be sent a reminder about the expiry of your road tax; nor will the DVLC be able to tell you if there is a possible safety defect in your vehicle.

Whoever you bought the vehicle from should also write to the DVLC. They should tear off the bottom part of the registration document and send it to the DVLC. If they do not do this they commit an offence.

The Motorist and the Law

***Must I tell the DVLC if I change my name or address?***

Yes. The DVLC must be told if you change your name (e.g. by marriage), or if you change address. To do this, you simply fill in the back of the registration document and post it to the DVLC. If you do not, you will be committing an offence.

***Can I get a replacement registration document?***

Yes. If you lose your registration document you can apply for a replacement. Complete form V62 (obtainable from local vehicle licensing offices and main post offices) and send it to the DVLC, Swansea SA99 1AR. There is a fee of £2.

The same applies if the registration document is stolen. But if it is the car that is stolen – not the registration document – you need not tell the DVLC. Report the theft to the police, who will automatically tell the DVLC.

***What if my car is written off or scrapped?***

If your car is written off there are two possibilities. Either the insurance company will buy the wreckage from you, or you will hold on to the wreckage yourself (in which case they may deduct a few pounds, for the scrap value, from your settlement cheque).

If the insurance company takes the vehicle you must transfer the vehicle to them. You do this in the usual way – complete the tear-off part of the registration document and send it to the DVLC. The rest of the document goes to the insurance company.

If you are left with the wreckage you should send the registration document to the DVLC and tell them that the vehicle has now been broken up. On the other hand, if you transfer the vehicle to someone else (e.g. a scrap merchant) you follow the usual procedure on transfer of a vehicle – complete the tear-off part of the registration document and send it to the DVLC. The person you have sold the vehicle to should then send the rest of the registration document to the DVLC, in the usual way.

### Can I find out the names of previous owners of my car?

You can find out about previous keepers (remember, this may not be the same as the owner) of your car. Write to Enquiries, Record Section, at the DVLC, Swansea SA99 1AN. There is no fee. It can take some time before you receive a reply.

### Will the DVLC tell me who owns a particular vehicle?

Usually, no. As a member of the public you have no right of access to the records at the DVLC, so you cannot insist on being told who owns a particular car or vehicle. However, in certain circumstances you may be able to find out this information. If you can convince the DVLC that you have a valid and sufficient reason for wanting the information they will give it to you (the fee is £2). For instance, if you want to trace a witness to an accident they might give you the name of the keeper of the vehicle that the witness was in at the time. In practice you may find it better to have your solicitor write this letter for you. Bear in mind that the DVLC will want a good and substantial reason. Mere curiosity to know who owns a particular car will not be enough.

### How do I transfer personal numberplates?

There are complicated rules to follow. What you should do depends on whether you are buying personalized numberplates from someone else, or whether you are trying to transfer your own personalized number-plates to a different vehicle:

*When you buy numberplates*, from a dealer or another motorist. The important point to realize is that the numberplates must be on another vehicle. You cannot have numberplates without a vehicle. However, the person selling you the numberplates will have to allow the local vehicle licensing office to inspect that vehicle. All you need to do is to complete form V317) obtainable from local vehicle licensing offices or main post offices), but make sure that the seller signs the form on the reverse side.

*If you are transferring the numberplates to another car.* Again, you apply on form V317. You should take, or send, the registration documents for both vehicles – the old (donor) vehicle and the new (receiving) vehicle – to the local vehicle licensing office. If the new vehicle has not yet been registered you should take the application form for first registration of the vehicle (form V55 – see above). You will also have to take MOT certificates (if needed) and tax discs for both vehicles. Finally, you will need the fee (£80). The local vehicle licensing office may then ask to inspect the old (donor) vehicle, and perhaps even the new (receiving) vehicle.

Problems arise if the old (donor) vehicle is unlicensed, and will not pass another MOT test, in which case there are restrictions on when the numberplates can be transferred. You can only transfer the number-plates from this old vehicle if you were the registered keeper (i.e. your name was in the registration document) when the last licence expired, and in addition you must apply within six months of that tax running out. It follows that you cannot buy an old vehicle, which has not been taxed for some time, off a scrap heap and expect to be able to transfer the numberplates.

The rules on transfer of personalized and cherished numberplates are complicated. There are notes attached to form V317 that you should read; if you need more information telephone a local vehicle licensing office.

### Can I alter the position of the numberplates on my car?

Probably not. There are detailed regulations on the location of number-plates (i.e. height from the ground, etc.), and also on their dimensions. In particular the numberplates must be flat, and facing squarely to the

---

## WHAT'S THE PENALTY?

*For altering a registration document*

*For the buyer not notifying the DVLC*

*For the seller not notifying the DVLC*

*For not notifying the DVLC of a change of name or address*

*For not having numberplates or for having dirty numberplates*
MAXIMUM PENALTY: a £400 fine
LIKELY PENALTY: a £15 fine. For numberplate offences you may get a £12 fixed penalty ticket instead (see p. 217)

*For failure to produce a registration document to the police see p. 242*

*(For more on penalties see p. 216)*

---

front/rear. It follows from this that it is not legal, for example, to take off an existing numberplate and put stick-on letters on your bonnet. Bear in mind also that there are rules on the lighting of numberplates, and if you move the plates you will have to make sure that your new plates do not break those rules.

### What is the system of vehicle index marks?

Since 1904 all vehicles have had to have a registration number. Since 1963 we have operated a seven-digit system (with a single letter at the beginning, or the end, of the number), as follows:

*If the letter is at the end of the number*

| | |
|---|---|
| A – 1 January 1963 | M – 1 August 1973 |
| B – 1 January 1964 | N – 1 August 1974 |
| C – 1 January 1965 | P – 1 August 1975 |
| D – 1 January 1966 | R – 1 August 1976 |
| E – 1 January 1967 | S – 1 August 1977 |
| F – 1 August 1967 | T – 1 August 1978 |
| G – 1 August 1968 | V – 1 August 1979 |
| H – 1 August 1969 | W – 1 August 1980 |
| J – 1 August 1970 | X – 1 August 1981 |
| K – 1 August 1971 | Y – 1 August 1982 |
| L – 1 August 1972 | |

*If the letter is at the beginning of the number*

| | |
|---|---|
| A – 1 August 1983 | C – 1 August 1985 |
| B – 1 August 1984 | D – 1 August 1986 |

In addition the letters in the numberplate indicate where the vehicle was registered. To find out where, look at the last two letters and then refer to the chart in Appendix 2 (p. 304). For instance, the number B123 AHT shows that the vehicle was registered between 1 August 1984 and 31 July 1985 at Bristol.

# Seat Belts

### Must I always wear a seat belt when I am driving?

Yes. The general rule is that, as the driver of a vehicle, you must wear a seat belt, unless you are reversing (or unless you come within one of the exemptions mentioned on p. 273).

### Must a passenger always wear a seat belt?

A front-seat passenger will normally have to wear a seat belt. A rear passenger does not have to wear a seat belt, even if one is fitted (although it is possible there will soon be a change in the law).

The only exception for front-seat passengers applies when there is more than one front passenger seat (e.g. in a minibus, when there may be two separate front passenger seats). In this case the passenger in the middle seat need not wear a belt, but the other passenger must. If no one is sitting in the other passenger seat, the middle passenger must then wear a seat belt – usually, of course, this will mean having to move over to the other passenger seat.

### What if my passengers won't wear a seat belt; can I be prosecuted?

No – unless your passenger is under fourteen years old. If the passenger is fourteen or more you cannot be prosecuted – though your passenger can be!

### When do children have to wear seat belts?

If a child is a front-seat passenger it must wear a seat belt: the rules are the same as for adults (see above). A child under one year old must be in an approved child safety seat if it is travelling in the front of the car. Incredibly there is no legal requirement for a child in the back of a car to be in a safety seat.

## Can I apply to be exempted from the seat belt laws?

Yes, but only on certain grounds. Some drivers are automatically exempted; for instance, delivery drivers (e.g. postmen/women and milk roundsmen/women), taxi drivers and garage staff driving under trade plates who are checking out a vehicle for faults. But the exemptions are very narrowly defined – and apply on as few occasions as possible. For example, the delivery drivers exemption applies only if the vehicle is made or adapted for delivery, so it would not apply to a newsagent delivering papers from an ordinary car, but it would apply to milk deliveries from a milk float. Also, the delivery must be 'local', so the exemption would not apply on a long journey between the main depot and the area in which the goods were to be delivered. Similarly the taxi drivers exemption applies only when the taxi is actually being hired.

In addition there is a general exemption for all drivers when reversing (this also applies to a qualified driver accompanying a learner when the learner is reversing). Other exemptions include:

- the police (when protecting or escorting someone)
- firemen/women (when putting on their special clothing and equipment)
- if the seat belt has become damaged, or is defective (or if there is an inertia reel mechanism which has locked because the vehicle has been used on a hill). But see below.

It is possible to apply for exemption from the seat belt laws because of a medical condition. To do this you will need a medical certificate from a doctor, confirming that it is inadvisable on medical grounds for you to wear a seat belt. Doctors are wary about giving out these certificates. If you have a medical certificate, and are warned that you may be prosecuted for not wearing a seat belt, you must normally produce your certificate to the police station within seven days (see p. 239).

A doctor can charge for supplying a certificate of exemption under the seat belt rules. However, there is an alternative: if you are registered as disabled with the Department of Employment, or receiving certain DHSS benefits (a mobility allowance, attendance allowance, or war or industrial injuries constant attendance allowance) you can apply for a free examination at a DHSS Medical Boarding Centre. To apply for the free examination fill in the form at the back of a pamphlet called *Seat Belts: The Law and You* which can be obtained from the DHSS, or from a CAB. It also provides a useful summary of all the other rules on seat belts.

### What if my car does not have seat belts?

Most cars must have them: any car which was made after July 1964 and first registered after January 1965 must have seat belts. Most goods vehicles had to have seat belts as from April 1967; dual-purpose goods and motor car vehicles should have had them since October 1979.

If you have a vehicle that does not need seat belts (e.g. if it is a car made before July 1964) you cannot be prosecuted for failing to wear a seat belt – even if belts are in fact fitted!

### What if a seat belt is damaged?

There is a legal duty to maintain seat belts. For instance, the belt must be readily adjustable, and there must be no visible faults (fraying in the belt which might affect its performance). If the belt is damaged there is no need to wear it (see above). Bear in mind, however, that an offence may well be committed if the seat belt is damaged – realistically, the only defence is to show that the defect arose after the journey had begun.

---

## WHAT'S THE PENALTY?

*For not wearing a front seat belt*

*For the driver of a vehicle when a person under fourteen is not wearing a front seat belt*

*For a defective seat belt*

MAXIMUM PENALTY: a £100 fine

LIKELY PENALTY: a £20 fine. You may get a £12 fixed penalty ticket instead (see p. 217)

*(For more on penalties see p. 216)*

---

### I was injured in an accident, but was not wearing my seat belt. Can I still claim compensation?

Here we are dealing with the question of compensation following an accident. We are not concerned with criminal liability (i.e. have you committed a criminal offence by not wearing a seat belt?), but with whether failure to wear a seat belt can be held against you in any damages claim. Are you barred from claiming damages because you were not wearing a seat belt?

The answer is that the courts take a dim view of someone who does not wear a seat belt. The courts' approach is to say that wearing a seat belt can reduce the severity of injury, so if you do not bother to wear a seat belt you cannot expect to recover all your damages in full. In other words, you must expect a deduction from those damages because of your failure to wear the seat belt. There is no hard-and-fast rule, but in practice, if you were a front-seat passenger who failed to wear a fitted seat belt, you could expect to lose about 25 per cent of your damages. The same would apply if you were the driver (not wearing a belt) and you were claiming damages from another negligent driver.

Relatively few people realize that they can lose a quarter of their damages in this way. Obviously the loss of a quarter of your damages after an accident will be a much more serious penalty than any fine that may be imposed for not having worn a seat belt!

### Are rear seat belts compulsory?

No. It is not yet compulsory to fit rear seat belts (or to wear them if they are fitted). However, it can only be a matter of time before the fitting and wearing of rear seat belts is made compulsory. When it became compulsory to wear front seat belts there was a saving of 350 lives, and 4,500 serious injuries, in the first year. Apart from that there was a massive financial saving – about £120 million (enough to run four whole health districts for a year!). The experts argue over how many lives would be saved by making it compulsory to use rear seat belts – but the minimum figure would seem to be about 350 lives saved each year.

## Crash Helmets

### When can I ride my motorbike without a crash helmet?

You cannot. Only if you were driving on private property (i.e. not on the public highway) could you avoid the requirement to wear a crash helmet. The only other possible way of avoiding prosecution is if you are a Sikh – Sikhs are exempted from the crash helmet regulations while wearing turbans.

The helmet must be of an approved type. In fact there are now detailed regulations prohibiting the sale of non-approved helmets. In addition the helmet must be properly done up; it is an offence to wear it unfastened, or only partly fastened.

Pillion passengers must also wear crash helmets. Sidecar passengers need not.

## WHAT'S THE PENALTY?

*For not wearing a crash helmet on a motorbike*
MAXIMUM PENALTY: a £100 fine
LIKELY PENALTY: a £15 fine. You may get a £12 fixed penalty ticket instead (see p. 217)

*For more than one passenger on a motorbike*

*For a passenger sitting sideways on a motorbike*

*For a passenger not on a proper seat on a motorbike*
MAXIMUM PENALTY: one penalty point (plus an endorsement) and a £400 fine. Disqualification possible
LIKELY PENALTY: one penalty point (plus an endorsement) and a £25 fine. You may get a £24 fixed penalty ticket (plus one penalty point) instead (see p. 217)

*(For more on penalties see p. 216)*

# Speeding

## Is there a general 70 m.p.h. speed limit?

No! Most people think there is, but there is not. The 70 m.p.h. limit applies only to motorways and dual carriageways. Other main roads have a general speed limit of 60 m.p.h.

## When is there a 30 m.p.h. limit?

The general rule is that there is a 30 m.p.h. limit if there are street lights no more than 200 yards apart. If the lights are more than 200 yards apart there will not be a 30 m.p.h. limit – unless one has been imposed, in which case there should be signs.

In effect the 30 m.p.h. limit applies to built-up areas. But it does not follow that every built-up area is subject to a 30 m.p.h. limit – or that areas that are not built up do not have a 30 m.p.h. limit. Where the 30 m.p.h. limit applies is called a 'restricted area'.

## What if there are no signs imposing a 30 m.p.h. limit to be seen?

If you are in a restricted area (i.e. street lights no more than 200 yards apart – see above) 30 m.p.h. signs are not necessary. You will not be able to use the absence of signs as a defence.

On the other hand, if you are not in a restricted area (i.e. street lights are more than 200 yards apart) there must be 30 m.p.h. signs. So if you cannot see the signs (e.g. they were never there, or they have been knocked down in an accident or removed by vandals) you cannot be prosecuted.

The Motorist and the Law

### What if some of the street lights are broken?

If the street lights are no more than 200 yards apart you will automatically be in a 30 m.p.h. limit area. The fact that some of the street lights are broken will be irrelevant. This would be so even if some of the street lights had been knocked down.

### What speed limits are there for commercial vehicles?

Different speed limits apply to different types of goods vehicle. See the table on p. 70.

One point to note is that small vans (i.e. vans that are derived from cars, such as an Escort van) are treated as if they were cars. Thus the normal speed limit is 60 m.p.h., and 70 m.p.h. on motorways and dual carriageways. They are not subject to the normal restrictions on goods vehicles.

### What types of radar trap are there?

There are numerous electrical gadgets the police use.

Hand-held radar guns are popular. The main types are the MuniQuip, the Kustom and the MPH K-15. All these work on the basis of the Doppler effect (i.e. the radar beam is bounced off the car, and the frequency of the signal bounced back shows the speed of the car). Usually these guns are accurate up to 500 yards or so, and you would have great difficulty in convincing magistrates otherwise! But these guns can give false readings as a result of, for instance, low batteries, poor contact through the car light socket, interference from a radio, reflection from some other vehicle, and interference from TV transmitters and overhead cables, etc. In one famous case a hand-held radar gun was produced in court – when pointed at the magistrates it showed a speed of 175 m.p.h.!

Another type of speed trap is based on the Truvelo equipment. This uses two pieces of pressure-sensitive wire that are placed on the road, about two yards apart. When a car goes over it the speed can be calculated. A more popular alternative is Vascar. This is an on-board system, fitted to the police car. It is usually extremely accurate – provided the police operator has been properly trained, and measured the speed of the right car!

If you are prosecuted for speeding, and the evidence against you is based on a speed trap, you may feel that the equipment was inaccurate. By all means raise this defence before the magistrates, but do not expect to get very far with it. While magistrates may be sympathetic to these claims, the higher courts have made it quite clear that magistrates must not override clear-cut scientific evidence. If you want to show that the radar equipment was wrong it will be for you to produce clear evidence to that effect. This is extremely difficult to do.

### What evidence is needed for a speeding conviction?

It needs more than the word of just one police officer. There must be either two police officers, or one police officer plus radar equipment.

If the evidence came from one police officer alone, it would simply be your word against the officer's. However, if the police officer's opinion is backed up by other evidence (e.g. a speedometer, stopwatch, radar meter or Vascar) you can be convicted.

It follows therefore that, if you pass a stationary police motorcyclist, you cannot be got for speeding – provided you slow down by the time the motorcyclist catches up with you! This is because it is your word against the police officer's. On the other hand, if the police motorcycle was not stationary, the officer could have used the supporting evidence of the motorcycle's speedometer to bring a speeding charge. Or your saying sorry when stopped by the police motorcyclist would be sufficient to justify prosecuting you – you would have just provided the necessary corroboration!

### Must I be warned if I am going to be prosecuted for speeding?

Yes. You must be given a Notice of Intended Prosecution, or warned at the time. See p. 243 for the warning that has to be given. If you are not given a warning (or if you are not given a Notice of Intended Prosecution within fourteen days) you cannot be prosecuted.

### Is it legal to warn other motorists of a speed trap?

Perhaps! In 1907 there was a case involving a motorist who warned other motorists about police speed checks. He was prosecuted for obstructing the police – and acquitted. This was on the basis that he was merely reminding drivers that they should keep within the speed limits, and telling them that the police were checking. But, theoretically, if he had known that those other vehicles were travelling over the speed limit he could have been guilty of obstructing the police.

Surprisingly this case still seems to be law. The courts have made it clear that they dislike this case intensely, but – for the time being – it remains the law. So the answer would seem to be that you can flash your headlights at oncoming cars and so warn them of speed traps; but, if those cars are clearly speeding, you are not acting legally and are guilty of the offence of obstructing the police in the execution of their duty.

## WHAT'S THE PENALTY?

*For speeding on the motorway*

MAXIMUM PENALTY: three penalty points (plus an endorsement) and a £1,000 fine. Disqualification possible

LIKELY PENALTY: three penalty points (plus an endorsement) and a fine. The level of the fine will depend upon the extent of your speeding (and surrounding circumstances – weather, road conditions, amount of traffic, etc.). Generally the fine will be in the region of £1.75 or £2.25 per m.p.h. over the speed limit (but more for heavy vehicles). The court may consider disqualification if the limit was exceeded by more than 30 m.p.h. You may get a £24 fixed penalty ticket (plus three penalty points) instead (see p. 217)

*For speeding anywhere other than on a motorway*

MAXIMUM PENALTY: three penalty points (plus an endorsement) and a £400 fine. Disqualification possible

LIKELY PENALTY: three penalty points (plus an endorsement) and a fine. The level of the fine will depend upon the extent of your speeding, etc. (see above). Generally the fine will be in region of £1.50 or £2.00 per m.p.h. over the speed limit (but more for heavy vehicles). The court may consider disqualification if the limit was exceeded by more than 30 m.p.h. You may get a £24 fixed penalty ticket (plus three penalty points) instead (see p. 217)

*(For more on penalties see p. 216)*

# Traffic Lights and Traffic Signs

### What is the sequence of traffic lights?

The sequence is:

- *red:* this means stop. Wait behind the stop line on the carriageway
- *red and amber:* this also means stop. Do not pass through or cross the stop line until the green light shows
- *green:* this means you can go on, if the way is clear
- *amber:* this means stop, at the stop line. You can only go on if the amber light appears after you have crossed the stop line – or if you are so close to it that you may cause an accident by stopping.

### What happens if I don't have sufficient time to stop?

You are probably going too fast! As far as the red light is concerned, there is a total ban on your going over the stop line (i.e. the white line across the road, probably a few feet in front of the traffic lights themselves). If you have already passed that white line when the lights change to red you need not stop. You can carry on, though you should obviously take great care. However, if you are straddling the white line at the time the lights change to red (i.e. part of your car is over the line, and part is not) you must stop. As far as the law is concerned you would be committing an offence if you then allowed the rest of your vehicle to cross the white line. Although it may be impracticable for you to stop in time, the answer is that you must have been going too quickly in the first place.

In practice it is the change to amber (from green) that causes most problems. If you are approaching the lights, and find that the lights change from green to amber, you must stop. Basically the law treats the amber in the same way that it treats a red light: you must stop before you reach the white line. However, there is an exception – when the vehicle 'cannot safely be stopped' before passing the white line. So you can carry on over the white line if it would be unsafe to stop. Unfortunately it is not clear exactly what the phrase 'cannot safely be stopped' means. Presumably it covers the situation in which you would have to brake fiercely, and so run the risk of other vehicles driving into the back of your vehicle, or of your skidding. Bear in mind that, if you say you had to go through the amber light because you could not otherwise stop safely, the police may argue that you were going too quickly in the first place! – in which case you could face a careless-driving charge. In any event there is a catch-all provision which you may fall foul of: anyone using traffic lights must 'proceed with due regard to the safety of other users of the road'. So, if you were going so fast that you could not stop in time, it may be said that you were not proceeding with due regard to the safety of other road users.

### What does it mean when the lights change from red to red and amber?

Traffic lights go from 'red' to 'red and amber'. This is not the 'go' signal – you cannot roar away as soon as the amber light shows! The amber light is no more than a warning to you that the lights are about to change to green. But in the meantime it is as though the red light only was showing – there is a total prohibition on you crossing the white line in front of the traffic lights. If you move off while the lights are red and amber (i.e. before they change to green) you will be committing an offence.

One point to note is that all these traffic light rules are by reference to the stop line in front of the lights. Sometimes there may be a gap of a few yards between the stop line and the traffic lights. None the less it is the stop line that matters. For instance, if you have already crossed over the stop line, but have not yet reached the traffic lights, you need not stop if the lights change to red (subject, of course, to your proceeding with 'due regard to the safety of other road users' – see above). If there is no stop line painted on the road (or if it is scrubbed out) you should treat the traffic light as the stop line.

### Do emergency vehicles have to stop at traffic lights?

Emergency vehicles can jump the lights, but only if it is safe to do so. In fact the exemption for emergency vehicles (i.e. the fire, police and ambulance services) is not as wide as some police car drivers seem to think it is! What the law says is that, if the red traffic light would 'hinder' the emergency vehicle, the vehicle can jump the light, but only if the driver takes care. Firstly, drivers of these vehicles must not cause danger to other traffic. Secondly, they must behave just as if they were at a give way sign (i.e. between a major and a minor road) – in other words, they can cross the lights provided they do not cause danger to any other driver, and provided that no other driver has to swerve, or change speed, in order to avoid an accident. If they are sure they can do this safely they can jump the red light. In fact this exemption does not apply just to official vehicles of the emergency services – as the regulations are worded, it is probably the case that a private individual who is acting as ambulance, fire brigade or police could claim the exemption (e.g. a doctor going to the scene of an accident, or perhaps even the owner of a private car taking a seriously ill relative to hospital).

In practice the drivers of emergency vehicles who do wrongly jump the lights are unlikely to be prosecuted. If they are prosecuted, the chances are they will simply get an absolute discharge (i.e. they will be found guilty but no other penalty will be imposed – see p. 237). On the other hand, they would probably face a fine (plus endorsement and penalty points) if they had acted carelessly or recklessly.

### What if the traffic lights are broken?

This is a tricky question. Strictly speaking the regulations do not cover this situation – there is no exemption saying you can ignore traffic lights if they are broken or faulty. However, the probable answer is that, if you have reasonable grounds for thinking that the lights are faulty, you cannot be prosecuted for ignoring them. The logic behind this is that if traffic lights are defective the traffic light regulations themselves cannot apply. In any event, if you do decide to cross in defiance of the lights you must make sure you do so with care – if you don't you could face a careless-driving charge.

### What about temporary lights at roadworks?

From the legal point of view these are no different from fixed, permanent, traffic lights. The usual rules apply.

### What is the difference between a stop sign and a give way sign?

At a stop sign you must stop. At a give way sign you need not stop.

As far as a stop sign is concerned, you must always stop at the white line. This is so even if you can see that the other road is perfectly clear, and that there is no oncoming traffic. If you do not stop you will commit an offence. Remember that 'stop' means stop! If there is a stop sign it is not good enough simply to reduce your speed to a crawl, and check that it is safe to proceed. You must actually stop.

With the give way sign you can cross the dotted line without stopping – but only if it is safe to do so. In particular this means that you must be able to enter the other road without causing any other motorist to change speed or swerve to avoid an accident. Note that there is no need for an accident actually to occur for an offence to be committed – if another vehicle has to slow down because you have pulled out you have broken the give way rules. For instance, say you are at a crossroads and pull out – safely – to the centre of the road so that you can cross to the other side. If by straddling the middle of the road you block the carriageway, you will be committing an offence.

### Can I be prosecuted if I did not see the traffic sign, or if the traffic sign was damaged?

Your failure to see the traffic sign (whether it be traffic light, stop sign or white line on the road, etc.) is irrelevant – it is up to you, as a motorist, to keep your eyes open and proceed safely. Obviously, if the sign could not be seen from the road (e.g. a bush had grown up in front of it), that would be a different case: you would then be well advised to defend any charge, and argue that the sign was invalid.

The same applies if a sign is damaged. There are detailed regulations setting out the design and appearance of traffic signs, and if these are breached (e.g. because part of the sign has been broken off, or because the sign has been twisted round) the sign has no legal effect – and you therefore cannot be prosecuted for disobeying it. The AA or RAC may be able to give you advice on the detailed rules about traffic signs.

### What is the difference between a single white line and a double white line?

Single white lines do not normally have any legal significance. They are merely marks on the road that are designed to help and assist drivers. You will not be committing an offence if, for instance, you cross a single white line in the middle of the road. However, this assumes that you are driving in a safe and careful manner – if you are not, you could well face a careless-driving charge.

On the other hand, double white lines must be obeyed. There are two possibilities:

● when there are *two solid white lines* you cannot cross either of those lines
● when there is *one solid white line and one dotted white line* you cannot cross the solid white line if it is on your side of the road. If the dotted white line is on your side of the road you may cross both the white lines.

As always, there are a few exceptions. You can cross double white lines if:

● you are turning right
● you are overtaking a stationary vehicle
● there would otherwise be an accident
● you are signalled to do so by a police officer or traffic warden.

Note in particular that you can cross the white line to overtake a stationary vehicle. Not all motorists realize that this exception applies: so, if there is a large vehicle stationary on your side of the road, you can cross the white line to overtake it. But this would not be the case if there was an extremely slow-moving vehicle in front of you; if the vehicle is not stationary the exception does not apply. You must simply wait patiently until you have reached the end of the white lines.

We have all seen car drivers who overtake before the white lines begin, but who have reached the white lines by the time they have finished passing the cars. These motorists are breaking the law. Motorists who choose to overtake do so at their own risk. It is for them to make sure that it is safe to do so and that they will be able to complete their overtaking manoeuvre before they reach double white lines. If they misjudge the situation (or if the cars in front do not let them back in) they will be guilty of an offence – the simple answer is that they should never have overtaken in the first place.

How much of the vehicle has to be over the white line for the offence to be committed? The answer is that the vehicle is treated as crossing the line as soon as one of its tyres touches it. There is no need for the whole tyre to be over the line, let alone the whole vehicle. Merely touching the solid white line is enough!

As with all traffic signs there are detailed regulations which set out the size and layout of white lines on the road. If a mistake is made when the

lines are painted, so that they do not comply with the legal requirements, a motorist cannot be prosecuted for breaking those white-line
rules – provided the mistake was not just trivial. For example, in one
case double white lines were painted too close together – they were only
6 centimetres apart, whereas they should have been at least 9 centimetres apart. The court held that this was a trivial oversight, and the
motorist could not avoid conviction for crossing the double white lines.
The AA and RAC can give advice on these regulations.

### What about parking when there are double white lines?

Most motorists do not realize that double white lines prohibit parking as
well as overtaking. In fact, in some ways, the prohibitions on parking
when there are double white lines are more strict than those on
overtaking.

If there are double white lines you cannot park or stop your car.
Surprisingly this is so even if there is a dotted white line on your side of
the road. Though you can overtake if the dotted white line is on your
side of the road, you cannot park. The only exceptions are for stopping
to allow someone to get into the car (or to get out of it), to load or
unload, or for emergency services, etc.

### What about signals from a police officer or a traffic warden?

Failing to comply with traffic directions given by a police officer or traffic
warden is a specific offence. It applies to traffic being directed at a
junction and to motorists who do not obey the instructions being given.

The motorist must observe the traffic directions – even if the police
officer is not in uniform (compare the position with the power of the
police to stop vehicles – see p. 238 – when the police officer must be in
uniform).

A traffic warden whose signals have been disobeyed can demand that
offending motorists give their name and address. But traffic wardens
cannot demand to see motorists' documents (i.e. the registration book,
MOT and insurance certificates, and driving licence), whereas a police
officer can demand to see all these documents (see p. 238).

## WHAT'S THE PENALTY?

*For disobeying traffic lights*

*For disobeying a stop sign*

*For crossing double white lines*

*For disobeying a police officer's or a traffic warden's traffic sign*
MAXIMUM PENALTY: three penalty points (plus an endorsement) and a £400 fine. Disqualification also possible
LIKELY PENALTY: three penalty points (plus an endorsement) and a fine of £25 (perhaps £50 for disobeying a police officer's signals). You may get a £24 fixed penalty ticket (plus three penalty points) instead (see p. 217)

*For disobeying any other traffic sign*
MAXIMUM PENALTY: a £400 fine
LIKELY PENALTY: a £20 fine. You may get a £12 fixed penalty ticket instead (see p. 217)

*(For more on penalties see p. 216)*

### Who is to blame for an accident at traffic lights?

As always, it depends on the facts. When we talk about blame we are not concerned with criminal liability (e.g. can someone be prosecuted by the police for jumping the lights?), but with the question of who is to pay for the damage caused. This is a *civil* claim – suing for damages caused by the negligence of a motorist – completely separate from the question of prosecution. A motorist – or, more likely, the motorist's insurance company – will have to pay compensation (i.e. for the damage and injury caused) only if he or she was negligent. See p. 177 for more information on the negligence laws.

If you have the traffic lights in your favour, and you are then involved in an accident, the court will almost certainly award you full compensation from the other driver:

*A lorry wanted to turn right at a crossroads. The lorry driver went through the traffic lights when they were green, although immediately afterwards they turned to amber. He waited for the oncoming traffic to clear. As he began to pull away he could see a car approaching about twenty-five yards away. The lorry driver knew that the lights would be showing red to that car driver, so he assumed the car would stop. The car didn't – and the lorry drove straight into it. The owners of the lorry claimed compensation from the car driver. Held: the car driver was mainly to blame, since he had crossed red lights. However, the court that originally heard the case decided that the lorry driver was also partly to blame – the judge said that, before pulling away, he should have waited to see if the car would stop. So he found the lorry driver 10 per cent to blame. However, the appeal court would have none of this. In their view the lorry driver was totally blameless. It was unrealistic to expect the lorry driver (and any other road user) to expect that any oncoming vehicle would jump the lights! The lorry driver was quite blameless, and therefore full compensation had to be paid by the car driver.* Hopwood (1975)

In short, if you enter the traffic lights at green, and then wait to turn right, you can reasonably expect that oncoming vehicles will slow down and stop at the red light. However, this assumes that any oncoming car does have enough time in which to stop. If it is obvious that the car cannot slow down in time you will be partly to blame for the accident if you pull away in front of it.

Problems can arise when two vehicles approach from opposite directions when the lights are changing. When this happens it is possible for both drivers to be acting legally – in the sense that neither is 'jumping' the lights – and yet for an accident to occur. For instance, one motorist may not have sufficient time to slow down when the lights change to amber, and the other can be travelling through when the lights change to green. When this happens who is to blame? As always, each case must be decided on its own merits, and the court will try to apportion blame between the two motorists. Often this will mean that a 50/50 award is made – both drivers are found half to blame for the accident and get half the normal value of their claim (i.e. for injury, loss of earnings, damage to their vehicle, etc.) from the other. In other words, they both end up paying each other and claiming off each other!

However, a 50/50 apportionment will not be made if it seems that one of the motorists almost jumped the lights, by hurrying on when the lights changed from green to amber. That motorist is likely to be found more to blame for the accident:

*A lorry and a car collided at a crossroads. The lorry had crossed when the lights changed from green to amber, although it was probable that the lorry could have stopped in time. The car had crossed when the lights had just changed from red and amber to green. Held: the lorry driver was more to blame than the car, so the car driver got two thirds of his damages from the lorry driver and the lorry driver only got one third of his damages from the car driver. (In practice, of course, these claims would have been met by their insurance companies.)* Godsmark (1960)

The point to note about this case is that the car driver was held one third to blame, even though he had crossed when the lights had changed from red and amber to green. In other words, he had crossed when the light was green. You should always take care when approaching a junction when the lights have changed – you should keep an eye on cars that are still crossing. If those other vehicles have jumped the lights you will clearly not be to blame if there is an accident – but, as this case shows, it will be different if they have hurried through as the lights were changing.

All too often a motorist involved in a traffic lights accident will say that the lights were not working properly, and argue that they were out of adjustment. The courts are very wary about accepting such an argument, and will need clear independent evidence (e.g. police tests) before they are convinced – if they believed these claims too readily lots of negligent car drivers would try and put the blame on to faulty traffic lights.

See also the cases involving crossroads accidents – when a vehicle from a side road crashes into a vehicle on the main road (see p. 183).

# Tyres

### What are the rules on worn tyres?

Bald – or even partly bald – tyres are illegal. If any part of the tread of a tyre is worn down to the bottom of the groove, the tyre is illegal (even if it is the spare tyre that you have just taken out of the boot – but see p. 291).

It is not uncommon for a front wheel to be out of alignment or tracking; when that happens one side of the tyre wears out more quickly than the other. It is therefore possible to have a tyre which is badly worn down in one place, yet which has a lot of tread on the rest of the surface. Such a tyre is illegal.

Also, having the tyres at the wrong pressure can be illegal. If a tyre is so flat (or over-inflated) that it is 'unsuitable having regard to the use' to which the vehicle is being put, an offence is committed. In practice this provision is used against motorists who have extremely flat tyres.

In addition the tread across three quarters of a tyre's width must be at least 1 mm deep. The tread pattern on the remaining quarter (i.e. which need not be at least 1 mm deep) must still be visible.

---

## WHAT'S THE PENALTY?

*For worn or defective tyres*

MAXIMUM PENALTY: three penalty points (plus an endorsement) and a fine of £1,000 (£2,000 for a goods vehicle). Disqualification also possible

LIKELY PENALTY: three penalty points (plus an endorsement) and a fine of £40. There will be a separate penalty for each defective tyre. You may get a £24 fixed penalty ticket (plus three penalty points) instead (see p. 217). But if you did not know of the defect see p. 228

*(For more on penalties see p. 216)*

---

No part of the tyre ply or cord must be visible. In addition no cut more than 25 mm wide (or 10 per cent of the width of the tyre, whichever is greater) deep enough to reach the ply or cord is allowed.

Not surprisingly other obvious defects are also illegal: for instance, cuts, bulges and tears will nearly always be illegal.

Each defective tyre is a separate offence. A motorist who has two defective tyres will face two charges – and so two fines!

### What about knobbly tyres?

Scrambling motorbikes use knobbly tyres – tyres that have large knobs as the tread. Some farmers also use them on bikes that they use around their farms. The legality of these tyres is open to question, because at speed the knobs distort and grip is lost. Prosecutions have been brought against motorcyclists using these tyres; some have been convicted, and some have not. Generally it seems that the courts are prepared to acquit motorcyclists if they can show that they were riding carefully and, in particular, at a low speed.

### Are mini spare tyres legal?

In this country nearly all vehicles have a conventional spare wheel and tyre. But car manufacturers are anxious to save space and money, so they sometimes fit mini wheels as spares. These wheels are only designed to be driven for a short time, but they have the big advantage of being smaller and cheaper than normal wheels. Such wheels have been legal in many other countries. In the UK they are likely to become legal in 1986. Until a test case is brought on the point no one knows whether they are legal or not.

Incidentally, one point to note is that it is not a legal requirement that you carry a spare wheel in your car. If you do have one of these mini tyres as your spare you cannot be prosecuted unless you are in fact using it as the spare. Similarly, if you have a conventional spare tyre which is defective (e.g. it is partly worn), you will not be committing an offence until you actually use the defective tyre. Merely having it in your boot is not an offence.

### What is the difference between radial and cross-ply tyres?

In the old days all tyres were cross-plys. However, these days most new vehicles have radial tyres (on which the tread goes both across and along the tyre). Radial tyres are much safer: they give better grip and also use less petrol.

It is not a good idea to mix the two types of tyre. In any event it is illegal to have different types of tyre on the same axle, or to use radial-ply on the front and cross-ply at the back. It would be legal – although most unwise – to have radial tyres at the back and cross-plys at the front. It is more sensible (and safer) to have only one type of tyre on all four wheels. Make sure that the spare is of the same type – otherwise you will be committing an offence when you use it.

*Practical motoring:* **How can I avoid excessive tyre wear?**

Make sure that your tyre pressures are correct. They should be checked once a week – but make sure you check them when the tyres are cold, otherwise the readings will not be correct. If you drive with your tyres under-inflated they will soon wear out; this is because the tyre will be less rigid, and the extra bending increases the heat in the tyre, which in turn causes it to wear more quickly. When checking the pressures have a quick look for any nails, stones or glass caught in the tread and remove them, since they can become embedded in the rubber, and cause damage.

If the tyres are wearing unevenly find out why. It may be because the wheels are out of alignment, or it could be that the front wheels need to be balanced; it could also be that the brakes or suspension are out of adjustment. Either way, find out what the problem is and fix it.

*Practical motoring:* **What is aquaplaning?**

If a road is very wet there may be a continuous film of water all over the surface. It may be so bad that the tyre tread cannot cope, and becomes unable to penetrate the water and grip the road. When this happens your car will be sliding along the surface of the water, rather than gripping the road. The first you will probably know about this is when your steering begins to feel light; this is because your steering is in fact having no effect (nor will your brakes). When this happens, slow down – but do it as smoothly as possible. In particular do not apply the brakes suddenly since this may cause a skid. Simply take your foot off the accelerator and slow down gradually. The faster you go, the more chance there is of aquaplaning.

# Unsafe Vehicles

### Where will I find the laws on unsafe vehicles?

As you would expect, there are numerous laws setting out detailed requirements as to safety in vehicles. Unfortunately these laws are not collected in one convenient place. You would have to look through numerous road traffic acts, other acts and lots of regulations. As far as vehicle safety is concerned the most important rules are set out in what are called the Construction and Use Regulations, which are extremely detailed and lay down numerous minute requirements as to vehicle design and maintenance.

In particular, refer to:

- brakes (p. 37)
- goods vehicles (p. 69)
- lights (p. 150)
- MOT test (p. 171)
- noise (p. 187)
- police checks (p. 238)
- seat belts (p. 272)
- tyres (p. 290).

Many of the other regulations are much too numerous and detailed to mention in this book. For instance, there are detailed regulations on exhaust emissions, the design and location of bumpers, etc. If you have detailed queries of this sort you will have to consult one of the motoring organizations, such as the AA or RAC.

### What happens if I own a vehicle that is in bad condition?

It is not an offence to have an old banger, or a car that is slow and inefficient. But it is an offence to have a car that is dangerous, or which is otherwise unsafe (i.e. because it breaks the various regulations). If you have an old car you should check that it meets all the legal requirements.

If your vehicle breaks any of the numerous specific regulations dealing with such things as brakes, tyres, steering, lights, etc. you can be convicted. These laws are enforced strictly, and you will not be able to argue that you did not know of the defect (e.g. you did not know that one of the headlights was broken – but see p. 228).

Even if you do not break one of the specific regulations there is a catch-all provision that you might well fall foul of. Under the Construction and Use Regulations it is an offence to have a vehicle in a 'dangerous condition', which means that it must not be in such a condition that it is likely to cause danger or nuisance to anyone else. This can be an extremely wide-ranging offence. For instance, suppose you are a motorcyclist and decide to fit an extension piece to your exhaust; if the rest of the exhaust system is in good condition you will not be breaking the exhaust rules. However, if the extension pieces stick out at all it might be argued that the hot exhaust could cause a nuisance or danger to pedestrians and other road users (because of the heat and gases). Therefore you could be caught under the dangerous condition law – even though you had not broken the exhaust laws.

Similarly, if you remove the radiator grill from your car, you may be guilty of having a vehicle in a dangerous condition, because pedestrians may be able to put their hand in through the opening, and so touch the rotating fan blades. However, this is not a hard-and-fast rule – it all depends on the particular facts. In one case a Mini driver had removed the grille and yet was found not guilty, because the fan in a Mini is not at the front of the engine and so could not be touched by a pedestrian!

If you break one of the specific safety requirements (e.g. your car has defective brakes) the police can choose to prosecute you for either of two offences: they can either charge you for breaking the brake laws (see p. 37) or simply prosecute you for having a vehicle in a dangerous condition. They do not have to opt for the specific offence under the brakes rules. But they cannot prosecute you twice!

Do not forget that the police can often carry out spot checks on vehicles (see p. 241). For insecure loads on goods vehicles see p. 74.

### *What is a Vehicle Defect Rectification Scheme?*

In some parts of the country the police operate a Vehicle Defect Rectification Scheme. If you are found to have an unsafe vehicle, or one that is in bad condition, the police can give you the chance of fixing the defect (or scrapping the vehicle) as an alternative to being prosecuted.

The rules are simple. You will be reported for the offence, but you will be told that if you fix the defects (or scrap the vehicle) you will not be prosecuted. If you decide to accept this offer you will be given a written notice with details of your name and address, and details of the vehicle. The defects in the vehicle will be listed. You must then do one of two things: either have the defects fixed or have the vehicle scrapped within fourteen days. Strictly speaking, if you decide to have the defects fixed you must do so 'forthwith' – in other words, as soon as you possibly can – though in practice you would probably be allowed up to fourteen days. However, the best advice is to have the defects fixed straight away. You can do the work yourself or you can ask a garage to do it. Either way, you must have the work passed by an MOT garage. Take the vehicle to an MOT station, who will check that the defects have been fixed. Having done that, they will then stamp the written notice that was given to you by the police.

If you do not follow the rules – you fail to have the defects fixed or you do not scrap the vehicle – the police will prosecute you.

The Vehicle Defect Rectification Scheme is a marked change in the police approach to road safety. The idea is to encourage people to have safer vehicles. Many of the people who drive old bangers are hard-up: that is why they have vehicles that are not properly repaired. If they are prosecuted it is difficult for them to afford to pay the fine and also to have the vehicle mended. In practice, many people were found to pay the fine, but to continue to drive an unsafe vehicle. The advantage of the Vehicle Defect Rectification Scheme is that it encourages motorists to spend money on keeping their vehicles in good condition.

The Vehicle Defect Rectification Scheme is not nationwide. In 1986 there were only six police areas that were operating it (Nottinghamshire, Kent, Lancashire, Leicestershire, Gloucestershire and the West Midlands). So if you are stopped outside one of these areas there is no possibility of your being given the opportunity to have the defect fixed instead of being prosecuted. Bear in mind that, even if you are stopped in one of these areas, the Vehicle Defect Rectification Scheme is operated entirely at the discretion of the police. They can, if they prefer, simply prosecute in the usual way.

Nottinghamshire (which was the first to introduce the Vehicle Defect Rectification Scheme) is taking this Scheme one stage further with the introduction of a Driver Rectification Scheme, whereby some motorists who are involved in minor accidents (in which no one is injured) are given the opportunity to take eight hours' intensive tuition with police instructors as an alternative to being charged with careless driving. If they take the course they are not prosecuted. Once again, the idea is to improve the standards of road safety rather than simply prosecute.

### Is it illegal to sell a defective vehicle?

If you sell a vehicle that is in a dangerous condition you may well be committing an offence (see p. 58).

### What is the difference between 'using' a car, 'causing' an offence and 'permitting' an offence?

A person who drives a car may not be the person who owns the car, or who authorized its use. The law must make sure that the responsible person can be prosecuted, and so it is not enough merely to prosecute for 'driving' in a way that is against the law (e.g. having defective brakes). All these eventualities are covered by the following:

● *using*. Someone can be 'using' a car even if they are not driving. So if they are parked they will still be using it. Similarly a car can be used even if it is in such a bad condition that it won't go. On the other hand, if the car has been stripped or damaged to such an extent that it would never go (e.g. the engine has been taken out, or all the wheels have been taken off), that would probably not count as using
● *causing*. This covers a person telling someone else to use a vehicle, all the while knowing it to be defective. For example, an employer who tells an employee to use a vehicle, knowing its brakes to be defective, can be prosecuted for causing the vehicle to be used with defective brakes
● *permitting*. This is similar to causing, but the permission to use the car can be implied. The police simply have to show that the owner knew the car was being used, or deliberately turned a blind eye to its use.

For most motorists, of course, these legal niceties do not apply. Most motorists own and drive their own cars, so there is no need for 'causing' or 'permitting' to be used.

### Who is to blame if an accident is caused by an unsafe vehicle?

Nearly always, the owner or driver of the unsafe vehicle (as you would expect). When we talk about blame we are not concerned with criminal liability (e.g. can someone be prosecuted by the police for having a car in a dangerous condition?), but with the question of who is to pay for the damage caused. This is a *civil* claim – suing for damages caused by the negligence of a motorist – completely separate from the question of prosecution. A motorist – or, more likely, the motorist's insurance company – will have to pay compensation (i.e. for the damage and injury caused) only if he or she was negligent. See p. 177 for more information on the negligence laws.

The usual rule is that someone who drives a car in an unsafe condition will be liable for any accident it causes. Quite simply if you choose to take an unsafe vehicle on the roads you do so at your own peril. Only exceptionally will you be able to avoid blame. However, if you can show that the accident was caused by a mechanical defect – that you could not have known about – the court will have reluctantly to find that you were not negligent, and so no damages can be awarded against you. However, the courts bend over backwards to avoid doing this because they think it unfair that the victim should go uncompensated. In practice, therefore, it is almost unheard of for a court to allow the driver of an unsafe vehicle to blame it all on an unforeseen mechanical defect:

*A lorry's brakes failed when it was going downhill. The lorry crashed, and killed a man who was getting out of his car. The widow sued, wanting compensation for the death. In defence the owners of the lorry (in practice their insurance company) argued that the accident was not their fault. Expert evidence showed that it was caused by failure of a brake pipe which had corroded. The pipe could not be seen, even on normal inspection – it would have been necessary to remove the whole pipe from the lorry to inspect it. The lorry was only five years old, although it had done 150,000 miles. Held: the owners of the lorry were to blame. The court said it would only excuse the lorry owners for any blame if they could conclusively prove that they had done everything in their power to avoid this sort of thing happening (e.g. carrying out regular checks, making sure the vehicle was not used for loads that might be unduly corrosive, cleaning the underneath of the vehicle regularly, etc.). The widow was entitled to full compensation.* Henderson (1970)

*A bus crashed, killing four passengers. Expert evidence showed that the crash was due to a burst tyre. This was probably caused by a heavy blow to the tyre in normal use. Evidence was given that the bus company regularly checked tyres, although it did not remove them from the wheel rims. Held: the bus company was to blame. Their drivers should have known when tyres received bad knocks, and there should have been a system for reporting this to the bus company.* Barkway (1950)

So, in theory, as the owner of a defective vehicle you may be able to argue that you were not negligent in any way – that an accident wasn't your fault. In practice the courts do everything they can to avoid such a finding and you are almost certainly bound to have to pay compensation. When an accident is caused by a mechanical fault it is usually the case that the vehicle should have been checked and examined more regularly. Certainly, if the vehicle has not been checked regularly it would be extremely difficult for you to avoid liability. On the other hand, you may be able to say that you had the car serviced and checked – in which case it may be that the negligent garage will have to compensate anyone injured by the dangerous vehicle. For instance, if brake pads are not properly replaced the negligent garage will be to blame. In the case of an accident involving a new car the blame might pass to the car dealer it was bought from, or even the manufacturer (see 'Buying and Selling a Car', p. 44).

---

## WHAT'S THE PENALTY?

*For driving a vehicle in a dangerous condition*

MAXIMUM PENALTY: three penalty points (plus an endorsement) and a fine of £1,000. The maximum fine will be £2,000 for goods vehicles. Disqualification possible

LIKELY PENALTY: three penalty points (plus an endorsement). A fine of perhaps £50. The fine may be considerably more for a commercial vehicle. You may get a £24 fixed penalty ticket (plus three penalty points) instead (see p. 217)

*(For more on penalties see p. 216)*

---

# Appendix 1
# AA and RAC Legal-Advice Schemes

Both the RAC and the AA provide comprehensive legal services for their members. These are highly recommended.

The two schemes differ slightly in details. The current terms are set out below. Members should check with the RAC and the AA that these terms have not been changed in the meantime. Do bear in mind that both the AA and the RAC need ample warning if they are to be able to help with a motoring prosecution. Be sure that you comply with the time limits set out in the two schemes.

## AA Legal Services

### *The services available to members*

**1. Free legal representation**
The Association will pay the fee of its designated solicitor appointed for the representation of a member being prosecuted for a motoring offence, whether a plea of guilty or not guilty is made.

Upon application being made, the Association may support, in whole or in part, appeals against conviction and/or sentence on what is considered by the Association to be an important point of law or where the decision is contrary to the interests of members generally. (NB In such cases, the onus is upon the member to ensure that Notice of Appeal is served and lodged within the required period).

**Important conditions**
**a.** 'Designated solicitor' means such solicitor appointed by the Association and includes the fees of Counsel who may be instructed at the entire discretion of the Association.
**b.** 'Members' means all members of the Automobile Association (excluding Restricted Members, Fordcare Members and 5-Star Limited Membership class) who have paid the appropriate subscription before the date of the alleged offence and includes drivers who are in the paid employment of a member present in the vehicle at the time of the alleged offence.
**c.** 'Motoring offence' means an offence prosecuted in a Magistrates Court or its equivalent under the statutes governing the use or ownership of motor vehicles in

the United Kingdom, Republic of Ireland, Channel Islands and Isle of Man. (NB Excluding theft of motor vehicles or similar offences).

**d.** The member must complete and return to the Association a Free Legal Representation form in time for the designated solicitors to be properly instructed and co-operate throughout with those solicitors.

**e.** No other expenses of any kind (e.g. fees of a witness or expert, travel expenses or fees to solicitors instructed privately) will be reimbursed by the Association except with the prior consent of the Manager, Legal Services.

**f.** Special additional conditions may apply in the Republic of Ireland.

## 2. Claims recovery service

The Association will provide free advice to members on claims against other parties arising out of accidents involving a motor vehicle belonging to the member or for which he is responsible.

Negotiations to settle such claims may be undertaken in appropriate cases by solicitors designated by the Association after payment of a registration fee. The member will be indemnified in respect of those solicitors' costs, including all reasonable disbursements incurred by those solicitors such as police and medical reports, Counsel's fees, etc.

When such negotiations do not achieve a satisfactory settlement, and where there appears to the Association to be a reasonable prospect of a successful recovery being made in court proceedings, the Association will consider indemnifying the member in respect of his own legal costs in bringing such court proceedings.

## Important conditions

**a.** The service is available to those members who would be entitled to Free Legal Representation and have paid the appropriate subscription before the date of the accident, although Restricted Members may seek advice only in connection with a claim.

**b.** The accident must occur on the roads of the United Kingdom, Republic of Ireland, Channel Islands or the Isle of Man.

**c.** Negotiations in respect of the **defence** of claims made against a member are not undertaken.

**d.** The service extends to accidents involving foreign registered vehicles in this country.

**e.** The members must complete and return the Accident Report Form, incorporated within the Claims Recovery Service Booklet, to the Association and co-operate throughout with the solicitors instructed in the case.

## 3. Free legal advice

The Association will provide free advice on legal problems considered by the Association to arise directly from the use or ownership of a motor vehicle.

In such cases as the Association considers appropriate, and with the member's consent, attempts will be made to negotiate a satisfactory settlement in cases involving disputes with garages, motor dealers, etc.

Upon application being made, the Association may support, in whole or in part, claims which are considered by the Association to involve important points of law, or where the interests of members generally are being prejudiced.

**Important conditions**
**a.** The service is available to all members, excluding the 5-Star Limited Membership class.
**b.** The Association cannot give advice or act on behalf of members where the Association or a subsidiary company may be involved.
**c.** It is not usually possible to provide legal advice if the position is not governed by the laws of the United Kingdom, Republic of Ireland, Channel Islands or Isle of Man.

**4. Leaflets**
A range of leaflets has been prepared covering many topics of law in Great Britain which are raised by members most frequently. Copies are available on request from your Regional Headquarters or any AA Centre . . .

## How to obtain service

If you are writing to the AA for advice or assistance, address all correspondence to Legal Services at your Regional Headquarters.

Preliminary advice and guidance may be obtained by telephoning any of the Breakdown Service Centres listed . . . Most of these operate a 24 hour service. Similarly, you may telephone or call at any of the AA Centres listed . . . for preliminary advice and guidance.

**1. Free legal representation**
As soon as you think you may be prosecuted for a motoring offence, ask for a Free Legal Representation form which should be completed and returned to your Regional Headquarters . . . , together with the summons and any other relevant information.

It is important that all the papers are received at least 14 days before the court hearing date, otherwise it may be necessary for you to seek an adjournment from the court. Legal Services staff will advise you if this is necessary.

**2. Claims recovery service**
Following an accident, please contact your Regional Headquarters as soon as possible since delay may prejudice your claim. If general advice only is required, you will be sent a booklet containing helpful information to guide you.

In order that negotiation of your claim can be arranged, you should complete the Accident Report Form contained in the booklet and return the form together with all relevant information to your Regional Headquarters.

Legal Services staff will consider your description of the accident and advise whether reasonable grounds exist for making a claim. If so, you will be invited to pay a registration fee, following which the papers will be passed to solicitors designated by the Association . . .

### 3. Free legal advice

Please telephone or write to your Regional Headquarters.

Often only preliminary guidance can be given by telephone, and you may be asked to write providing full details.

Legal problems are often complex and may need research before advice can be given.

# RAC Legal Services

## *Legal*

**Free Legal Representation.** The recipient of a summons for a motoring offence is entitled to the benefit of legal representation by solicitor (or, at the option of the Legal Department, by counsel) appointed by the Legal Department in any court of summary jurisdiction in the United Kingdom (including the Isle of Man and the Channel Islands) or Eire on the following terms:

**1.** Application must be made to the Legal Department in Croydon at least 10 days before the hearing date on the RAC's printed form.

**2.** The date of the alleged offence must have been within the currency of membership.

**3.** The summons must be for a motoring offence arising out of the use or ownership of a vehicle covered by membership or of a type covered by the personal membership of the defendant or his or her spouse. Representation is also extended to a member's personal full time chauffeur in the course of his or her duties. Taxis, minicabs and PSVs are excluded.

**4.** The following are excluded: drink, drugs or excess alcohol offences; trade plate offences or those arising out of the use of a vehicle being tested or demonstrated or delivered by the motor trade; goods vehicle operators' licensing offences and those relating to hours of work or failure to keep records; criminal charges; illegal driving instruction offences.

**5.** The RAC reserves the right to refuse legal representation in cases in which the Legal Committee considers it desirable to do so.

**6.** Travelling expenses incurred by the solicitor are covered but not the cost of tracing or securing the attendance of witnesses, or fees of expert witnesses.

**7.** The RAC shall be entitled to reimbursement from the member of any costs resulting from his or her failure to keep an appointment or from the arrangement of adjournments to suit his or her convenience.

**8.** If a member wishes to stipulate that counsel shall be briefed, counsel's fees and any additional solicitors' fees involved must be borne by the member.

**9.** A member may if he or she so desires instruct his or her own solicitor. In such cases the RAC will pay an amount equal to the fee which a solicitor appointed by the Legal Department would have received if he or she had been instructed in the normal way, any balance will be the responsibility of the member. Completion of the RAC's printed application form is required for record purposes and a receipted solicitor's account must be provided. This concession applies only to representation on summonses and not to assistance with negotiations.

**Manslaughter.** The benefit of the Free Legal Representation Scheme extends to manslaughter charges, arising out of driving, both in the Magistrates' and Crown Courts. Experienced counsel will be briefed at the Crown Court, but it is to be understood that the conduct of the defence, including the selection of counsel, is left to the Legal Department.

**S.1. Road Traffic Act, 1972.** In cases of causing death by reckless driving the Free Legal Representation Scheme operates in respect of the preliminary hearing before the Magistrates but not at the Crown Court. The Legal Committee has a discretion to authorise contributions towards the cost of defences at the Crown Court.

**Removal of Disqualification.** The Legal Committee is prepared to consider authorising applications by solicitor for the removal of disqualifications imposed on members. Full details of the proceedings at which the disqualification was imposed, any previous convictions and reasons for requiring the return of the licence must be submitted . . .

**Financial Assistance.** The RAC is prepared to entertain applications for financial assistance towards the cost of legal representation in respect of cases not falling within the scope of the Free Legal Representation Scheme. Such applications are considered on their merits by the Legal Committee after full investigation of the facts.

**Appeals.** If a member suffers a conviction or sentence which appears to be a gross miscarriage of justice or wrong in law, the Legal Committee will consider the support of, or financial assistance towards, the conduct of an appeal. It is important to remember that notice of appeal may have to be lodged within 21 days of the date of conviction. In Scotland the time limit is in some cases only ten days.

**Inquests.** Representation either by solicitor or counsel at the discretion of the Legal Department will be provided for the member in respect of the death of his or her passenger in a traffic accident if the member is not entitled to have such representation arranged by his or her insurers. The benefit of such representation will also be given to the relatives of a member who is fatally injured while travelling in the member's private vehicle.

**Free Consultation with Solicitor.** Members are entitled to consult a solicitor of the Legal Department in Croydon or, by special arrangement in London, for the purpose of obtaining advice and assistance, where relevant, on any legal matter relating to the use or ownership of private motor vehicles, whether of a civil or criminal nature, free of charge. In the first instance, members should phone or write to the Legal Department in Croydon. Should a personal interview with a Solicitor subsequently be deemed necessary this may be arranged by prior appointment.

**Personal Injury and Accidental Damage Claims.** In civil claims for damages for personal injuries or uninsured losses arising during the currency of membership out of road traffic accidents in the United Kingdom and Eire in which members are involved as drivers or passengers in private motor vehicles, or commercial vehicles covered by membership, the RAC will, under its Claims Recovery Service, appoint a solicitor of its choice to advise and conduct negotiations up to the point at which litigation becomes inevitable. The RAC reserves the right to charge a small non-recoverable registration fee, but will otherwise bear the cost except disbursements (e.g. on police and medical reports) or such costs as are customarily recoverable from a third party or his insurers. The conduct of litigation or special enquiries is not covered.

# Appendix 2
# Vehicle Index Marks

To find out where a vehicle was registered, take the last two letters of the numberplate and refer to the chart below. For instance, a vehicle with the number C789 MNO was registered at Chelmsford (see also p. 271).

## Index Marks

These are listed in order Great Britain (England, Scotland and Wales) followed by Northern Ireland and Republic of Ireland.

### England, Scotland and Wales

| Index Mark | Office | Index Mark | Office |
|---|---|---|---|
| AA | Bournemouth | BA | Manchester |
| AB | Worcester | BB | Newcastle upon Tyne |
| AC | Coventry | BC | Leicester |
| AD | Gloucester | BD | Northampton |
| AE | Bristol | BE | Lincoln |
| AF | Truro | BF | Stoke-on-Trent |
| AG | Hull | BG | Liverpool |
| AH | Norwich | BH | Luton |
| AJ | Middlesbrough | BJ | Ipswich |
| AK | Sheffield | BK | Portsmouth |
| AL | Nottingham | BL | Reading |
| AM | Swindon | BM | Luton |
| AN | Reading | BN | Manchester |
| AO | Carlisle | BO | Cardiff |
| AP | Brighton | BP | Portsmouth |
| AR | Chelmsford | BR | Newcastle upon Tyne |
| AS | Inverness | BS | Inverness |
| AT | Hull | BT | Leeds |
| AU | Nottingham | BU | Manchester |
| AV | Peterborough | BV | Preston |
| AW | Shrewsbury | BW | Oxford |
| AX | Cardiff | BX | Haverfordwest |
| AY | Leicester | BY | London NW |

The Motorist and the Law

| Index Mark | Office | Index Mark | Office |
|---|---|---|---|
| CA | Chester | DY | Brighton |
| CB | Manchester | | |
| CC | Bangor | EA | Dudley |
| CD | Brighton | EB | Peterborough |
| CE | Peterborough | EC | Preston |
| CF | Reading | ED | Liverpool |
| CG | Bournemouth | EE | Lincoln |
| CH | Nottingham | EF | Middlesbrough |
| CJ | Gloucester | EG | Peterborough |
| CK | Preston | EH | Stoke-on-Trent |
| CL | Norwich | EJ | Bangor |
| CM | Liverpool | EK | Liverpool |
| CN | Newcastle upon Tyne | EL | Bournemouth |
| CO | Exeter | EM | Liverpool |
| CP | Huddersfield | EN | Manchester |
| CR | Portsmouth | EO | Preston |
| CS | Glasgow | EP | Swansea |
| CT | Lincoln | ER | Peterborough |
| CU | Newcastle upon Tyne | ES | Dundee |
| CV | Truro | ET | Sheffield |
| CW | Preston | EU | Bristol |
| CX | Huddersfield | EV | Chelmsford |
| CY | Swansea | EW | Peterborough |
| | | EX | Norwich |
| DA | Birmingham | EY | Bangor |
| DB | Manchester | | |
| DC | Middlesbrough | FA | Stoke-on-Trent |
| DD | Gloucester | FB | Bristol |
| DE | Haverfordwest | FC | Oxford |
| DF | Gloucester | FD | Dudley |
| DG | Gloucester | FE | Lincoln |
| DH | Dudley | FF | Bangor |
| DJ | Liverpool | FG | Brighton |
| DK | Manchester | FH | Gloucester |
| DL | Portsmouth | FJ | Exeter |
| DM | Chester | FK | Dudley |
| DN | Leeds | FL | Peterborough |
| DO | Lincoln | FM | Chester |
| DP | Reading | FN | Maidstone |
| DR | Exeter | FO | Gloucester |
| DS | Glasgow | FP | Leicester |
| DT | Sheffield | FR | Preston |
| DU | Coventry | FS | Edinburgh |
| DV | Exeter | FT | Newcastle upon Tyne |
| DW | Cardiff | FU | Lincoln |
| DX | Ipswich | FV | Preston |

| Index Mark | Office | Index Mark | Office |
|---|---|---|---|
| FW | Lincoln | HU | Bristol |
| FX | Bournemouth | HV | London (Central) |
| FY | Liverpool | HW | Bristol |
|  |  | HX | London (Central) |
| GA | Glasgow | HY | Bristol |
| GB | Glasgow |  |  |
| GC | London SW | JA | Manchester |
| GD | Glasgow | JB | Reading |
| GE | Glasgow | JC | Bangor |
| GF | London SW | JD | London (Central) |
| GG | Glasgow | JE | Peterborough |
| GH | London SW | JF | Leicester |
| GJ | London SW | JG | Maidstone |
| GK | London SW | JH | Reading |
| GL | Truro | JJ | Maidstone |
| GM | Reading | JK | Brighton |
| GN | London SW | JL | Lincoln |
| GO | London SW | JM | Reading |
| GP | London SW | JN | Chelmsford |
| GR | Newcastle upon Tyne | JO | Oxford |
| GS | Luton | JP | Liverpool |
| GT | London SW | JR | Newcastle upon Tyne |
| GU | London SE | JS | Inverness |
| GV | Ipswich | JT | Bournemouth |
| GW | London SE | JU | Leicester |
| GX | London SE | JV | Lincoln |
| GY | London SE | JW | Birmingham |
|  |  | JX | Huddersfield |
| HA | Dudley | JY | Exeter |
| HB | Cardiff |  |  |
| HC | Brighton | KA | Liverpool |
| HD | Huddersfield | KB | Liverpool |
| HE | Sheffield | KC | Liverpool |
| HF | Liverpool | KD | Liverpool |
| HG | Preston | KE | Maidstone |
| HH | Carlisle | KF | Liverpool |
| HJ | Chelmsford | KG | Cardiff |
| HK | Chelmsford | KH | Hull |
| HL | Sheffield | KJ | Maidstone |
| HM | London (Central) | KK | Maidstone |
| HN | Middlesbrough | KL | Maidstone |
| HO | Bournemouth | KM | Maidstone |
| HP | Coventry | KN | Maidstone |
| HR | Swindon | KO | Maidstone |
| HS | Glasgow | KP | Maidstone |
| HT | Bristol | KR | Maidstone |

| Index Mark | Office | Index Mark | Office |
|---|---|---|---|
| KS | Edinburgh | MP | London NE |
| KT | Maidstone | MR | Swindon |
| KU | Sheffield | MS | Edinburgh |
| KV | Coventry | MT | London NE |
| KW | Sheffield | MU | London NE |
| KX | Luton | MV | London SE |
| KY | Sheffield | MW | Swindon |
| | | MX | London SE |
| LA | London NW | MY | London SE |
| LB | London NW | | |
| LC | London NW | NA | Manchester |
| LD | London NW | NB | Manchester |
| LE | London NW | NC | Manchester |
| LF | London NW | ND | Manchester |
| LG | Chester | NE | Manchester |
| LH | London NW | NF | Manchester |
| LJ | Bournemouth | NG | Norwich |
| LK | London NW | NH | Northampton |
| LL | London NW | NJ | Brighton |
| LM | London NW | NK | Luton |
| LN | London NW | NL | Newcastle upon Tyne |
| LO | London NW | NM | Luton |
| LP | London NW | NN | Nottingham |
| LR | London NW | NO | Chelmsford |
| LS | Edinburgh | NP | Worcester |
| LT | London NW | NR | Leicester |
| LU | London NW | NS | Glasgow |
| LV | Liverpool | NT | Shrewsbury |
| LW | London NW | NU | Nottingham |
| LX | London NW | NV | Northampton |
| LY | London NW | NW | Leeds |
| | | NX | Dudley |
| MA | Chester | NY | Cardiff |
| MB | Chester | | |
| MC | London NE | OA | Birmingham |
| MD | London NE | OB | Birmingham |
| ME | London NE | OC | Birmingham |
| MF | London NE | OD | Exeter |
| MG | London NE | OE | Birmingham |
| MH | London NE | OF | Birmingham |
| MJ | Luton | OG | Birmingham |
| MK | London NE | OH | Birmingham |
| ML | London NE | OJ | Birmingham |
| MM | London NE | OK | Birmingham |
| MN | (not used) | OL | Birmingham |
| MO | Reading | OM | Birmingham |

| Index Mark | Office | Index Mark | Office |
|---|---|---|---|
| ON | Birmingham | RL | Truro |
| OO | Chelmsford | RM | Carlisle |
| OP | Birmingham | RN | Preston |
| OR | Portsmouth | RO | Luton |
| OS | Glasgow | RP | Northampton |
| OT | Portsmouth | RR | Nottingham |
| OU | Bristol | RS | Aberdeen |
| OV | Birmingham | RT | Ipswich |
| OW | Portsmouth | RU | Bournemouth |
| OX | Birmingham | RV | Portsmouth |
| OY | London NW | RW | Coventry |
| | | RX | Reading |
| PA | Guildford | RY | Leicester |
| PB | Guildford | | |
| PC | Guildford | SA | Aberdeen |
| PD | Guildford | SB | Glasgow |
| PE | Guildford | SC | Edinburgh |
| PF | Guildford | SCY | Truro (Isles of Scilly) |
| PG | Guildford | SD | Glasgow |
| PH | Guildford | SE | Aberdeen |
| PJ | Guildford | SF | Edinburgh |
| PK | Guildford | SG | Edinburgh |
| PL | Guildford | SH | Edinburgh |
| PM | Guildford | SJ | Glasgow |
| PN | Brighton | SK | Inverness |
| PO | Portsmouth | SL | Dundee |
| PP | Luton | SM | Glasgow |
| PR | Bournemouth | SN | Dundee |
| PS | Aberdeen | SO | Aberdeen |
| PT | Newcastle upon Tyne | SP | Dundee |
| PU | Chelmsford | SR | Dundee |
| PV | Ipswich | SS | Aberdeen |
| PW | Norwich | ST | Inverness |
| PX | Portsmouth | SU | Glasgow |
| PY | Middlesbrough | SV | Spare |
| | | SW | Glasgow |
| RA | Nottingham | SX | Edinburgh |
| RB | Nottingham | SY | Spare |
| RC | Nottingham | | |
| RD | Reading | TA | Exeter |
| RE | Stoke-on-Trent | TB | Liverpool |
| RF | Stoke-on-Trent | TC | Bristol |
| RG | Newcastle upon Tyne | TD | Manchester |
| RH | Hull | TE | Manchester |
| RJ | Manchester | TF | Reading |
| RK | London NW | TG | Cardiff |

| Index Mark | Office | Index Mark | Office |
|---|---|---|---|
| TH | Swansea | VF | Norwich |
| TJ | Liverpool | VG | Norwich |
| TK | Exeter | VH | Huddersfield |
| TL | Lincoln | VJ | Gloucester |
| TM | Luton | VK | Newcastle upon Tyne |
| TN | Newcastle upon Tyne | VL | Lincoln |
| TO | Nottingham | VM | Manchester |
| TP | Portsmouth | VN | Middlesbrough |
| TR | Portsmouth | VO | Nottingham |
| TS | Dundee | VP | Birmingham |
| TT | Exeter | VR | Manchester |
| TU | Chester | VS | Luton |
| TV | Nottingham | VT | Stoke-on-Trent |
| TW | Chelmsford | VU | Manchester |
| TX | Cardiff | VV | Northampton |
| TY | Newcastle upon Tyne | VW | Chelmsford |
| | | VX | Chelmsford |
| UA | Leeds | VY | Leeds |
| UB | Leeds | | |
| UC | London (Central) | WA | Sheffield |
| UD | Oxford | WB | Sheffield |
| UE | Dudley | WC | Chelmsford |
| UF | Brighton | WD | Dudley |
| UG | Leeds | WE | Sheffield |
| UH | Cardiff | WF | Sheffield |
| UJ | Shrewsbury | WG | Sheffield |
| UK | Birmingham | WH | Manchester |
| UL | London (Central) | WJ | Sheffield |
| UM | Leeds | WK | Coventry |
| UN | Exeter | WL | Oxford |
| UO | Exeter | WM | Liverpool |
| UP | Newcastle upon Tyne | WN | Swansea |
| UR | Luton | WO | Cardiff |
| US | Glasgow | WP | Worcester |
| UT | Leicester | WR | Leeds |
| UU | London (Central) | WS | Bristol |
| UV | London (Central) | WT | Leeds |
| UW | London (Central) | WU | Leeds |
| UX | Shrewsbury | WV | Brighton |
| UY | Worcester | WW | Leeds |
| | | WX | Leeds |
| VA | Peterborough | WY | Leeds |
| VB | Maidstone | | |
| VC | Coventry | XA | Spare Marks |
| VD | *Series withdrawn* | XB | |
| VE | Peterborough | XC | |

| Index Mark | Office | Index Mark | Office |
|---|---|---|---|
| XD | Spare Marks | YB | Taunton |
| XE | | YC | Taunton |
| XF | | YD | Taunton |
| XG | | YE | London (Central) |
| XH | | YF | London (Central) |
| XJ | | YG | Leeds |
| XK | | YH | London (Central) |
| XL | | YJ | Brighton |
| XM | | YK | London (Central) |
| XN | | YL | London (Central) |
| XO | | YM | London (Central) |
| XP | | YN | London (Central) |
| XR | | YO | London (Central) |
| XS | | YP | London (Central) |
| XT | | YR | London (Central) |
| XU | | YS | Glasgow |
| XV | | YT | London (Central) |
| XW | | YU | London (Central) |
| XX | | YV | London (Central) |
| XY | | YW | London (Central) |
| | | YX | London (Central) |
| YA | Taunton | YY | London (Central) |

## Northern Ireland and Republic of Ireland

| Index Mark | Office | Index Mark | Office |
|---|---|---|---|
| Z | Dublin | ZS | Dublin |
| ZA | Dublin | ZT | Cork |
| ZB | Cork | ZU | Dublin |
| ZC | Dublin | ZV | Dublin |
| ZD | Dublin | ZW | Kildare |
| ZE | Dublin | ZX | Kerry |
| ZF | Cork | ZY | Louth |
| ZG | Dublin | | |
| ZH | Dublin | AZ | Belfast |
| ZI | Dublin | BZ | Down |
| ZJ | Dublin | CZ | Belfast |
| ZK | Cork | DZ | Antrim |
| ZL | Dublin | EZ | Belfast |
| ZM | Galway | FZ | Belfast |
| ZN | Meath | GZ | Belfast |
| ZO | Dublin | HZ | Tyrone |
| ZP | Donegal | JZ | Down |
| ZR | Wexford | KZ | Antrim |

| Index Mark | Office | Index Mark | Office |
|---|---|---|---|
| LZ | Armagh | IN | Kerry |
| MZ | Belfast | IO | Kildare |
| NZ | Londonderry | IP | Kilkenny |
| OZ | Belfast | IR | Offaly |
| PZ | Belfast | IS | Mayo |
| RZ | Antrim | IT | Leitrim |
| SZ | Down | IU | Limerick |
| TZ | Belfast | IV | Limerick |
| UZ | Belfast | IW | Londonderry |
| VZ | Tyrone | IX | Longford |
| WZ | Belfast | IY | Louth |
| XZ | Armagh | IZ | Mayo |
| YZ | Londonderry | | |
| ZZ | Dublin | AI | Meath |
| | | BI | Monaghan |
| IA | Antrim | CI | Laois |
| IB | Armagh | DI | Roscommon |
| IC | Carlow | EI | Sligo |
| ID | Cavan | FI | Tipperary (N. Riding) |
| IE | Clare | GI | Tipperary (S. Riding) |
| IF | Cork | HI | Tipperary (S. Riding) |
| IH | Donegal | JI | Tyrone |
| IJ | Down | KI | Waterford |
| IK | Dublin | LI | Westmeath |
| IL | Fermanagh | MI | Wexford |
| IM | Galway | NI | Wicklow |

# Appendix 3
# Code of Practice for the Motor Industry

This Code of Practice was drawn up by the Society of Motor Manufacturers and Traders (SMMT), the Motor Agents Association (MAA) and the Scottish Motor Traders Association (SMTA) in consultation with the Director-General of Fair Trading. If you have a complaint, read through this Code, which sets out the proper standards one should expect from any member of the motor industry – although it will of course only be binding on members of the above associations. For details of their arbitration scheme refer to the Appendix at the end of the Code.

## 1 New Car Sales

1.1 Dealers must bear in mind that in sales of goods to consumers they are responsible under the Sale of Goods Act 1979 for ensuring that the goods are of merchantable quality and fit for the purpose for which they are required. Statements whether oral or in writing which are in apparent conflict with this principle must be avoided.

1.2 Manufacturers relying on dealers to carry out a standard Pre-Delivery Inspection shall provide dealers with a standard check list for the particular model of car. Dealers must ensure that these inspections are carried out properly and a copy of the PDI check list shall be given to the customer.

1.3 The car must be delivered in condition which is to the manufacturer's standard. Each car must conform fully to all legislation affecting its construction, use and maintenance. This paragraph does not affect any legal responsibilities which may be placed on manufacturers and users to ensure this.

1.4 The benefit and limitations of any treatment over and above that already provided by the manufacturer which is recommended by the dealer in order to inhibit the growth of rust or other corrosion should be explained to the customer.

1.5 Order forms are intended to help both parties to the contract by spelling out the terms and conditions on which business is being done. Such terms and conditions must be fair and reasonable and set out clearly, together with a statement of the circumstances under which the order can be cancelled.

1.6 All documents must be legible.

1.7 Order forms must contain details of all charges additional to the car price so that the customer may understand clearly the total price he has to pay to put the car on the road.

**1.8** Manufacturers and dealers should ensure that the manufacturer's handbook relating to the model of car being sold is available to the customer at the time of sale of the car and for a reasonable length of time thereafter.

**1.9** The terms of the manufacturers' warranties should be drawn to the attention of the customer and any relevant document published by the manufacturer must be handed over to him.

## 2 Car Manufacturer's Warranties (or Guarantees hereafter called Warranties)

**2.1** A manufacturer's warranty is a simple and straightforward way for the customer to have faults of manufacture appearing within certain times (or before the car has done a certain mileage) put right at little or no cost to the customer without the necessity of his pursuing legal rights against the seller.

**2.2** The warranty must not adversely affect the consumer's remedies against the seller under the Sale of Goods Act and must include a statement making this clear to the consumer.

**2.3** The warranty must include a statement advising the customer that it is in addition to any other remedies he may have under the contract of sale.

**2.4** The warranty will not extend to cover defects arising from a failure by the customer to have the car serviced in accordance with the manufacturer's recommendations.

**2.5** The terms of the warranty must be easily understandable particularly in relation to any items specifically included in or excluded from its provisions. Manufacturers and dealers should also give advice to customers as to who is responsible and what to do if they have a problem regarding parts and accessories not covered by the manufacturer's warranty.

**2.6** The manufacturer should permit the transfer of the unexpired portion of any warranty to a second or subsequent owner.

**2.7** The manufacturer should make clear that rectification work may be done under warranty by any of his franchised dealers. Manufacturers and dealers will take steps to ensure that warranty work is carried out rapidly and effectively.

**2.8** Manufacturers will operate fair and equitable policies to permit the extension of warranty in the event of a car being off the road for an extended period for rectification of warranty faults, or of the repetition outside warranty of a fault which had previously been the subject of rectification work during the warranty period.

### Vehicle off road for warranty work

**2.9** There is no automatic right to a loan car or contribution towards hiring charges in circumstances where a customer's own car is off the road for repair under warranty. Whether there is any such right will depend on the normal legal rules relating to damages.

**2.10** Manufacturers must give clear advice to their dealers as to the circumstances in which a loan car or contribution towards hiring charges should be provided. Such guidance should take full account of the legal position and should be made available to customers on request.

**2.11** Where a loan car is made available, this will merely be as reasonable alternative transport rather than an exact replacement for the car which is off the road.

## 3 Used Car Sales

**3.1** Used cars sold to customers must conform to legislation affecting the construction and use of cars and should, where appropriate, be accompanied by a current Department of Transport Test (MOT) Certificate.

**3.2** Dealers must bear in mind that sales of used cars are subject to the Sale of Goods Act 1979 and attention is specifically drawn to the conditions of merchantable quality and fitness for purpose contained in this Act. If, however, defects are specifically brought to the attention of the customer or the customer examines the car before the contract is made there is no condition of merchantable quality as regards those specific defects or ones which that examination ought to reveal. Dealers should therefore reveal defects on an approved checklist. See 3.5. The format and use of the checklist are determined and approved by the trade associations or the manufacturer of the car concerned. Dealers should provide all reasonable facilities to enable prospective customers or their nominees to carry out an examination of the car prior to sale, in order that any defects which ought to be revealed at the time of sale are made known to both parties.

**3.3** Dealers are reminded of the legal requirement that when selling a used car subject to a printed guarantee or warranty, that guarantee or warranty must not purport to take away or diminish any rights which the consumer would otherwise enjoy in law. The warranty document must also include a statement advising the consumer that the warranty is in addition to his statutory or common law rights.

**3.4** If a printed guarantee or warranty is not used, then any specific promises which the dealer is willing to make in relation to the used car should be set out in writing.

**3.5** Used cars will be subject to a pre-sales inspection in accordance with an approved checklist. The checklist must be completed before the car is offered for sale and displayed in a prominent place in the car. A copy of the checklist shall be given to the customer for his retention.

**3.6** All descriptions, whether used in advertisements or in negotiations regarding the sale of used cars should be honest and truthful. Terms which are likely to be misunderstood by the customer or which are not capable of exact definition should be avoided.

**3.7** Copies of relevant written information provided by previous owners regarding the history of cars should be passed on to the customer. This may include service records, repair invoices, inspection reports, handbooks and copy of warranties, as applicable.

**3.8** Reasonable steps will be taken to verify the recorded mileage of a used car and dealers will use their best endeavours to obtain a signed statement from the previous owner as to the car's mileage. Dealers should pass on any known facts about an odometer reading to a prospective customer.

**3.9** Unless the dealer is satisfied that the quoted mileage of a used car is accurate, such mileage should not be quoted in advertisements, discussions or negotiations or in any documents related to the supply of the used car. Where the car's mileage cannot be verified the customer should be informed. The law requires that any disclaimer used must be as bold, precise and compelling as the car's mileage reading itself and as effectively brought to the prospective customer's attention.

## 4 Replacement Parts, Accessories and Petrol

**4.1** Dealers must bear in mind that in sales of goods to consumers they are responsible under the Sale of Goods Act 1979 that the goods are of merchantable quality and fit for the purpose for which they are required. Statements, whether oral or in writing, in apparent conflict with this principle must be avoided.

**4.2** Whenever goods are offered for sale a clear indication of cash price must be available to the customer.

**4.3** Terms must not be used in advertisements if they are likely to be misunderstood by the customer or if they are not capable of exact definition.

**4.4** With offers of promotions or trading stamps, any restrictions which are attached to sales other than cash sales must be clearly stated.

**4.5** A dealer must not display any notices or make any statements which might mislead a consumer about his legal rights in relation to the purchase of faulty goods.

## 5 Repairs and Servicing (excluding work carried out under a car manufacturer's warranty)

**5.1** Dealers must bear in mind that when supplying parts or accessories in connection with repairs or servicing work for consumers, they have a similar responsibility to that which exists under a contract for the sale of goods to ensure that the goods are of merchantable quality and fit for the purpose for which they are required and that work is performed in a proper and workmanlike manner.

**5.2** Manufacturers accept a responsibility for ensuring the reasonable availability of spare parts to the distribution chain.

**5.3** Spare parts should be readily available from the manufacturer from the time that a new model is offered for sale continuing throughout its production and for a reasonable period thereafter.

**5.4** Dealers will provide at least an estimate of the cost of labour and materials for all major repairs and manufacturers' recommended servicing. A firm quotation should be offered wherever possible. It must be made clear to the customer whether an estimate or quotation is being made and whether it is inclusive of VAT and where applicable the rate at which this is chargeable. Quotations should always be in writing identifying the dealer. If requested, estimates will be in writing. It should be remembered that an estimate is a considered approximation of the likely cost involved whereas a quotation constitutes a firm price for which the work will be done. If a charge is to be made for the estimate or quotation this must be made known to the customer before his instructions are accepted. Any dismantling costs which are necessary to arrive at such estimates or quotations should be notified to the customer in advance on the clear understanding whether or not dismantling costs are to be charged on an estimate or quotation which is refused. If, during the progress of any work, it appears that the estimate will be exceeded by a significant amount, then the customer should be notified and asked for permission to continue with the work.

5.5   Parts replaced during service or repair will be made available for return to the customer until the customer has taken delivery of the car unless a warranty claim is involved or unless the parts have to be submitted to the supplier because replacement parts are being supplied on an exchange basis. Dealers should notify customers in advance of work being done what their arrangements are in regard to retention and disposal of parts replaced.

5.6   Invoices should be clearly written or typed and give full details of the work carried out and materials used. The amount and rate of VAT should be clearly indicated. Dates and recorded mileages should always be noted where applicable.

5.7   Dealers should exercise adequate care in protecting customers' property while it is in their custody, and must not seek by disclaimers to avoid their legal liability for damage or loss. Dealers should carry adequate insurance to cover their legal liability and should strongly advise customers to remove any items of value not related to the car.

5.8   Repairs must be guaranteed against failure due to workmanship for a specific mileage or time period which should be stated on the invoice. Dealers are advised to ensure that they are adequately insured against consequential loss claims arising from any such failure.

5.9   A dealer's rules as to the method of payment he will require on completion of the work should always be notified to the customer before the work is accepted.

5.10   When it is necessary to sub-contract work, the dealer will agree to be responsible for the quality of the subcontractors' work. Any estimate given to the customer must include the sub-contracted work and in the event of any increase in charge for the work, the principles in para 5.4 must apply.

5.11   Dealers must make it clear whether or not servicing will be carried out in accordance with the appropriate manufacturer's recommended service schedule.

5.12   While a dealer's contractual responsibility is limited to the exact terms of the customer's instructions or, for standard services, the schedule prepared by the manufacturer or other body or person, he should make it a general rule to advise the customer of any defects which may become apparent while the work is being carried out.

## 6 Advertising

**6.1** All advertising by manufacturers and dealers must comply with the codes and standards set by the Advertising Standards Authority and the Independent Broadcasting Authority, and with the requirements of the Trade Descriptions Acts and the Energy Act (e.g. concerning fuel consumption figures). In particular, references to credit facilities must conform to the appropriate legal requirements current at the time.

**6.2** Advertisements must not contain any references to guarantees or warranties which would take away or diminish any rights of a customer nor should they be worded as to be understood by the customer as doing so.

**6.3** Advertisements must not contain the words 'guarantee' or 'warranty' unless the full terms of such undertakings as well as the remedial action open to a customer are either clearly set out in the advertisement or are available to the customer in writing at the point of sale or with the product.

**6.4** Claims and descriptions in advertisements should not be misleading. In particular any comparison with other models of different manufacturers should be based on a similar set of criteria and should not be presented in such a way as to confuse or mislead the customer.

**6.5** In principle, a price quoted should be a price at which the customer can buy the goods. Manufacturers and dealers should therefore quote prices for new cars, whether in advertisements or in showrooms, inclusive of the price of any extras known to be fitted to the car together with the appropriate VAT (quoting the rate applicable) and Car Tax. If the price excludes delivery charges or number plates, such exclusions must be clearly specified.

**6.6** Advertisements for used cars must quote prices inclusive of VAT and they should state that the prices are inclusive.

**6.7** In the description of used cars, terms likely to be misunderstood by the customer or which are not capable of exact definition should be avoided. For example, if the word 'reconditioned' is used, the nature of the reconditioning must be carefully explained.

**6.8** In the description of a used car, any year must be either:
(a) the year of first use, or
(b) the year of first registration, or
(d) the last year that the car complied with the manufacturer's specification of a model sold as new during that calendar year whichever is the earliest.

**6.9** Where an advertisement quotes the price of one model in any model range but depicts another, the actual price of that other model should also be shown.

**6.10** Where a manufacturer advertises a rust-proofing process, information about the process and its limitations should be made freely available.

## 7 Handling Complaints

7.1 Manufacturers and dealers must ensure as appropriate that effective and immediate action is taken with a view to achieving a just settlement of a complaint. To this end there will be, from the point of view of the customer, an easily identifiable and accessible arrangement for the reception and handling of complaints. In addition, manufacturers must give every assistance to their dealers in handling complaints under warranty, or those in which the manufacturer is otherwise involved.

**7.2** When complaints are raised through a third party (e.g. the Automobile Association, the Royal Automobile Club, a Trading Standards Officer or a Citizens Advice Bureau), willing guidance must be given to that body and every attempt should be made to re-establish direct communication with the complaining customer and to reach a satisfactory settlement with him.

**7.3** In the event that a complaint is not resolved, manufacturers and dealers must make it clear to a customer that he has a right to refer the complaint to the appropriate trade association.

**7.4** Manufacturers and dealers will give every assistance to the association concerned while it is investigating a complaint. The SMMT, the MMA and the SMTA will establish liaison as necessary.

**7.5** Where conciliation has failed to resolve a dispute the SMMT, the MAA and the SMTA have agreed to co-operate in the operation of low cost arbitration arrangements which will be organised by the Chartered Institute of Arbitrators. Details of the arbitration arrangements are set out in the Appendix. Customers must always be advised that they have the option of taking a claim to the Courts.

**7.6** The award of the arbitrator is enforceable in law on all parties.


## 8 Monitoring

**8.1** As Subscribers to the Code of Practice, dealers should ensure by the clear display of appropriate symbols or other means that customers are informed of dealers' adherence to the industry's Code of Practice.

**8.2** All manufacturers and dealers should maintain an analysis of justified complaints relating to any of the provisions of the Code of Practice and should take action based on this information to improve their service to the customer.

**8.3** The SMMT, the MAA and the SMTA will analyse all complaints about the Code of matters referred to the association for conciliation or arbitration. The results of such analyses will be published in the Annual Report of the relevant association.


## Appendix 1: Complaints and Arbitration

1 A customer who has a complaint about the quality of the goods or service to his motor car should in the first place and at the earliest opportunity refer it to the dealer concerned.

2 The complaint, preferably in writing, should be addressed to a senior executive, a director, a partner or the proprietor. Some dealers will have an executive specially appointed to deal with complaints.

3 If the complaint relates to warranty on a new car and the dealer is unable to

resolve the matter, the customer should take his complaint direct to the manufacturer concerned.

4 If attempts to reach a satisfactory solution fail, the customer has a right to refer his complaint to one of the trade associations who subscribe to the Code of Practice for the Motor Industry, if the dealer concerned is a member of that association. Any such complaint must be in writing.

(a) if the complaint refers to a manufacturer's warranty or lies against a dealer who is a member the address is:

The Customer Relations Department,
Society of Motor Manufacturers & Traders Ltd,
Forbes House,
Halkin Street
London SW1X 7DS.

(b) if the complaint lies against a dealer who is also a member situated in any part of the United Kingdom except Scotland the address is:

The Conciliation Service,
Motor Agents Association Ltd,
73 Park Street,
Bristol BS1 5PS.

(c) if the complaint lies against a dealer who is a member situated in Scotland, the address is:

Customer Complaints Service,
Scottish Motor Trade Association,
3 Palmerstone Place,
Edinburgh EH12 5AQ.

5 All complaints referred to the appropriate trade association (SMMT, MAA or SMTA) within a reasonable time of the cause for complaint arising will be considered.

6 If the trade association fails to resolve the complaint, its members will agree to go to arbitration except in those cases where the trade association is of the opinion that it would be unreasonable for the member to be required to do so.

7 Parties to arbitration will be asked to pay the registration fee laid down by the Chartered Institute of Arbitrators. When, later, the arbitrator makes his award, he will consider whether the registration fee should be returned to the successful party.

8 The parties will also be asked to sign an application for arbitration which will be sent, together with the registration fee, to:

The Chartered Institute of Arbitrators,
75 Cannon Street, London EC4N 5BH.

9 In order to keep costs as low as possible, the arbitration will normally rely on documents. In these cases, none of the parties to the dispute may be present nor may they be represented by any other person.

10 The trade association will submit to the Chartered Institute of Arbitrators all the documentary evidence in their possession that they consider relevant to the case. The Chartered Institute of Arbitrators will advise the parties to the dispute of the written evidence they have available on which to base their judgement and invite the parties to submit any further evidence which they consider relevant.

11 The President of the Chartered Institute of Arbitrators will appoint a single arbitrator and will make all the necessary arrangements for the arbitration to be conducted as speedily as possible.

12 In suitable cases, the Arbitrator has the right to conduct an oral arbitration and the parties may then attend to present their evidence. Legal representation may only be employed if the Arbitrator so directs.

13 The Arbitrator will have the power to direct any party to provide him and to the other party(ies) any additional document or information he considers to be relevant to the matter under dispute.

14 The award of the Arbitrator will be published in writing to the parties to the dispute and to the relevant association.

15 The award of the Arbitrator is enforceable in the Courts by any party.

# Index to Cases

| Name | Year | Page | Full Name of Case | Full Reference |
|---|---|---|---|---|
| Jankovic | 1970 | 215 | Jankovic v Howell | 1970 CLY 1863 |
| Jones | 1969 | 67 | Jones v Lawrence | 1969 3 All ER 267 |
| Jungnikel | 1966 | 41 | Jungnikel v Laing | 1966 111 SJ 19 |
| Kite | 1983 | 68 | Kite v Nolan | 1983 RTR 253 |
| Kozimor | 1962 | 214 | Kozimor v Adey | 1962 106 SJ 431 |
| Lancaster | 1979 | 75 | Lancaster v H B & H Transport | 1979 RTR 380 |
| Minter | 1983 | 68 | Minter v D & H Contractors | 1983 The Times 30 June |
| Moore | 1968 | 160 | Moore v Maxwells | 1968 1 WLR 1077 |
| Mulligan | 1971 | 210 | Mulligan v Holmes | 1971 RTR 179 |
| Nettleship | 1971 | 140 | Nettleship v Weston | 1971 RTR 179 |
| O'Dowd | 1951 | 185 | O'Dowd v Fraser-Nash | 1951 95 SJ 269 |
| Parkinson | 1973 | 212 | Parkinson v Parkinson | 1973 RTR 193 |
| Powell | 1966 | 181 | Powell v Moody | 1966 The Times 10 March |
| Prudence | 1966 | 67 | Prudence v Lewis | 1966 The Times 21 May |
| Scott | 1960 | 206 | Scott v Clint | 1960 The Times 28 October |
| Smith | 1982 | 33 | Smith v Sudron | 1982 NLJ 415 |
| Snow | 1969 | 214 | Snow v Giddins | 1969 113 SJ 229 |
| Stevens | 1970 | 203 | Stevens v Kelland | 1970 RTR 445 |
| Thompson | 1973 | 41 | Thompson v Spedding | 1973 RTR 312, CA |
| Thorp | 1957 | 31 | Thorp v King | 1957 The Times 23 February |
| Wadsworth | 1978 | 183 | Wadsworth v Gillespie | 1978 CLY 2534 |
| Waller | 1968 | 202 | Waller v Levoi | 1968 112 SJ 865 |
| Watson | 1971 | 203 | Watson v Heslop | 1971 115 SJ 308 |
| Whitehead | 1962 | 119 | Whitehead v Unwins (Yorks) | 1962 The Times 1 March |
| Wood | 1948 | 119 | Wood v General Accident | 1948 SJ 720 |

# Index

# FOR THE BEST IN PAPERBACKS, LOOK FOR THE

In every corner of the world, on every subject under the sun, Penguin represents quality and variety – the very best in publishing today.

For complete information about books available from Penguin – including Pelicans, Puffins, Peregrines and Penguin Classics – and how to order them, write to us at the appropriate address below. Please note that for copyright reasons the selection of books varies from country to country.

**In the United Kingdom:** For a complete list of books available from Penguin in the U.K., please write to *Dept E.P., Penguin Books Ltd, Harmondsworth, Middlesex, UB7 0DA*

**In the United States:** For a complete list of books available from Penguin in the U.S., please write to *Dept BA, Penguin, 299 Murray Hill Parkway, East Rutherford, New Jersey 07073*

**In Canada:** For a complete list of books available from Penguin in Canada, please write to *Penguin Books Canada Ltd, 2801 John Street, Markham, Ontario L3R 1B4*

**In Australia:** For a complete list of books available from Penguin in Australia, please write to the *Marketing Department, Penguin Books Australia Ltd, P.O. Box 257, Ringwood, Victoria 3134*

**In New Zealand:** For a complete list of books available from Penguin in New Zealand, please write to the *Marketing Department, Penguin Books (NZ) Ltd, Private Bag, Takapuna, Auckland 9*

**In India:** For a complete list of books available from Penguin, please write to *Penguin Overseas Ltd, 706 Eros Apartments, 56 Nehru Place, New Delhi, 110019*

**In Holland:** For a complete list of books available from Penguin in Holland, please write to *Penguin Books Nederland B.V., Postbus 195, NL–1380AD Weesp, Netherlands*

**In Germany:** For a complete list of books available from Penguin, please write to *Penguin Books Ltd, Friedrichstrasse 10 – 12, D–6000 Frankfurt Main 1, Federal Republic of Germany*

**In Spain:** For a complete list of books available from Penguin in Spain, please write to *Longman Penguin España, Calle San Nicolas 15, E–28013 Madrid, Spain*